Secret Messages _____

Modern War Studies _____

Secret Messages

Codebreaking and
American Diplomacy,
1930–1945

David Alvarez

 UNIVERSITY PRESS OF KANSAS

Published by the University Press of Kansas (Lawrence, Kansas 66049), which was organized by the Kansas Board of Regents and is operated and funded by Emporia State University, Fort Hays State University, Kansas State University, Pittsburg State University, the University of Kansas, and Wichita State University

Library of Congress Cataloging-in-Publication Data

Alvarez, David J.

   Secret messages : codebreaking and American diplomacy, 1930–1945 / David Alvarez.

     p. cm. — (Modern war studies)

   Includes bibliographical references and index.

   ISBN 0-7006-1013-8 (cloth : alk. paper)

     1. World War, 1939–1945—Cryptography. 2. Cryptography—United States—History—20th century. 3. World War, 1939–1945—Diplomatic history. 4. United States—Foreign relations—1933–1945. I. Title. II. Series.

D810.C88 A48 2000

940.54'8673—dc21

                                            99-049798

British Library Cataloguing in Publication Data is available.

Printed in the United States of America

10 9 8 7 6 5 4 3 2 1

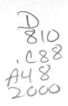
THIS ONE IS FOR GRANT.

CONTENTS

ACKNOWLEDGMENTS _____

The research for this book was completed while I held an appointment as scholar-in-residence at the National Security Agency's Center for Cryptologic History. I owe a special debt to David Hatch, the center's director, for inviting me to spend a year at NSA and for shepherding me through the agency and its culture. Everyone at the agency made me feel welcome, but several individuals deserve special thanks. The history staff, Bob Hanyok, Tom Johnson, Sharon Maneki, and David Mowry all contributed to making the year the most professionally rewarding of my career. At NSA's National Cryptologic Museum, Jack Ingram and Larry Sharpe opened their library and facilities to me. Robert Louis Benson generously shared his voluminous knowledge of wartime signals intelligence operations and arranged for the agency to declassify for me portions of his multi-volume history of the VENONA program. Although it supported this project, the National Security Agency did not review or approve the manuscript. The end result does not necessarily reflect the official position of the National Security Agency or the United States government.

The bibliography identifies the many veterans of the Signal Intelligence Service and its wartime successors who reminisced about their experiences and provided insight into personalities and operations. One in particular deserves special mention. Cecil Phillips took a special interest in my project and went out of his way to facilitate the research by introducing me to his former colleagues at Arlington Hall and by illuminating various cryptanalytic operations, especially those of the Russian section in which he served with such distinction. His untimely death is a great personal loss to those who knew him and a professional loss to intelligence historians who benefited from his counsel.

At the National Archives John Taylor once again guided me through the intelligence records of the United States government, a task he has patiently performed since, as a callow graduate student, I first appeared at his desk at "old archives" more than twenty-five years ago.

Several colleagues contributed significantly to the completion of this project. Ralph Erskine generously shared the results of his research in the archives of the Government Code and Cypher School and was always available to discuss the finer points of wartime signals intelligence. Every chapter is better for his advice. Carl Boyd and John Ferris reviewed the entire manuscript, and their thoughtful comments were invaluable. David Kahn read several chapters and was a constant source of advice and encouragement. Steve Budiansky provided information from his work in OP-20-G records. Frode Weirud patiently responded to my questions concerning cipher machines and signals intelligence operations in Scandinavia.

My home institution, Saint Mary's College of California, provided a sabbatical during which I finished writing this project.

My family lived with this book for two years and patiently endured its demands, including two moves across the continent. My wife, Donna, remained cheerful and supportive throughout the ordeal. This book could not have been begun, let alone finished, without her understanding and encouragement.

ABBREVIATIONS

ANCIB	Army-Navy Communications Intelligence Board
BSC	British Security Coordination
DESAB	Deutsches Satzbuch
FBI	Federal Bureau of Investigation
FCC	Federal Communications Commission
FECB	Far East Combined Bureau
GCCS	Government Code and Cypher School
IIC	Interdepartmental Intelligence Conference
MID	Military Intelligence Division
MIS	Military Intelligence Service
ONI	Office of Naval Intelligence
OSS	Office of Strategic Services
OTP	one-time-pad
RCA	Radio Corporation of America
RID	Radio Intelligence Division
sigint	signals intelligence
SIS	Signal Intelligence Service
SRI	signal radio intelligence
SSA	Signal Security Agency
TICOM	Target Intelligence Committee

INTRODUCTION ———————————

For some time historians have been aware that signals intelligence (sigint), the interception and decryption of the secret messages of foreign governments, played a crucial role in the Second World War. Names such as Ultra, Magic, and Enigma are now a necessary part of the vocabulary of any historian seeking to explain the course of the war. No consideration of the Battle of Matapan in the Mediterranean or the Battle of Midway in the Pacific, the campaign in New Guinea or the campaign in North Africa, combat in the air above Britain or in waters below Japan's Inland Sea is now complete without reference to special intelligence provided by decrypted messages. In London, Washington, and command centers around the globe, admirals and generals diverted ships, concentrated divisions, and directed air squadrons in reaction to the pieces of paper passed to them by the codebreakers. There can be little doubt that signals intelligence contributed significantly to the military defeat of the Axis. Indeed, entire books have been devoted to illuminating the role of codebreaking in combat operations.[1]

The centrality of signals intelligence in military and naval operations in both the European and Pacific theaters has become so evident that historians may be tempted to exaggerate the contributions of the codebreakers. Awed by the seemingly miraculous achievements of American and British cryptanalysts, historians may too easily assume that decrypted messages guided every decision, both tactical and strategic, and that diplomats and politicians were as well served by signals intelligence as were admirals and generals. In fact, the study of signals intelligence has been skewed toward its manifestations in the realm of military affairs. There has been little attempt to determine whether codebreaking was as central to

1

the formulation of diplomatic policy as it was to the development of military policy.[2]

To a certain extent this deficiency reflects a lack of imagination. Diplomatic historians, for example, have exhibited a curious reluctance to investigate systematically the place of intelligence of any type in wartime foreign policy. The secrecy that has surrounded signals intelligence in general and diplomatic signals intelligence in particular has also discouraged an appraisal of the role of codebreaking in wartime diplomacy. Long after acknowledging their successes in military and naval cryptanalysis, the United Kingdom and the United States continued to withhold details concerning their diplomatic signals intelligence. In Washington, revelations were limited to confirming that American codebreakers successfully read important Japanese diplomatic communications enciphered by the famous PURPLE cipher machine. Authorities, however, deflected questions about American efforts against German and Italian ciphers, and they were particularly reticent concerning possible operations against Allied and neutral governments. As a result, even intelligence historians remained uncertain about the organization, scope, and achievements of diplomatic cryptanalysis. In such a situation the path of least resistance was to assume that the influence of American and British signals intelligence in the military field was echoed in the diplomatic field.

The situation began to change in the 1990s with decisions by American and British authorities to declassify and release records concerning prewar and wartime signals intelligence. This welcome, though belated, openness reached a high point in 1996 when the National Security Agency transferred to the National Archives 1.3 million pages of American cryptologic materials covering the period 1914–1945. Unprecedented in its size and scope, this release of top secret documents (along with important though less extensive releases in the United Kingdom) transformed the field of intelligence history. The hundreds of boxes of decrypted messages, operational directives, organizational charts, section reports, committee minutes, and internal histories provided historians with a documentary base for the comprehensive study of wartime signals intelligence.

This book is an effort to describe American efforts to intercept and decrypt the secret diplomatic communications of foreign governments in the period 1930–1945. The opening date coincides with the creation of the U.S. Army's Signal Intelligence Service (SIS). Since SIS and its various organizational reincarnations remained through the end of the Second World War the U.S. government's principal instrument for diplomatic codebreaking, this book is also an operational history of that service. The focus throughout is on diplomatic signals intelligence. There is no attempt to describe American codebreaking operations in the military or naval spheres, since these efforts have been addressed by other histories and their existence is generally well known. Less well known and much less well understood are American codebreaking efforts against diplomatic targets. If this book makes any contribution to an understanding of the prewar and war years, it will be by illuminating this especially dark corner of intelligence history.

Chapter One

Antecedents

Americans came late to codebreaking. In fact, they were among the last to arrive. Almost as soon as people began to write, they sought ways of hiding the meaning of what they wrote from curious or hostile eyes. Secret writing appears in ancient Egyptian hieroglyphs, Mesopotamian cuneiform tablets, eleventh century Chinese ideographs, Viking runes, and Celtic inscriptions, and it served the needs of Spartan generals, Roman emperors, Vedic poets, and Irish monks. Not surprisingly, efforts to conceal the meaning of a communication encouraged efforts to circumvent the concealment, and the practice of cryptanalysis followed in the wake of cryptography. The prophet Daniel, who read the writing that appeared mysteriously on the wall at Belshazzar's feast, may have been the first cryptanalyst, although only isolated instances of cryptanalysis appear in the literary and historical record until the flourishing of Arab civilization in the ninth and tenth centuries. The Arabs were the first to frame and apply systematic methods of reading secret words and alphabets. By the early Renaissance the practice had spread to the West, where the courts and chancelleries of popes, kings, and dukes now included functionaries skilled in the making and breaking of codes and ciphers. Over the centuries the skills of both makers and breakers evolved as governments and individuals recognized that secret communications were a useful tool in public and private affairs. By the eighteenth century, most major European powers (and some minor ones) routinely intercepted mail passing through their territories and passed it to so-called Black Chambers, where clerks skilled in the arts of opening envelopes and reading ciphers revealed secrets that shaped the future of rulers and ruled.[1]

None of this had the slightest impact on the new nation that emerged on the North American continent at the end of the eighteenth century.

Although heavily influenced in culture, language, taste, and (though they would be loathe to admit it) political and legal arrangements by their connections with Europe, the citizens of the United States of America self-consciously repudiated those institutions that reminded them of repression and unrestrained authority. In a society that considered organized police forces and a standing army threats to liberty, there was no room for Black Chambers. To be sure, cryptology played a modest role in the American Revolution and the early years of the Republic, but it was transitory and episodic. A year before he would sign the Declaration of Independence, Elbridge Gerry, a Massachusetts revolutionary, collaborated with a fellow Harvard graduate, Elisha Porter, to decipher a message. The message revealed that Dr. Benjamin Church Jr., chief of medical services for George Washington's revolutionary army, was passing information to the British. In the fall of 1781, James Lovell, a Boston schoolteacher and delegate to the Continental Congress, deciphered several messages between the British commander in New York, General Henry Clinton, and his second in command, General Charles Cornwallis, who was then at Yorktown, Virginia, hoping to escape encirclement by Washington's army and French warships.[2]

These episodes suggest the amateur and unsystematic approach to codebreaking that characterized American activities in this field well into the twentieth century. Codes and ciphers and their solution occasionally surfaced in personal and political intrigues: a cipher message figured prominently as evidence in the treason trial of Aaron Burr, a former vice president of the United States; telegraphers in the War Department cipher office next door to the White House occasionally decrypted Confederate messages during the Civil War; two editors at the *New York Tribune* solved cipher telegrams revealing efforts by Democrats to purchase electoral votes in the closely fought Hayes-Tilden presidential election of 1876.[3] The U.S. government, however, had no organization dedicated to the surveillance of communications and the solution of codes and ciphers. When in the course of operations the armed services encountered cryptograms, they had to depend on the initiative, effort, and good luck of personnel on the scene. During the so-called Philippine Insurrection (1899–1901), General Frederick Funston, the officer commanding U.S. Army forces in Luzon, sat down with a Spanish intelligence officer who was working with the Americans to solve several cipher messages sent by the insurrectionist leader, Emilio Aguinaldo, to his field commanders. When, in 1916, an American expeditionary force crossed into northern Mexico to punish the forces of revolutionary general Pancho Villa for their depredations against American citizens and property, the army frequently intercepted messages of the regime in Mexico City or the forces contesting its rule. Some of these were solved by a young infantry captain, Parker Hitt, who discovered an interest in cryptology after participating in a technical conference at the army's Signal School on military cryptography; others were read by Victor Weiskopf, a Justice Department investigator working along the border.[4] Despite (or, perhaps, because of) these experiences, no one in Washington thought that the interception and decryption of secret messages was sufficiently useful to the United States government to require some system and organization. The First World War, however, compelled people in Washington and elsewhere to change what they thought about a lot of things.

By the time the United States entered the war on 6 April 1917, signals intelligence had become an important element in the diplomacy and military operations of both the Allies and the Central Powers. Indeed, the interception and decryption by British codebreakers of a German diplomatic message (the so-called Zimmerman Telegram) inviting Mexico to ally with Germany and reconquer Arizona, New Mexico, Texas, and other territories lost to the United States in the War of 1848 was the proximate cause of American belligerency. The United States, however, was as ill prepared for signals warfare as it was for trench warfare. Aside from the odd officer, like Parker Hitt, who pursued the subject as a hobby, neither the army nor the navy had any personnel knowledgeable in cryptanalysis, and neither service had a program to impart such knowledge.[5] In desperation the army turned to the private sector. George Fabyan, an Illinois businessman who made a fortune in textiles and spent it on intellectual enthusiasms, had endowed a private research center, the Riverbank Laboratories, on his estate in Geneva, Illinois, where investigators conducted research in chemistry, genetics, physics, and veterinary medicine. The laboratories included a cipher department, where a handful of researchers combed Shakespeare's plays and sonnets for evidence to support Fabyan's belief that the works were in fact authored by Francis Bacon. For all its eccentric purpose, Riverbank's cipher department was the only place in the country pursuing systematic cryptanalysis. As a patriotic gesture upon the declaration of war, "Colonel" Fabyan (the title was an honorific) offered the facilities of his cipher department to the United States government. In the spring and summer of 1917, the department solved encrypted messages intercepted by the Army, Navy, and Justice Departments, including messages exposing a conspiracy by expatriate Hindus in the United States to foment armed rebellion in India. In October 1917 the War Department sent four officers to Riverbank for six weeks of instruction in codes and ciphers. The program was so successful that in January 1918 the department sent another sixty officers for training.[6]

From the start the army considered the connection with Riverbank a temporary expedient and worked to develop its own cryptologic service. In June 1917 it established a cipher office in its Military Intelligence Branch. Known as MI-8, this office was entrusted to a newly commissioned first lieutenant, Herbert Yardley, a brash, fast-talking midwesterner who had developed an interest in cryptology while working as a code clerk at the State Department. To fill the quiet hours of the code room's night shift, Yardley tried to solve the various encrypted messages that came into the department from its embassies and consulates around the world. His efforts were so successful that he submitted a lengthy memorandum to the official responsible for the department's communications detailing the weaknesses in the codes that protected the government's diplomatic secrets. After the declaration of war, Yardley convinced Major Ralph Van Deman, the officer responsible for jump-starting the army's cryptologic program, that he was just the man to take charge of the army's new cipher office. At first the new lieutenant's command consisted of two civilian clerks working from a makeshift office on the mezzanine of the War College library, but as American military and diplomatic authorities began to appreciate the importance of the work, the staff gradually increased until by the end of the war it numbered 151 cryptologists, clerks, and translators and occupied the top floors of a building in northwest Washington, D.C.[7]

Staff shortages and special duties, such as responsibility for compiling codes and ciphers for the army and processing all military intelligence communications, delayed Yardley's plans to study foreign diplomatic communications. Only in the summer of 1918 did MI-8 turn seriously to diplomatic operations.[8] Not surprisingly, the early focus was on Germany. With the help of information provided by British cryptanalysts, who had been working Berlin's diplomatic traffic for almost four years, MI-8 was soon reading several German diplomatic systems. Independently, Yardley's staff solved ciphers used by German agents in North America, including one carried by Lothar Witzke (alias Pablo Waberski), the only German agent condemned to death by an American court during the war. A Spanish diplomatic code, photographed during a clandestine entry into the Spanish consulate in Panama, provided clues that led to the solution of other cryptosystems used by Madrid to communicate with its embassies and consulates. During the war MI-8 also solved Argentine, Brazilian, Chilean, Costa Rican, Cuban, Mexican, and Panamanian diplomatic codes.[9]

There is no evidence that any of this effort had the slightest impact on American diplomacy during the war or during the negotiations at the Versailles Peace Conference. The affairs of Spain and a handful of minor Latin American governments did not engage the attention of the State Department or the White House. Furthermore, there was no formal mechanism for transmitting the results of MI-8's work to the president and his diplomatic advisers; indeed, it is unlikely that President Woodrow Wilson ever saw any foreign messages decrypted by Yardley's office. Wilson's temperament, characterized by complete confidence in the righteousness of his vision of America and its role in the world, a reluctance to accept evidence at odds with that vision, and a distaste for espionage and the seamier aspects of international affairs made the president resistant to the influence of *any* intelligence, let alone that from a new source like signals intelligence.

Of course, signals intelligence was in its infancy in the United States. Few in military and diplomatic circles understood its methods, and even fewer grasped its potential. One who did was General Marlborough Churchill, the director of military intelligence. In December 1918, only weeks after the armistice that ended the fighting on the western front, General Churchill urged the army chief of staff to continue MI-8 and its cryptanalytic operations after the war. In making this recommendation, Churchill did not consult MI-8's chief, who was in Paris performing cryptologic chores for the American delegation to the peace conference, but he could count on Yardley's enthusiastic support.

Upon his return to Washington in April 1919, Yardley, who had little interest in exchanging the glamour and excitement of intelligence work for the mundane duties of the State Department's cipher office, prepared for General Churchill's signature a memorandum that reviewed the wartime accomplishments of MI-8 and suggested the contributions that a cryptanalytic organization could make to American military and foreign policy in peacetime. The memorandum recommended the creation of a civilian cryptanalytic agency "to carry out the program of deciphering promptly all foreign code and cipher messages submitted to it, of solving new codes, of developing new methods and of training an adequate personnel." It also recommended that the agency's expenses, estimated at one hundred thousand dollars in the first year, be shared by its two most likely clients, the State Department and the War Department. On 17 May 1919 the acting secretary of state, Frank Polk, approved the recommendation, as did the army chief of staff, General Peyton March, three days later.[10] Herbert Yardley's wartime service as chief of MI-8 made him the natural choice to lead the new agency, which was designated the Cipher Bureau. Because the State Department was restricted in its ability to spend money in the District of Columbia, Yardley established his new office in New York City. By the end of August 1919, a staff of twenty, most of whom had served in MI-8 during the war, were ensconced with their files behind locked doors in a four-story townhouse on East Thirty-eighth Street. A plaque on the street entrance informed the curious that the men and women who worked inside were employees of the "Code Compilation Company."[11]

The Cipher Bureau maintained contact with the army's Military Intelligence Division (MID) by means of ordinary and registered mail. Occasionally, Yardley would travel to Washington for conferences with MID or State Department officers, and less frequently officials would visit the Cipher Bureau. Once or twice a week, envelopes full of intercepted messages would arrive at the bureau's offices. Verbatim texts of decrypted and translated messages would be collected and forwarded to MID as a "bulletin." The decrypts were mainly diplomatic and of little immediate interest to army intelligence. MID passed copies of the decrypts to the office of the undersecretary at the State Department. These copies were prefaced with the stereotypical phrase: "We learn from a source believed to be reliable that . . . "; the subsequent text would faithfully translate the message, but in indirect discourse. At State the messages were available to the secretary of state, the undersecretary, and senior officers in the regional bureaus.[12]

In his memoirs Yardley claimed that his Black Chamber solved the codes and ciphers of twenty governments, including Britain, France, Germany, and Japan.[13] The Cipher Bureau's greatest achievement was against Japan. MI-8 had briefly studied Japanese systems at the end of the war, but without success. When the Cipher Bureau was established, Yardley impetuously announced to MID that he would read Tokyo's diplomatic messages within a year or resign. It was a close thing. The attack against Japanese communications was constrained not so much by the difficulty of the cryptosystems (which were rather simple) but by the absence of personnel familiar with the Japanese language. Without any knowledge of Japanese, Yardley personally applied himself to the problem. With the help of an assistant, Frederick Livesey, who had a special aptitude for languages, he broke into the first code in December 1919, although it would be a while before plain-language values of enough code groups were identified to allow messages to be read. This initial success convinced MID to allow Yardley to hire a Protestant minister who had worked as a missionary in Japan to advise the cryptanalysts and translate the messages. The worthy parson resigned when it finally dawned on him that he was employed in espionage, but by then Livesey had picked up enough of the language to muddle through. The first translated Japanese diplomatic messages reached the War Department in February 1920. By May the Cipher Bureau had cracked four more Japanese diplomatic codes. By September it added the solution of two military attaché codes to its achievements.[14]

Between 1920 and 1926, the Cipher Bureau solved more than two dozen Japanese cryptosystems. This success proved especially valuable during the Washington Conference on the Limitation of Armaments, which convened on 12 November 1921. After four months of deliberations, the conference, attended by delegations from Britain, China, France, Italy, Japan, and the United States, adopted limitations on naval construction. By decrypting the messages passing between Tokyo and its delegation, the Cipher Bureau provided the American delegation and its chief, Secretary of State Charles Evan Hughes, an insight into Japan's negotiating strategy. When, for instance, the Japanese delegation rejected the American proposal for a 10:6 naval tonnage ratio between the United States and Japan and insisted that Tokyo could accept nothing below a 10:7 ratio, Hughes patiently maintained his position, knowing from the decrypts that Tokyo had authorized its delegation to accept the lower ratio rather than alienate the United States. MID was so pleased with the work of Yardley's office during the conference that it distributed cash bonuses to the staff.[15]

The Washington Conference was the high point in the history of the Cipher Bureau. Indeed, an insistent critic might argue that the bureau's notable achievements during the conference were an aberration in an otherwise modest record. Yardley's boasts about solving the codes and ciphers of a score of governments obscure the fact that many of these successes came against the simple ciphers of minor powers, such as Costa Rica, the Dominican Republic, El Salvador, and Liberia, whose diplomatic affairs were, at best, of only marginal interest to the War and State Departments. Some of the successes claimed for the Cipher Bureau by Yardley, for example, the reconstruction of a Brazilian code, were actually achieved by MI-8 during the First World War. Except in the case of Japan, the successes against major powers, such as the partial reconstruction of a British code and the solution of French and German systems, all occurred in the first two years of the bureau's existence. In the case of Germany, the codes dated from the First World War, and most had been read by MI-8 before the armistice. The American Black Chamber registered no successes against the systems of the Weimar Republic that governed Germany during the 1920s. After the Washington Conference, Japan was the only significant power whose messages were regularly read.

The Cipher Bureau's record is seen in its true proportions when it is compared with the achievements of its foreign counterparts. For example, in the period 1926–1928, when Yardley's office was producing only Japanese diplomatic decrypts, the signals intelligence unit of the German Defense Ministry was decrypting the diplomatic or military traffic of Belgium, Britain, Czechoslovakia, France, Italy, Poland, Romania, the Soviet Union, the United States, and Yugoslavia. During the 1920s, Britain's cryptanalytic service, the Government Code and Cypher School (GCCS), successfully attacked the communications of a range of major and minor powers, including Afghanistan, France, Greece, Italy, Japan, Persia, the Soviet Union, Spain, Turkey, and the United States.[16] In this context the Cipher Bureau's achievements, with their narrow focus on Japan, appear unremarkable. Indeed, by mid-decade even Yardley's success against Japan had begun to lose its luster.

The problem was primarily one of intercept. Cryptanalysis requires messages, lots of messages. Without traffic the most skillful codebreakers are helpless. Unfortunately, when the State and War Departments agreed to fund the Cipher Bureau, they made no provision for acquiring traffic. During the war, Washington imposed censorship on all international communications, and copies of all foreign diplomatic cables entering or leaving the country had been automatically provided to MI-8 by the censorship authorities. To monitor the relatively few messages then transmitted by radio, in 1918 the army established an intercept station at Houlton, Maine, and deployed, mainly along the Mexican border, several so-called mobile tractor units. After the war, however, these sources of raw traffic dried up. Cable censorship ended in 1919, and the intercept facility in Maine closed the following year. The mobile units were neglected and fell into disuse.

Initially the Cipher Bureau relied for its traffic on informal understandings with private cable companies in Washington and New York that voluntarily passed to Yardley's office copies of cables sent and received by foreign diplomatic and consular missions. This relationship began to un-ravel in 1921, in large part because the companies worried about the legal ramifications of continued collaboration. The United States was a signa-tory of the International Radio Telegraph Convention of 1912, which pro-hibited disclosure of the contents of a cablegram to anyone other than the person to whom the message was addressed. Although the strict letter of the treaty may have allowed an exception for "competent authority," the cable companies were not inclined to expose themselves, especially in the absence of any clear and present threat to the national security. Yardley's principal source of traffic began to dry up as one company after another declined to cooperate further with the Cipher Bureau. By January 1923, the flow of cable messages had declined to a trickle, and to fill their day the cryptanalysts were reduced to studying Japanese messages from the First World War. By the fall of 1924, the problem was so serious that months might pass without the bureau receiving a single message. The Army Sig-nal Corps made an effort to alleviate the problem by organizing radio in-tercept stations at Fort Sam Houston, Texas, and the Presidio at San Fran-cisco, California, but these stations operated only intermittently and were hampered by poor equipment and inexperienced personnel.

In all of 1926 the Cipher Bureau received only eleven radio inter-cepts, and cryptanalytic work in the New York offices came to a standstill. The situation improved the next year when the army delivered to Yardley 428 messages, 150 of which the codebreakers decrypted and circulated in the bulletin. Even in these "improved" circumstances, the bureau was sending to Washington only two or three translations a week, all of them Japanese. This output seems especially pathetic when compared with the production of foreign services. Less fastidious about privacy rights, Euro-pean governments allowed their cryptanalytic agencies to obtain cable-grams from postal and cable authorities and to establish networks of inter-cept stations to collect radio messages. More aggressive collection paid off in solutions. In 1927, for example, the cryptanalytic service of the German war ministry distributed, on the average, twenty-eight translations a week, ten times the weekly total of Yardley's Cipher Bureau. In Britain the Gov-ernment Code and Cypher School averaged sixty-nine translations a week throughout the 1920s.[17]

As traffic dried up, so did funds. Throughout American history, the peacetime military has always had to struggle to extract money from a parsimonious Congress, and the Roaring Twenties were no different. Mili-tary preparedness bored the handful of civilians who thought about it. In the years immediately after the "war to end all wars," the country expected to return to its prewar posture of noninvolvement in world affairs and the modest military establishments that complemented that posture. The focus was on controlling military expenditures and arms races, and the high-profile disarmament conferences in Washington (1921) and Geneva (1926) were politically popular in the United States in large part because they spoke to both the hearts and the wallets of Americans. The army's MID saw its contingency funds, the source of the Cipher Bureau's funding, cut from $2.5 million in 1919 to $150,000 in 1923.[18] In such an environment even a productive Cipher Bureau would have been hard-pressed to defend its budget against pressures for economy; a bureau whose output had declined to a handful of translations every month was defenseless. By the summer of 1923, at a time when Britain's GCCS employed ninety-four men and women, twenty-four of them codebreakers, the Black Chamber's budget had been cut to $35,000 (68 percent of its appropriation in 1920) and the staff reduced to seven, including Yardley.[19] In 1925 the budget was $25,000, the staff was down to six, and Yardley had moved his operation to cheaper premises in two large rooms in an office building on Vanderbilt Avenue.[20]

By 1928 the American Black Chamber was moribund; the next year it was dead. If a scarcity of messages and money seriously weakened Yardley's enterprise, a surfeit of morality finally killed it off. In March 1929 Herbert Hoover moved into the White House as the thirty-first president of the United States. Next door to the presidential mansion, Henry Stimson occupied the office of the secretary of state in the ornate pile known as the Old State, Navy, War Building. The new secretary of state knew nothing about the Cipher Bureau, and the officials in the department who did refrained from informing him for several weeks. Perhaps they were anxious about his reaction; perhaps, given the somnolent state of the Cipher Bureau, they had no translations to show him.

In May, Joseph Cotton, the undersecretary of state whose office received the decrypts from New York, informed Stimson that the department was subsidizing a codebreaking organization. The secretary of state was appalled by the news. An upright man who believed that relations between states should be governed by the same courtesy and mutual respect that governed relations between individuals, Stimson thought it was unethical for his government to read secretly the messages of foreign ambassadors, who were, after all, guests of the United States. He also believed that it was inappropriate for the State Department to engage in covert intelligence activities of any sort. If such activities were necessary, they should be left to the War Department. Stimson promptly ordered his undersecretary to discontinue subsidies to the Cipher Bureau.[21] Since the State Department was by then covering almost all of the bureau's expenses, Stimson's decision was the final blow. The American Black Chamber ceased operations in 1929.

The army could have saved the American Black Chamber, but it chose not to. Even before the State Department withdrew its financial support from the bureau, the army had decided to abandon the Cipher Bureau. By the first week in April 1929, fully a month before Stimson learned of Yardley's organization, MID, the War Plans Division, and the Signal Corps had agreed on a plan to consolidate the army's code compilation and code solution activities in a new Signal Corps unit, the Signal Intelligence Service (SIS).[22] Until then, these programs had been divided between the Signal Corps in Washington and the Cipher Bureau in New York. The new unit would have sections devoted to code and cipher compilation, code and cipher solution, radio intercept, and secret inks. Aside from the preparation of new cryptosystems for the army, the emphasis was to be on training rather than operations. Army authorities, perhaps recalling the scramble to train personnel for radio intelligence work in 1917 and the professional embarrassment of turning to civilians for assistance, were adamant that the primary function of SIS was to prepare personnel in cryptanalysis and radio intercept, so that in the event of a military emergency the army would have a pool of specialists ready for service. In his directive establishing SIS, the adjutant general was explicit concerning the new organization's responsibilities in the area of cryptanalysis: "In time of war the solution of all secret or disguised enemy messages or other documents that may be intercepted by the Army, or forwarded by other agencies to the Army for solution; and in peace time the necessary research work, and the organization and training of personnel to render this service capable of immediate operation in time of war." Should anyone remain uncertain about the section's mission, the adjutant general reiterated: "The ultimate peacetime objective of this activity [solution] is the training of sufficient personnel to the end that they will be expert in solving enemy code and cipher messages in war."[23] Signal Corps officers understood that cryptanalysts and radio intercept operators would best train by collecting and studying real encrypted messages, and these efforts might well turn up information of interest to military intelligence. But such information was regarded as "a by-product of the training work and not as the function of the Signal Communication [*sic*] Service in peacetime."[24]

There can be no doubt that despite pressure to economize and the moral fastidiousness of the secretary of state, the army in 1929 wanted a cryptanalytic service. It just didn't want the one it had in New York. MID agreed to pay the salaries of the remaining Cipher Bureau staff until 1 November 1929, but the army did not expect to absorb any of them into SIS. Herbert Yardley was offered a position at a salary substantially below that he enjoyed in New York, with the expectation that the invitation would be declined. It was. If the other employees were offered similar deals, none accepted. The army preferred to "reorganize from the very bottom, with no entanglements from the past."[25] Ostensibly, the army wanted to start fresh because the Cipher Bureau had always been a purely operational service, and its staff was unsuited for the training mission of SIS. One cannot escape the impression, however, that senior officers had lost confidence in the Cipher Bureau in general and its director in particular.

In the first two years of the Cipher Bureau's existence, Yardley received several letters of commendation from the War Department for his work, but there were no commendations after the spring of 1921. General Marlborough Churchill, the director of military intelligence who had sponsored the idea of a peacetime cryptanalytic service and served as Yardley's patron, was long gone, as were many of the officers who were aware of the wartime contributions of radio intelligence. In 1929 few officers were sufficiently knowledgeable about radio intelligence to understand the constraints under which the Cipher Bureau labored. All they knew was that the bureau produced only diplomatic translations, and not many of those. How was Yardley's organization serving the interests and needs of the War Department?

As production of even diplomatic translations fell off after the Washington Conference, army officers may well have wondered what those civilians up in New York were doing with their time. There were rumors that, in between the occasional decryptions, Yardley speculated in real estate and advised businesses on commercial codes. Since Yardley received a salary twice as large as that of the next most senior bureau employee and had lived, at least for a time, in the townhouse occupied by his organization, there was more than a little suspicion that the Cipher Bureau had become a sinecure for its increasingly disinterested director. In the end the army decided that its cryptologic activities needed to be reorganized and redirected and that Herbert Yardley was not the man for the job. The army had someone else in mind.

A slim, dapper individual who took snuff and favored bow ties and two-tone shoes, William Friedman wanted to be a geneticist but instead became the world's most famous cryptologist. The first step along the road to fame occurred in 1915 when George Fabyan, the successful business-man who sponsored the Riverbank Laboratories, a private research insti-tute on his Illinois estate, asked the chair of the genetics department at Cornell University to recommend someone to establish a genetics re-search program at Riverbank. The professor recommended Friedman, who was pursuing a graduate degree in the department. The young gradu-ate student visited Riverbank and, after touring the facilities, admiring the vegetarian bears, and discussing his interests with Fabyan in the main house where all the furniture hung from the ceiling on chains, left with a job. When, in September 1915, Friedman arrived to begin work, he found that his boss, never one for halfway measures, had converted the estate's old windmill into a bachelor apartment for his new employee and had con-structed and furnished a complete genetics laboratory, along with green-houses and other facilities. Surrounded by the latest equipment and sup-ported by an eccentric millionaire, the erstwhile graduate student was left to pursue his own research program without regard for practical or com-mercial applications.[26]

The new director of the genetics program had hardly begun his work when he found his interest drawn to the activities of Riverbank's cipher department, or at least to the activities of Elizebeth Smith, a banker's daughter from Indiana who had been recruited by Fabyan from Chicago's Newberry Library to join the team searching Shakespeare's plays for Baconian ciphers. Soon Friedman was as fascinated by the work of the de-partment as he was by its staff. Having convinced Fabyan to entrust the daily work of the genetics program to a research assistant, he embarked on an intensive study of cryptography under the welcome tutelage of Elizebeth Smith. Friedman had found his métier and his future wife. When, at the outbreak of war in April 1917, Fabyan offered the services of his cipher program to the U.S. government, he made Friedman director of the expanded program. Friedman directed a staff of more than twenty-five in analyzing encrypted messages submitted by various government agen-cies, and he personally solved the messages in the famous Hindu conspir-acy case. He also prepared the syllabus for the cryptologic training course established at Riverbank for army officers, wrote the course manuals, delivered most of the lectures, and supervised the exercises. In June 1918 he accepted a commission as a lieutenant in the army and went to the head-quarters of the American Expeditionary Force to join the small team of officers working on German military ciphers.

After the armistice and his return to civilian life, Friedman considered his options. George Fabyan wanted him and Elizebeth back at Riverbank, and he promised higher salaries and complete freedom to prove or disprove the theory of Baconian ciphers in Shakespeare. The Friedmans returned to Riverbank in April 1919, but within a month William was corresponding with Herbert Yardley, whom he had probably met in France, about joining the postwar Cipher Bureau. Perhaps he had reservations about Riverbank, or maybe he preferred working in the practical world of government cryptanalysis to chasing phantom ciphers through the lines of *Love's Labour's Lost*. For whatever reason Friedman, in July 1919, accepted Yardley's offer of positions for both him and Elizebeth and agreed to report to New York on 1 August.[27] Something or someone intervened, however, to spoil this plan. In mid-August the Friedmans were still in Illinois, and a clearly irritated Yardley was moved to complain:

> Whether you should stay at Riverbank or come to New York is a question for you to decide, but I do feel that I have put off as long as I reasonably can the selection of someone to do the work I have in mind for you and Mrs. Friedman. However, I will, because I promised you that I would, delay action until the first of September. This will have given you two months to definitely make up your mind and I feel sure that you must agree that I have been fair to you.[28]

The decision to remain at Riverbank proved ill considered. George Fabyan was increasingly obsessed by the search for the Baconian ciphers, which he was now sure must be hidden in the Shakespearean plays. Despite his earlier assurances of intellectual freedom, he squelched any effort to disprove his pet theories and compelled an embarrassed Friedman to preside over lantern-slide presentations on the subject.[29] After a year of intellectual servitude, Riverbank's chief cryptologist sought escape in military service. The army, which had previously secured new codes and ciphers by hiring outsiders to produce them as required, had decided to institutionalize the process by establishing in the Signal Corps a special section to construct new cryptosystems. Learning of this plan, Friedman applied for a commission as a signals officer and sat for an interview with a panel of officers. He believed that his experience and earlier service prepared him for a commission as a senior officer, and he was deeply disappointed when the review board refused to grant him a commission higher than lieutenant, the rank he held during the war. Adding insult to injury, the board also found him deficient in certain technical areas, particularly electricity, on which all Signal Corps officers were expected to be conversant.

Too proud to sit for an examination, Friedman withdrew his application.[30] He had been the only candidate for the code compilation position, and the army now had no one with both the appetite and the aptitude for the work. Since the army needed new codes and Friedman needed a new job, both parties had reason to find a compromise. In December 1920 Friedman signed a contract with the army to revise the confidential staff code and to construct three field codes. Upon the completion of this contract, he accepted additional cryptographic work from the War Department. The prospects for long-term employment were sufficiently promising that in the spring of 1921 the Friedmans walked away from George Fabyan and Riverbank Laboratories and settled in Washington. In December of that year the Signal Corps hired Friedman as a full-time cryptographer.[31]

For the next eight years, William Friedman was the U.S. Army's resident expert on codes and ciphers. His grand title, chief cryptanalyst of the Signal Corps and director of the Code and Cipher Compilation Section, Research and Development Division, of the Office of the Chief Signal Officer, belied the modesty of his resources, which consisted of himself, a former prizefighter who provided clerical assistance, and a single room in the Munitions Building, a ramshackle "temporary" structure that had been built during the war. Since Herbert Yardley monopolized codebreaking in his semi-independent fiefdom in New York, Friedman's work was mainly cryptographic rather than cryptanalytic. He prepared new codes and ciphers for the army, tested systems invented by civilians and submitted for adoption by the government, served as technical adviser to the American delegations to international radio and telegraphy conferences, and taught a course on cryptology at the Signal School at Camp Vail, New Jersey. For his classroom text he prepared a monograph, the now-classic *Elements of Cryptanalysis,* that, by labeling various cipher systems and processes (Friedman invented the term "cryptanalysis"), established a taxonomy that is still used today.[32]

Friedman's role in the army's decision to abandon the Cipher Bureau and consolidate all cryptologic activity in the new Signal Intelligence Service remains obscure. He certainly was involved in the discussions, and there is some evidence that he advocated bringing everything "home" to the Signal Corps.[33] He was sufficiently pragmatic to understand the advantage of his own position. After eight years as the Signal Corps' chief cryptologist, he had established his professional credentials and was well known within the Munitions Building. He was the only person around with any experience in teaching cryptology, no small consideration in planning a new service whose mission was primarily training. On a personal level, his industriousness, quiet demeanor, and commitment to the Signal Corps would have impressed officers who nurtured certain reservations about Herbert Yardley. Of course, as a military service SIS would have a military officer as titular commander. No one, however, least of all Friedman, was surprised when he was appointed principal cryptanalyst and effective director of the new organization.

As his first order of business the new director had to find a staff to direct. The Signal Corps expected to employ four "junior cryptanalysts," but suitable candidates were not exactly thick on the ground. The army wanted college graduates who had a strong background in mathematics and the physical sciences and knowledge of French, German, Japanese, or Spanish. Friedman asked the Civil Service Commission to submit the names of individuals who had passed the government examination for "junior mathematician." Among the eight individuals identified by the commission, only two, Frank Rowlett and Bernardo Capo, were deemed suitable for employment with the Signal Intelligence Service. Capo, a native of Puerto Rico who spoke both French and Spanish, seems to have declined an offer of employment. Rowlett, a twenty-four-year-old math teacher at Franklin County High School in the hills of Appalachia, accepted. He had no idea what a "junior cryptanalyst" did, but he knew what a crypt was and guessed that the job had something to do with the military cemeteries the United States had established in Europe for Americans killed in the war. Rowlett's new bride, also a teacher, had a job in a town two hundred miles away from the town where he taught. Since the job with the army paid two thousand dollars a year, more than he and his wife earned together as teachers, they would no longer have to be separated. On April Fools' Day 1930, Rowlett reported for duty at the Munitions Building, the largest building the impressionable country boy had ever visited. He soon discovered that his new job had nothing to do with cemeteries.[34]

With Rowlett's arrival, Friedman was still short three cryptanalysts.

Of the six candidates initially rejected, some had been judged too old and some too weak in math or languages. As Friedman again reviewed the names provided by the Civil Service Commission, his attention returned to two who had almost made the cut the first time around. Solomon Kullback and Abraham Sinkov were friends from Brooklyn, where both had attended Boys' High School. Together they studied mathematics at City College of New York and completed master's degrees in that discipline at Columbia University. Both were teaching mathematics in New York City schools when Sinkov showed his friend an announcement for an examination for government mathematician. Since both were more interested in "doing math" than in "teaching it to kids who aren't interested in learning anything," the two sat for the test and did very well. While there had been no question about their competence in mathematics, the Signal Corps had had reservations about their language abilities. Sinkov had studied French only in high school, and his competency was judged "rather rudimentary." Kullback's background included some Spanish in high school, but the Signal Corps expected its first choice, Bernardo Capo, to cover this language, and preferred someone who knew Japanese. Capo, however, proved unavailable, and Friedman had neither the time nor the appetite to ask the Civil Service Commission to produce additional candidates. He decided to take a chance on the two friends from New York. On 10 April 1930 Abraham Sinkov reported to the Munitions Building. Eleven days later, Solomon Kullback arrived.[35]

Three of the four positions for junior cryptanalysts were filled, but the last remained vacant because the Civil Service Commission could not produce a mathematician who was also qualified in Japanese, the last of the languages that required coverage. Friedman was about to abandon the search when opportunity walked through the door. Having heard from the Civil Service Commission that the Signal Corps was looking for a Japanese linguist, Congressman Joseph Shaffer of Virginia asked the chief signal officer to interview his nephew, John Hurt, a high school language instructor from rural Virginia. Unwilling to alienate a member of the Congress that voted the War Department's appropriation each year, the chief signal officer sent the young man to William Friedman's office. As a gesture of personal courtesy and political expediency, the civilian director of SIS agreed to interview the nephew and to have a Japanese-speaking officer from military intelligence test his language competency.

The interview went well; the test went even better. As a boy Hurt had picked up bits of Japanese from a neighbor, a former missionary in the Far

East. While a student at the University of Virginia, he had extended his knowledge of the language when he shared a room with a student from Japan. A natural linguist, Hurt was proficient in French and German as well as Japanese. The intelligence officer admitted to Friedman that outside of Japan he had never encountered anyone with such a facility for the Japanese language. John Hurt's mathematical skills, however, did not measure up to his linguistic abilities; in fact, he had failed to graduate from both William and Mary College and the University of Virginia because he could not complete the math requirements. Fortunately, Friedman already had three mathematicians; what he needed was a Japanese linguist. Hurt accepted Friedman's offer of a position and joined Solomon Kullback, Frank Rowlett, and Abraham Sinkov on 13 May.[36]

While preoccupied with the search for potential codebreakers, Friedman did not neglect the administrative side of his operation. Even before Rowlett's arrival, he had hired Louise Newkirk Nelson, a stenographer from the Post Office Department, as "cryptographic clerk" and personal assistant. The former prizefighter, who had been a general dogsbody when Friedman represented the entire cryptologic capability of the Signal Corps, was fired for malfeasance. In his place Friedman employed Lawrence Clark, a nineteen-year-old student at George Washington University who had been working for the parks department of the city of Washington.

The War Department had created SIS to prepare new codes to protect the army's secret communications and train personnel in the arcane skills of cryptanalysis and radio direction finding. As he watched his staff settle into Room 3406 of the Munitions Building, Friedman might have been forgiven for wondering if the recruits—four high school teachers, a stenographer, and a gardener—were up to a task whose demands and pitfalls were all familiar to him, if to no one else. Friedman, however, was not one to hesitate in the face of a challenge. It was time to begin.

Chapter Two

Launching a Service

In the summer of 1930 the United States had a new signals intelligence service, but it would be some time before it had any signals intelligence. Whatever ambitions William Friedman nurtured for his fledgling service, its ability to monitor and penetrate the secret communications of foreign governments was constrained by the inexperience of its personnel, the insufficiency of its raw material, and the indifference of its patrons.

Solomon Kullback, Frank Rowlett, and Abraham Sinkov had qualified for government service as mathematicians, and John Hurt was a natural linguist, but, as Rowlett would later recall, "We didn't know anything about cryptanalysis."[1] This was a worrisome deficiency in a cryptanalytic service. Friedman intended to remedy the situation by placing his recruits on a regimen of formal instruction and on-the-job training. Since there were hardly a half dozen professional cryptologists in the entire country and no programs for training more, Friedman (who believed that cryptologic proficiency required a minimum of two years of training) had to rely on his own resources.

Friedman determined the syllabus, delivered the lectures, and wrote the texts for his one-room schoolhouse in cryptology. During his tenure at the Riverbank Laboratories, Friedman had published several monographs on the solution of codes and ciphers. After joining the War Department in 1920, he published *Elements of Cryptanalysis* (1923), a training pamphlet for use in the course in cryptology offered to reserve officers by the Army Extension Program. *Elementary Military Cryptography* (1930) and *Advanced Military Cryptography* (1931) were prepared for a more specialized audience. Along with Parker Hitt's *Manual for the Solution of Military Ciphers* (1916) and reprints of certain classic texts in cryptology, such as Friedrich Kasiski's *Die Geheimschriften und die Dechiffrir-kunst* (1863), these

publications served as textbooks for the novice codebreakers as they began studying their new craft.[2]

The curriculum was an expanded version of the short courses Friedman had occasionally offered at the Signal School in the twenties. The
early focus was cryptography, the various methods of encoding and enci-
phering messages, but rather quickly the students moved into cryptanalysis, the solution of encrypted messages. Friedman devised various
cryptanalytic problems and, dividing his small group into two teams, Hurt/
Rowlett and Kullback/Sinkov, set them to competing over their solution.
They began with simple substitution ciphers and then moved to more difficult polyalphabetic and transposition systems. To enhance the challenge
of the more advanced problems and to duplicate the conditions inside a
working cryptanalytic office where codebreakers often had only a handful
of messages to study, Friedman distributed just a few sample cryptograms
each day. The students progressed to the study of cipher devices such as
the U.S. Army's M-94, an instrument invented by Thomas Jefferson. The
syllabus concluded with a survey of some of the new cipher machines that
promised to revolutionize a field that for two thousand years had relied
on hand labor. Sample machines were purchased in Europe by American
military attachés, while inventors hoping for a lucrative contract from the
U.S. government provided others. Friedman's young staff analyzed the design and operation of such machines as the Kryha and Hagelin. They also
studied the commercial model of the Enigma machine, little imagining
that, in a more sophisticated version, this instrument would return to
haunt them in the future. A machine invented in 1919 by Arvid Gerhard
Damm, a colorful Swede who managed textile mills and devoted his spare
time to chasing circus equestriennes and designing mechanical furniture, malfunctioned so frequently that the group referred to it as "that
Damm machine." At one point the neophytes saved the State Department
from serious embarrassment by demonstrating the weakness of a cipher
machine offered to the department by Parker Hitt, until his retirement
in 1918 the army's leading expert in cryptology. On another occasion
Friedman accepted a challenge from "a group of technical men associated
with the motion picture industry in California" to test the security of a
cipher machine they had developed at the then by no means modest cost
of ten thousand dollars. Within three hours his junior codebreakers solved
two test messages enciphered by the machine, thereby sending the "technical men" back to their drawing boards and their banks.[3]

Understanding that no one learned to swim by reading descriptions of the breaststroke and inspecting pools, Friedman seized every opportunity to get his students wet in the real world of practical cryptanalysis. Within months of their appointment, he threw them into the deep end of the pool. He gave them some two thousand encrypted telegrams subpoenaed from Amtorg, the Russian trade office in New York, as part of a congressional investigation into communist propaganda in the United States. Congress suspected that the messages contained evidence of subversive activities. At the time, Russian ciphers were among the most sophisticated in the world, and the novice codebreakers were hopelessly out of their depth. After two months of effort they had read not a word of the messages, but the exercise allowed them to apply their lessons to a cryptanalytic problem whose solution could not be found in the back of a textbook.[4]

More rewarding were a collection of messages contributed by the Coast Guard. During the Prohibition era the Coast Guard patrolled American coastal waters to intercept vessels seeking to smuggle contraband liquor into the United States. To evade police surveillance, these rumrunners adopted a variety of stratagems, including the use of codes and ciphers in their ship-to-shore communications. In 1924 the Coast Guard began intercepting this radio traffic and established a small cryptanalytic unit to solve the rumrunners' ciphers. Friedman convinced the Coast Guard to share these encrypted messages with his office, an arrangement undoubtedly facilitated by the fact that the Coast Guard's chief cryptanalyst was Elizebeth Friedman, William Friedman's wife and an accomplished codebreaker in her own right. Since the smugglers used a variety of cryptosystems, ranging from simple substitution ciphers to sophisticated transpositions, their messages provided the War Department's junior cryptanalysts an instructive exercise.[5] At first the messages came from the files of intercepts already cracked by Elizebeth Friedman's competent unit, and Rowlett and company merely checked their own solutions against those of the Coast Guard. As their ability and confidence increased, the students were allowed to work with more current traffic, as yet unsolved, and they experienced the excitement of solving their first "real" messages.

Opportunities for practice sometimes appeared from unexpected sources. Because of his reputation as the country's leading cryptologist, Friedman received inquiries and requests for assistance from various government agencies. The State and War Departments asked SIS to test cryptosystems offered for sale to the government by independent inventors and entrepreneurs, and Friedman passed these requests to his young assistants to hone their skills. Law enforcement agencies often submitted cryptograms encountered in the course of criminal investigations. The solution of one such message led to the arrest of a ring of counterfeiters by the Secret Service; another solution enabled prison officials to foil an escape. Once the group cracked an enciphered note that had been enclosed with a bomb mailed to Senator Huey Long, a colorful, rabble-rousing politician from Louisiana.[6]

One message became enshrined in SIS lore. While censoring inmates' mail, prison officials in Ohio intercepted a letter addressed to a private residence and composed in some form of secret writing. Suspecting the worst but unable to penetrate the strange symbols on the page, the authorities forwarded the letter to Washington, where it eventually landed on Friedman's desk. As was his custom in such matters, Friedman asked his four assistants to try their hand at breaking the cipher. Kullback, Rowlett, and Sinkov eagerly gathered their pencils and graph paper, and with no small amount of seriousness began the frequency counts and statistical tests that were the tools of cryptanalysis. Only John Hurt hung back. Among the original quartet hired by Friedman, Hurt was the only one who had not qualified as a mathematician; indeed, he often exhibited an alarming incapacity to penetrate the mysteries of the multiplication tables. Although he endured Friedman's course on basic cryptology, he did not participate in the more advanced courses, realizing that his contribution to the work of SIS would be as a linguist and translator.[7] Consequently, Hurt did not take a seat with the others at the large table that served as a common work space in the small office. He walked about, providing encouragement, fetching materials, and occasionally glancing over the shoulders of his earnest colleagues as they beavered away on the mysterious letter. At one point he lingered behind Kullback's chair, his attention drawn for several minutes to some feature of the document. Then, without introduction, he pointed to the first characters on the page and casually intoned, "Dearest sweetheart Sarah." To the astonishment of everyone, Hurt had noticed the pattern of a monoalphabetic cipher.[8] His intuitive solution chagrined his colleagues who had been too engrossed in assembling the apparatus of scientific cryptanalysis to detect the simplest of all ciphers.[9]

Friedman's tutorial responsibilities were not limited to his four civilian students. Resources did not permit the Signal Corps to train and retain a standing cadre of specialists in cryptology. Nor, in an emergency, could the Corps expect to find in civilian life enough experts in codebreaking to meet the needs of the army. The handful of individuals knowledgeable in this arcane field were already working for the navy, the Coast Guard, or, in Friedman's case, the Army. To deal with this problem, the Signal Corps conducted courses in cryptology through the army extension program. Through home study, interested individuals, mainly reserve officers with an aptitude for the subject, gained at least an elementary knowledge of cryptanalysis and provided a pool from which the army could draw in an emergency. Additionally, the Signal School at Fort Monmouth, New Jersey, offered regular officers a two-week course in radio intelligence. In 1929 this course had been opened to signal reserve and military intelligence reserve officers on their annual two-week tour of active duty. The Signal Corps realized, however, that a longer, more comprehensive course of study was required to prepare a competent signal intelligence specialist. In 1930 the adjutant general had issued a directive creating a Signal Intelligence School within the new Signal Intelligence Service and authorizing the detail of one regular Signal Corps officer to that school for a full year's instruction in all aspects of radio intelligence.[10]

In September 1931, First Lieutenant Mark Rhoads reported to SIS to begin an assignment as the sole student in the new school. His only instructor was William Friedman, who offered the junior officer the same curriculum as that studied by his four civilians, with the addition of components dealing with radio direction finding and secret inks. Lieutenant Rhoads was an apt student, but Friedman believed that even twelve months of study was insufficient to train adequately a cryptologist. By the completion of the planned program, he had convinced the Signal Corps to expand the curriculum to two years. Rhoads continued for a second year, and another Signal Corps officer, First Lieutenant W. Preston Corderman, arrived as a first-year student in a school whose student body had now doubled to two. Thereafter, a new officer-student matriculated each year.

The expanded program devoted seven months to the study of cipher problems, six months to code problems, four months to cipher machines, three and a half months to code construction, and two weeks to secret inks. The students inspected the Coast Guard radio monitoring station at Fort Hunt, Virginia, and visited the accounting sections of various government agencies to observe the use of tabulating machines. The students were also encouraged to study foreign languages. For the first two years, Friedman provided all the instruction. After his graduation, Lieutenant Corderman remained to teach in the school, and thereafter all instruction was provided by recent graduates, although former schoolteachers Abraham Sinkov and Solomon Kullback occasionally lectured on mathematical and statistical applications in cryptanalysis.[11]

By the end of 1932, Friedman's four civilians had acquired, through study and practice, a fairly sophisticated understanding of the principles of cryptanalysis. The Signal Intelligence School was about to produce the first of what, with luck and continued support, would prove to be a steady stream of specialized radio intelligence officers. It was the moment for which Friedman had planned and prepared. SIS was poised to become an operational intelligence unit, and its cryptanalysts could begin to solve and translate the intercepted messages of foreign governments. Unfortunately, nobody noticed. Aside from the Justice Department, which might send over the rare secret message acquired during a criminal investigation, no agency of the U.S. government seemed to have the slightest use for the hard-earned skills of Friedman's cryptanalysts. They were craftsmen without customers.

It is unlikely that President Herbert Hoover was even aware of the Signal Intelligence Service, and his acquiescence in the closure of Yardley's Black Chamber in 1929 suggests that he would have been ambivalent, at best, about the new unit. The birth and early years of SIS coincided with the onset of financial collapse and economic depression in the United States, and Hoover would have had little time for diplomatic decrypts as the worsening economic crisis relegated foreign affairs to the margins of White House concerns. Secretary of State Henry Stimson, the man directly responsible for closing the Black Chamber, remained steadfast in opposing a practice he condemned as unethical and ungentlemanly. There would be no market for decrypts at the State Department so long as he was secretary. Indeed, there would be little market even afterward, since Stimson's distaste for radio intelligence permeated an organization that preferred to depend for its information upon the traditional channels of embassy reporting. This attitude persisted, at least for a time, during the early tenure of Stimson's successor, Cordell Hull, who in 1933 had been appointed secretary of state by the newly elected president, Franklin Roosevelt. In the spring of 1933, when the War Department tentatively raised the question of radio intelligence with the State Department, the diplomats flatly rejected any plans to intercept and read foreign diplomatic traffic.[12]

Since SIS was an army unit, more might have been expected of the War Department. Why go to the trouble and expense of establishing such

a unit if there is no intention of using it? The army, however, was as paro-
chial and resistant to change as any other bureaucracy, and, with only a
few exceptions, officers failed to discern the intelligence potential of the
small bureau tucked away in the recesses of the Signal Corps. Various factors contributed to this myopia. Friedman and his team were civilians in
an institution in which uniform and rank determined status and influence.
Furthermore, Yardley's Black Chamber and its predecessor, MI-8, had
focused largely on diplomatic rather than military cryptanalysis, an emphasis not likely to engage the interest of military officers. The Signal Intelligence Service also represented innovation in a service noted for conservatism and dominated by traditionalists. The latter problem is evident
in the annual report of the Signal Corps for 1931, in which the status of the
army's carrier pigeons received as much attention as the progress of the
new SIS. As late as 1939, the year German panzer armies smashed both
Poland and traditional theories of war, the U.S. Army still expected its cav-
alry squadrons to play a central role in communications intelligence by
raiding behind enemy lines to seize telegraph stations and tap telegraph
lines, a tactic that had worked well in the American Civil War.[13]

Whatever Friedman's intentions, the army established SIS not as an
intelligence agency but as a training cadre and an office for the compilation of military codes. Code and cipher solution was a distinctly secondary
concern, and one that in peacetime had only limited application. The directive establishing the service was quite explicit: "The ultimate peacetime objective of this activity [solution] is the training of sufficient personnel to the end that they will be expert in solving enemy code and cipher
messages in war."[14] There was no sense that the army might benefit in
peacetime from information extracted from decrypted foreign messages.
The attitude of the military intelligence bureau (G-2) was especially pa-
tronizing. This bureau exhibited little interest in radio intelligence. When
the commander of the Eighth Corps Area (Fort Sam Houston, Texas) forwarded to Washington Mexican messages intercepted by his signalmen,
G-2 returned the items and loftily commented, "There seems no need at
the present time for you to make interceptions in your Corps Area especially for the War Department. . . . If at any time the War Department de-
sires that special information be obtained by radio interception within
your Corps Area, you will be notified."[15] This attitude was so pervasive
that it infected the Signal Corps and the very leadership of the Signal Intelligence Service. At the end of 1931 the military head of SIS, Major D. M.
Crawford, confidently assured the chief signal officer that "the War De-

partment has no responsibility whatever for interception or solution of diplomatic codes."[16]

Given the attitudes and expectations of senior officers, the young cryptanalysts found little opportunity to exercise their solution skills. Most of their time was devoted to compiling new cryptosystems to protect the confidential communications of the army. No one appreciated the importance of such work more than Friedman, but he complained that the demands of code and cipher compilation left no time for the study and solution of foreign codes. The progress reports that he regularly submitted to his superiors were little more than updates on the status of particular compilation projects: printer's galleys for Army Field Code Number 2 have been returned by the Government Printing Office for proofreading; construction of Army Field Code Number 3 has begun; the supplement to Military Intelligence Code Number 5 has been completed, and SIS requests permission for its printing. At one point, Friedman and his small staff had six different codes in various stages of development.[17]

The work was tedious and time-consuming, although Friedman tried to turn the situation to advantage by having his team use their skills to test the security of the codes they were developing for the army. Machine processing was still in its infancy at the War Department, and compilation often required the printing and shuffling by hand of tens of thousands of cards. Two-part codes were especially tiresome.[18] The staff devised unorthodox procedures to expedite the work and relieve the tedium. To compile a fifty-thousand-group two-part code, Kullback, Rowlett, and Sinkov wrote all the plain-language meanings on one set of cards and all the code groups on a second set. They then took the second set into the vault, where they turned on the fans and proceeded to toss handfuls of cards into the air until they stood ankle deep in paper. The trio then wandered about the room, retrieving cards at random and assigning values to the plaintext items in the sequence in which the cards were retrieved. Unfortunately, a staff major in search of certain secret war plans stored in the vault wandered into the middle of this operation. Retreating in the face of a cyclone of file cards, the major stumbled into Friedman, who quickly explained the rather eccentric behavior of his subordinates. "You mean this is their work?" was the incredulous reaction. The major left the office, mumbling that code-making seemed to have unsettled the minds of certain civilians in the Signal Corps. This imaginative though rather unscientific code compilation procedure was finally abandoned when the janitor responsible for cleaning SIS's rooms reported to his supervisor that cards were unaccountably stuck to the ceiling of the vault.[19]

The demands of training and code compilation limited the solution activity of SIS but did not necessarily prevent it. Friedman could always justify such activity by maintaining that the solution of foreign messages in peacetime was necessary training for solution of such messages in war, and that the insights garnered from the study of foreign cryptosystems could be applied to the perfection of the army's own codes and ciphers. This activity, however, required traffic. Without foreign messages to study, Friedman's aspiring codebreakers would have nothing to distract them but those wretched military codes. Unfortunately, the army had made little provision to supply Friedman's office with any radio or cable traffic, and consequently the newly minted codebreakers had no encrypted messages to solve. Private cable companies had briefly made their foreign message files available to Herbert Yardley in the early years of the Cipher Bureau but had ended the practice for fear of liability should word leak to the public that they were sharing with the government the confidential correspondence of their clients. Their fears had only increased after 1927, when Congress passed the so-called Radio Act, which made it illegal to intercept any radio message without the permission of the sender, or to divulge the contents of a radio communication to anyone other than the addressee. Such restrictions had seriously compromised the work of Yardley's unit, and the failure to secure a reliable source of traffic contributed significantly to the decline and ultimate demise of the Cipher Bureau.[20]

On a theoretical level the army understood that communications intelligence required communications intercept. From its inception the Signal Intelligence Service was responsible for training personnel and developing equipment for the task of intercepting enemy communications in wartime. Toward this end the directive establishing SIS envisioned several intercept stations directly under the chief signal officer, with additional stations under local commanders in the Eighth (Texas) and Ninth (California) Corps Areas and the Hawaiian, Philippine, and Panama Canal Departments.[21] On the practical level, however, the army had taken few steps to implement this directive. In 1931 the Signal Corps began constructing an intercept facility at Battery Cove, Virginia, the site of the remote-controlled receivers that serviced the War Department's message center. The Signal Corps intended to use the facility to test high-speed radio receivers and, incidentally, to collect radio traffic. Operations, however, were retarded by technical and administrative problems. Outside of Washington, initiative was left to the corps area and department commanders. For these generals, radio intercept was an exotic subject that seemed tangential to their main mission and promised only to dissipate further the ener-

gies of their overstretched signal companies. Full-time intercept operations were out of the question, although signal officers could detail temporarily unoccupied radio operators to scan the airwaves for a few hours and
copy whatever transmissions they encountered. The results of such unsystematic and halfhearted efforts were, not surprisingly, negligible.

At first the fledgling SIS was little troubled by the absence of reliable
intercept facilities. During those early months the focus was on education,
and Friedman's untrained recruits could not have done much with raw
traffic even if they had it. By 1932, however, the lack of traffic was more
troublesome. Friedman had devoted two years to handcrafting from rough
material four cryptanalysts who now gave every promise of future achievement. For what purpose had he and his charges labored? He certainly had
not invested two years of emotional, intellectual, and physical energy to
have his pupils apply their hard-won specialist skills to proofreading the
printer's galleys for Army Field Cipher Number 4. For all the bows toward
training and code compilation, Friedman had always prepared for the day
when his staff would decrypt foreign messages. They were, after all, the
Signal *Intelligence* Service, and to produce intelligence he and his staff
needed intercepts. No one in SIS, least of all Friedman, needed reminding
that Yardley's Cipher Bureau had foundered, in part, because it lacked access to the raw traffic necessary to produce results.

The problem with regard to Japanese communications was especially
worrisome. In 1931, after the Mukden Incident, the Japanese army had occupied Manchuria. The following year Japan established the puppet state
of Manchukuo, to which it added territories seized from the Chinese provinces of Jehol and Chahar. This aggression marked the onset of warfare
between China and Japan that would wax and wane for the next fourteen
years. Japan now began to loom larger on the horizon of American war
planners. It also became an object of attention in Room 3406 of the Munitions Building. SIS had very little information about Japanese codes and
ciphers, and practically nothing about the systems used by the imperial
army. It wasn't even sure that the receivers currently available to the Signal Corps could adequately monitor Japanese military radio circuits. Even
if its receivers were satisfactory, the army lacked operators qualified to intercept Japanese communications.

In 1933 the army still had no facilities dedicated to intercepting for-
eign communications. The few intercepts that dribbled into the offices of
SIS were the product of private initiative. In San Francisco, Lieutenant
Colonel Joseph O. Mauborgne, a signal officer attached to the Ninth Corps

Area, set up a receiver in the basement of his quarters. While off duty in the evenings, he searched the airwaves for foreign stations, recording the call letters and frequencies of those he consistently heard and seeking to determine their locations and those of the stations with which they communicated. At a time when the Signal Corps had little experience with radio intercept and none at all with traffic analysis, Mauborgne's effort was pathbreaking. This conscientious officer (who made violins in his spare time and may have been the only career officer in the army to have been educated at the Art Institute of Chicago) also copied and mailed to Washington any traffic that, in his opinion, might interest the Signal Corps or army intelligence. Some of this material, mostly Japanese, found its way to Friedman's office.[22]

Mauborgne's initiative was modest in scope and obviously no substitute for a systematic intercept program. In 1932 the army had taken some tentative steps toward establishing such a program, although here, too, an individual provided the initial push. Captain John Ferriter, a Signal Corps officer in the Philippines Department, had developed an interest in radio intercept and its intelligence potential especially with regard to Japan. In Manila, Ferriter observed that high-frequency Japanese commercial stations were easily copied, but low- and intermediate-frequency transmissions of the sort used by the Japanese army were not readily heard. During a voyage to China in the summer of 1932, the young captain convinced the radio officer of his ship, the USNT *Chaumont,* to let him experiment with monitoring foreign stations, a project he continued during visits to U.S. Army detachments stationed in China under various treaty arrangements with the Chinese government. Upon his return to the Philippines, Ferriter submitted a report outlining the potential for radio intercept against Chinese, Japanese, and Russian military stations, identifying three locations in China (Peking, Chefoo, and Tientsin) as possible sites for intercept facilities and urging the army to establish a school to prepare radio operators for Far Eastern intercept operations.[23]

Ferriter's report received the enthusiastic support of the Philippines Department commander, who immediately forwarded it to Washington. At the War Department, Major Spencer Akin, an assistant to the chief signal officer, also endorsed the report. Akin understood that the young SIS was woefully unprepared to fulfill its mission, and he believed that the army should take steps in peacetime to prepare for any future diplomatic or military crisis, especially one involving Japan. He proposed that the Signal Corps organize, equip, and train a small unit for intercept operations against Japanese military communications and assign this unit to the U.S. Army contingent stationed at Tientsin, China. The Signal Corps accepted Akin's proposal but could convince neither the secretary of war nor the army chief of staff to authorize China-based intercept operations against Japan. A brief message informed the commander of the Philippines Department that "as a matter of basic national policy, the establishment of a high speed recording station with the American Forces in China is not deemed advisable."[24]

The army was not entirely insensitive to the importance of radio intercept. In the fall of 1932 the Signal Corps installed high-speed recording equipment in the Philippines, Panama, and Hawaiian Departments, in the Ninth Corps Area (San Francisco), and at the Signal School at Fort Monmouth, New Jersey. New equipment would prove useless, however, without personnel assigned to its operation. In the departments and corps areas, intercept remained the secondary task of signal companies preoccupied with routine communication duties, but at Fort Monmouth the Signal Corps moved to create a special unit dedicated solely to radio intercept. On 1 October 1933, Lieutenant Mark Rhoads, the first graduate of the Signal Intelligence School, assumed command of the Provisional Radio Intelligence Detachment. The young officer found a largely paper organization attached to the Fifty-first Signal Battalion. The twelve enlisted men nominally assigned to the detachment were not present to salute their new commander, since they were all on other duty. Lieutenant Rhoads managed to convince the battalion commander to allow one man to work full-time on intercept duties, and in the succeeding months he added an operator here or lost an operator there, depending on the vagaries of training and duty schedules. It was an unpromising start, and Rhoads was hard-pressed to establish even the most basic intercept program. In the first ten months of its operation, the Provisional Radio Intelligence Detachment intercepted only 381 foreign radio messages, including 145 Japanese, 63 Russian, 32 Colombian, 28 Brazilian, and 24 French.[25]

The intercept program at Fort Monmouth was a model of purpose and efficiency compared with the situation in the departments and corps areas, where intercept, always a peripheral concern, remained a haphazard affair. In the Philippines, concerned officers took it upon themselves to bring some order and energy to the effort. Undeterred by his failure to establish a monitoring station in China, Captain Ferriter had taken to socializing with officers from the U.S. Navy's Asiatic Fleet in an effort to learn what the navy was doing in the intercept field. In February 1933 Ferriter accompanied the department signals officer, Major Coles, and the department intelligence officer, Major Taylor, to the flagship of the Asiatic Fleet, then moored in Manila harbor, to seek an interview with fleet communications and intelligence officers. The naval officers were rather nonplussed to learn that the army officers, who had appeared unannounced, sought details about the navy's intercept work in the Far East. Captain Ferriter further alarmed his hosts by announcing that he had been studying Japanese communications on his own for some time and hoped to visit the navy's intercept station in Peking to observe its work against Japanese targets. Since the naval station in Peking was a closely held secret, the naval officers decided that the best course of action was to divert their visitors and seek the advice of senior authority. Explaining that only the commander in chief of the Asiatic Fleet could authorize disclosure of information concerning fleet communications and that even he could not do so without consulting the Navy Department in Washington, the naval officers politely but firmly hustled their unwelcome guests off the ship.

Several days later, the assistant fleet communications officer visited the Signal Corps office in Manila to ask Major Coles how he came to know about the navy's intercept work. Surprised at the question, Coles said that the work was common knowledge among army officers in the Philippines. Aghast, the naval officer hurried back to the flagship with the horrible news that the navy's most secret operations were apparently the subject of idle banter in army officer clubs. Worse was to come. In March, the irrepressible Captain Ferriter appeared unannounced at the navy's intercept station in the U.S. Marine compound in Peking. Without a trace of self-consciousness, Ferriter informed a flabbergasted duty officer that he had long been interested in intercept work and, being in town, thought he would drop by to see what the navy was up to. He added confidentially that with the help of an enlisted man in Manila he had been copying Japanese traffic and studying the ciphers that protected the messages. The army captain was clearly eager to talk shop, but before he could begin, the duty officer, unsure whether he was dealing with a spy, a madman, or just another addle-brained army officer, hustled him out the door. The marine promptly informed his commander that one of the navy's most secret facilities seemed to be, along with the Forbidden City, on the itinerary of army personnel touring Peking.

Priority messages were soon passing between Peking and Manila, and between Manila and Washington as the marine commander in Peking complained to the commander, Asiatic Fleet, who, in turn, complained to the Navy Department. The army chief of staff, who demanded to know who this Captain Ferriter was, why he was wandering unsupervised around China, and how he came to be in the army in the first place, ultimately apologized to the chief of naval operations for the irregular behavior of junior officers. He then informed the commander, Philippines Department, in no uncertain terms that all further interservice inquiries were to be handled through formal channels. The affair did not endear signal intelligence enthusiasts to the army's high command. It certainly did not endear Ferriter to anyone, and the good captain subsequently disappears from American sigint history.[26]

Between 1933 and 1936 the army made fitful attempts to establish an intercept service on solid footing, but such efforts were continually undercut by the absence of resources and the ambivalence of army commanders. In the fall of 1934, for example, the commander, Philippines Department, approved the establishment in his command of a monitoring station to cover Far Eastern radio circuits. The Signal Corps promptly dispatched four signal intelligence specialists to the Islands, including Mark Rhoads, the first commander of the Provisional Radio Intelligence Detachment. The chief signal officer assured the Philippines Department that additional specialists would be provided as soon as qualified personnel became available. Once operational, the new station was expected to forward to Washington copies of intercepted foreign traffic. Good intentions, however, foundered on the shoals of practical realities. The Signal Corps could not find additional trained operators to reinforce the small team sent to the Philippines, and could suggest only that the team train local personnel to assist it. The department commander, who assumed that an intercept station would mean an accretion, not a dilution, in his signals personnel, was loath to release radiomen for intercept work. In fact, the commander was inclined to assign the radio intelligence specialists to routine signals work in his undermanned command. Soon after his arrival, Lieutenant Rhoads fell ill and had to be evacuated home. The remaining officer in the team had to divide his attention between radio intercept and the department's general communications. The Signal Corps tried to help by sending out another specialist, Lieutenant W. Preston Corderman, who had been teaching in the Signal Intelligence School, but upon his arrival in the Philippines he was not given any intercept duties by the department signal officer.[27]

The situation was hardly better in other commands. Because of a lack of personnel, there was as late as the spring of 1936 still no formal radio intelligence detachment in the Ninth Corps Area (San Francisco), although three enlisted men had recently been issued a receiver and detailed to monitor Japanese traffic from an abandoned coastal fortification. The Hawaiian Department also lacked a separate radio intelligence detachment. A few men from the regular signal company had recently been detached to establish a station, but no intercept work had yet begun. In the Panama Department (Canal Zone), one operator spent part of each night listening to foreign stations and copying traffic. The intercept effort in the Canal Zone was constrained by the absence of any trained signal intelligence specialists and a shortage of radio operators of any sort. In early 1937 the Eighth Corps Area (Fort Sam Houston, Texas) still had no personnel engaged in radio intercept, although the problem was a result of lack of equipment more than lack of personnel.[28]

William Friedman was not inclined to wait patiently, his cryptanalysts filling their time by proofreading the latest army field cipher, until the army decided to bring some order to its intercept program. If the army could not provide traffic, he would find it elsewhere, and he knew just where to look. One morning, early in their training, Friedman had surprised his civilian apprentices by announcing that he was taking them on a field trip. Curious about their destination but reluctant to challenge their superior's habitual reserve with questions, Kullback, Rowlett, and Sinkov (Hurt was absent that day) followed him out the door of Room 3406. It was a short trip. Walking briskly ahead, Friedman led them down one flight of stairs and along a corridor, halting finally before a steel door marked Room 2742 and protected by a combination lock. From their general knowledge of the Munitions Building, the young men knew that the corridor was the territory of G-2 (military intelligence), but they had no idea who sat behind that massive door and what secrets would be revealed in Room 2742. Friedman consulted a slip of paper that he took from his suit pocket and, stepping close to the lock to obscure the view of his students, twirled the dial left and right. The heavy door swung open to reveal a second door that Friedman unlocked with a key from his chain. Foul air spilled into the corridor from a room whose interior was obscured in shadow. Friedman stepped into the darkness and, by the flickering light of a match, found and pulled the cord for an overhead light. He then threw the switches on two fans, which set off a veritable dust storm in what the apprentices later agreed was the dirtiest room they had ever seen. Turning to his students, who peered into the room from the relative security of the corridor, Friedman motioned them in and, with all the pride of a new homeowner, proclaimed, "Welcome, gentlemen, to the secret archives of the Black Chamber." The trio stood silently, unsure of how to respond. None of them had ever heard of the Black Chamber; at first, they thought their boss was referring to the dingy room in which they were standing.[29]

When Herbert Yardley's Cipher Bureau closed in 1929, its files were shipped to the War Department, where they were stored and largely ignored behind the steel door of Room 2742, Munitions Building. Worksheets, frequency tables, codebooks, and the intercepted diplomatic traffic of a dozen countries were all crammed into battered file cabinets that surrounded a small worktable in the dusty, windowless strong room. Walking among those cabinets, occasionally pulling out a drawer to thumb through a file, Friedman told his rapt audience about Yardley and the Black Chamber; when his story was over, he left them in the room to rummage in the papers. The apprentice cryptanalysts were flabbergasted by what they found: Japanese translations from the Washington Naval Conference, copies of Spanish codebooks, French diplomatic telegrams, commendations from the secretary of state. It was a humid summer day, and the fans did little but blow the dust about, but in their enthusiasm the students noticed neither the sweat dripping from their brows nor the dirt that smeared their white summer suits. When Friedman rejoined them at midday, he could tell from their faces and their excited questions that his field trip had been a success. He treated the trio to lunch at a nearby restaurant and then took them back to his office, where he explained his plans for them.

The plans certainly included the solution of foreign codes and ciphers. To gain access to such materials in the absence of an effective radio intercept organization, Friedman, in 1933, sent his analysts back to Room 2742 and the archive of the Black Chamber. This archive contained the largest collection of foreign messages available to SIS, even though none was more recent than 1929. The bulk of the messages were Japanese, as were most of the solutions, since Yardley had concentrated upon Japan and achieved his most notable successes against Japanese codes and ciphers. Friedman sent his men to study the Japanese material as much because of its availability as for any inherent importance to American intelligence. For several hours each week, John Hurt taught his colleagues the rudiments of the Japanese language. He and Solomon Kullback were assigned the task of organizing the Japanese materials (which were in some disarray) and determining the status of solution work at the time of the Chamber's demise. In order to acquire some background in Japanese cryptography, the whole group studied the messages that had been read by Yardley's unit. They moved on to the study of Japanese messages from the 1920s that had not been solved by the Cipher Bureau and then to the handful of current Japanese messages that dribbled into the War Department. Until late 1933, when the Provisional Radio Intelligence Detachment at Fort Monmouth began to intercept small amounts of traffic, almost all of the latter were collected by the home receiver installed in Lieutenant Colonel Joseph Mauborgne's basement in San Francisco.[30]

Working with these messages, Kullback and Hurt identified a system in which plaintext digraphs and, occasionally, entire words were replaced by two-letter or four-letter code groups. Known as a syllabary, similar systems had been solved by the Cipher Bureau in the twenties. Despite the sensational revelations in Yardley's memoir, *The American Black Chamber,* which in 1931 revealed the bureau's success against Tokyo's secret communications, the Japanese government had not yet completely revised its cryptographic practices, and many systems of a type known to be insecure remained in service. Once the system was identified as a syllabary similar to the versions present in the archives, it was only a matter of hours before Kullback and Hurt solved the code and translated the messages. The Japanese radiograms provided no information of value, but as the first foreign messages decrypted by the Signal Intelligence Service, their symbolic importance was lost on neither William Friedman nor the young cryptanalysts whom he had prepared for that moment.

More successes followed quickly. At the time, the Japanese foreign ministry had in service five cryptosystems of the two- and four-letter type that it used in rotation at intervals of three months. Having solved one, SIS took on the remainder and by 1935 had solved them all. Friedman had trained his disciples well. One by one, Tokyo's diplomatic systems succumbed to the analytical attacks of Kullback, Rowlett, and Sinkov and the linguistic insights of Hurt. By 1938, SIS was reading nine Japanese diplomatic systems, including the one Tokyo relied on for its most secret communications.[31]

In late 1932 Japan's foreign ministry, which had long relied on hand systems, adopted a cipher machine for its high-grade traffic. *The American Black Chamber* had appeared the previous year, but it is unlikely that Herbert Yardley's revelations influenced the foreign ministry's decision. A new cipher machine cannot be summoned into service merely by snapping one's fingers. Time is required for the development, testing, and production of a new machine. Bulky components have to be distributed to diplomatic missions by couriers traveling by steamship. Cipher clerks have to be trained in new procedures. There is a transition period in which the various missions shift over to the new system. The cipher machine that went into service at the end of 1932 was almost certainly the result of a decision made by Japanese foreign ministry officials before they had a chance to read Yardley's memoir.

In March 1933 SIS began to notice Japanese messages that appeared to be enciphered by an unidentified machine. Friedman's team dubbed the new machine RED. At first only a handful of messages were intercepted, although the number increased toward the end of the year as the machine became operational at more posts. SIS began a preliminary study of RED in early 1934 and by the fall of that year had embarked on a serious effort at solution. In November 1934, with advice from the U.S. Navy, which had solved a Japanese naval attaché cipher machine that exhibited similarities to the foreign ministry model, SIS read its first RED message, a notice from the foreign ministry in Tokyo to the Japanese ambassador in Buenos Aires confirming the arrival of a trade official.[32]

Solution of the RED machine provided SIS a privileged perspective on Japanese politics and diplomacy. Many of the decrypted messages concerned routine affairs: a report to Tokyo on a meeting of Japanese consuls in the United States; a circular to Japanese missions in South America concerning the distribution of official press releases; an advisory concerning Japan's interest in attracting the 1940 Olympic Games to Tokyo.[33] Some messages were as dramatic as newspaper headlines. On 12 August 1935, for example, SIS decrypted a RED message to all Japanese embassies: "This morning, while the head of the Division of Military Affairs, Lieutenant General Tetsuzan Nagata, was seated at his desk in the War Office, a lieutenant colonel, whose name is being withheld, rushed in and stabbed him with a sword. Lieutenant General Nagata died soon afterward."[34] A few radiograms were politically portentous. In October 1936 SIS decrypted a RED message from Tokyo to its ambassador in Washington, affirming Japan's intention "to take up the question of joining hands with all those countries who share with us the common opinion toward suppressing communistic activity" and revealing that "the Empire of Japan is arranging for agreements with other countries for the suppression of communism."[35] The next month, Japan joined Germany in the Anti-Comintern Pact.

By early 1936 SIS had been reading Japanese diplomatic correspondence for three years, and with the solution of the RED machine the files of translated messages were growing thicker each day. Aside from affirming the professional pride of the codebreakers, none of this made the slightest difference to anyone. The early cryptanalytic successes of Friedman's team had absolutely no impact on American foreign policy. Of course this was, in part, due to the recent nature and narrow scope of those successes. After his inauguration on 4 March 1933, President Franklin D. Roosevelt necessarily focused on measures to alleviate the social and financial dislocations of the economic depression then ravaging the country. In a White House preoccupied with bank holidays, farm prices, and unemployment, foreign affairs was often a secondary concern, but the new president did not entirely ignore developments abroad. In its first year the Roosevelt administration actively engaged several major diplomatic issues, including the Geneva Disarmament Conference, the London Economic Conference, the Pan American Conference in Montevideo, the recognition of the Soviet Union, and a regime crisis in Cuba. In the next two years the administration had to deal with the London Naval Conference, the Italo-Ethiopian crisis, and the outbreak of the Spanish civil war.[36]

Unfortunately, most of the work of SIS was irrelevant to these issues. In Room 3406 only Japanese ciphers had been studied, and only Japanese messages had been read. There had been no opportunity to study the communications of other governments such as Britain, France, Germany, Italy, the Soviet Union, and the Latin American republics, but these were the very governments with whom American diplomacy was most engaged in the period 1933–1936. Cryptanalysis could tell the White House and the State Department nothing about Moscow's minimal goals during the recognition negotiations, nothing about London's willingness to compromise on the number of light cruisers allowed under a new naval treaty, nothing about Mussolini's possible reaction to economic sanctions after his attack on Ethiopia. Cryptanalysis did not even tell American policy makers anything about the diplomacy of the one country, Japan, whose communications were read. Some Japanese initiatives, such as Tokyo's decision in March 1933 to withdraw from the League of Nations, occurred before SIS had progressed much in the study of Japanese codes. Other initiatives, however, such as Tokyo's denunciation in December 1934 of the Washington Naval Treaty and its negotiating position at the London Naval Conference, may have been picked up by SIS, but they were not communicated to American policy makers.

As late as 1936, not a single diplomatic message decrypted and translated by SIS had ever gone to the White House. Decrypts were not circulated to the State Department or within the War Department; indeed, no one in the former agency and only a handful in the latter even knew what Friedman's unit was doing. Codebreaking may have provided a rare insight into Japanese foreign policy, but it was an insight granted only to the six men and one woman who then constituted the Signal Intelligence Service. This curious situation reflected the ambivalence with which the army still viewed its radio intelligence service. As noted earlier, the army thought of that service as primarily a code compilation office and a cadre for the training of cryptologists for wartime. It saw little use for peacetime interception and solution of foreign communications, and it wasn't even sure that such activity was legal.

Friedman had been able to convince the Signal Corps that the solution of foreign codes and ciphers was a necessary component of the training program, but he had not been able to overcome its concern for the consequences should word of such illegal activity leak out. Preferring to distance himself from possible trouble, the chief signal officer at first made it clear that Friedman need not send him any decrypts, and he flatly prohibited the distribution of decrypts to anyone else. Gradually, however, as the months passed without a scandal and the wholesale purge of Signal Corps officers, professional interest overcame professional timidity, and resistance slackened slightly. By the end of 1934, Friedman was occasionally showing an intercept to the chief signal officer, who, in turn, might share it with the assistant chief of staff, G-2 (intelligence). In January 1935 Friedman systematized the reporting process by creating the *Bulletin,* a compilation of diplomatic translations. The first message in this series was dated 28 January 1935.[37] Still, dissemination rarely went beyond the chief signal officer and never beyond G-2. Since all the decrypts concerned diplomatic affairs, there seemed no need to circulate them within the War Department. Distribution to the State Department, while certainly more appropriate, was simply too risky given its past objections to radio intelligence and the questionable legality of radio interception.[38]

Although its impact was still limited, by 1936 SIS was a functioning, professional cryptanalytic service. That year, however, it faced an unexpected challenge to its institutional role. The original plans for a radio intelligence service envisioned the assignment of civilian cryptanalysts to the military departments in Hawaii, Panama, and the Philippines. Nothing came of those plans, in part because of the lack of trained personnel, and in part because department commanders were so indifferent to signals intelligence as to preclude even serious support for radio interception, let alone cryptanalysis of the results of such interception. In the spring of 1936, however, the Signal Corps learned that the military intelligence officer in Panama had hired a local amateur codebreaker to examine encrypted radio messages intercepted in that department. At the Washington headquarters of the Signal Corps, this initiative by another branch of the army was considered impudent and a clear infringement on the prerogatives of the chief signal officer. Fearing the decentralization (and loss of control) of signal intelligence activities that would result if every department or corps area intelligence officer decided to hire his own cryptanalyst, William Friedman offered to send one of his young assistants to Panama to perform any necessary cryptanalysis. He also may have hoped through such cooperation to encourage support for the Signal Intelligence Service among the influential department commanders. In July 1936 Abraham Sinkov was assigned to Panama, and the following spring Solomon Kullback was sent to Hawaii. Both were instructed to perform whatever duties the local commanders assigned them. Friedman apparently expected such duties to be light, for he planned to have both Sinkov and Kullback decrypt Japanese messages intercepted by the local monitoring stations.

The radio intelligence unit in the Panama Canal Zone (Monitoring Station 4) tried to intercept first Japan's diplomatic traffic to and from Central and South America and, second, the diplomatic communications of Latin American governments. Friedman initially expected Sinkov to work Japanese traffic on site, and toward that end he planned to forward to Panama relevant cryptographic materials. The SIS representative would also attempt to solve Latin American diplomatic messages, although he could expect little help, since Washington had done no work against the codes and ciphers of the Latin republics. Friedman soon abandoned the plan to attack Japanese traffic in Panama, deciding that the exchange of cryptanalytic materials between Washington and Panama risked compromising the security of operations that remained a closely guarded secret. He was probably encouraged in his decision by the unsettling news that the signal officer in Panama routinely submitted to the department commander Japanese messages solved by Sinkov. In any event, South American communications were more interesting than Japanese to the commander of the Panama Department, and within a year of his arrival Sinkov was devoting most of his time to these targets. Although constrained by the lack of traffic, Sinkov, by the end of 1937, had solved Mexican and Colombian polyalphabetic ciphers, entered a Brazilian code, and identified the use of polyalphabetic ciphers by the Venezuelan foreign ministry. In late 1937 the Signal Corps directed Monitoring Station 4 to copy whatever Italian traffic it could pick up, and by December Sinkov had identified two Italian diplomatic systems, although he could not read the messages.[39]

The signal intelligence detachment in Hawaii also covered Japanese diplomatic circuits, and Friedman originally expected Solomon Kullback to solve Japanese diplomatic messages intercepted by that station. To that end Friedman intended to forward relevant cryptographic materials from Washington. Once again, however, security concerns forced the abandonment of this plan. After learning that questions had been raised about the social contacts of one of the enlisted men in the detachment, Friedman decided not to send any Japanese cryptographic material to Hawaii. He instead directed his cryptanalyst to survey the Japanese messages intercepted by Station 5, select those whose indicators revealed they had been enciphered by the RED machine, and forward those messages to Washington for solution. Kullback also worked on minor Japanese diplomatic ciphers and embarked on a preliminary analysis of German diplomatic traffic occasionally intercepted by the Hawaiian station. In his free time (which seems to have been substantial), Kullback revised for publication his paper, "Statistical Methods in Cryptanalysis," and prepared for Friedman various observations on the solution of the Kryha cipher machine, a device that had recently appeared on the international market.[40]

The experiment with field cryptanalysis proved unrewarding, and in January 1938 Sinkov and Kullback were recalled to Washington. Both men had complained that their talents were wasted in the field, where facilities and relevant assistance for solution were lacking. Friedman agreed and, further, convinced the War Department that the decentralization of cryptanalytic work to the departments represented a security risk as well as a duplication of work pursued in Washington. The two analysts returned to the Munitions Building to discover some new faces at the old desks in Room 3406. Although the work of SIS had increased dramatically since its inception, its staff had not. In early 1936 William Friedman employed the same number of people as he had in 1930, all appeals for additional personnel foundering on the shoals of government frugality. Financial constraints began to loosen only in 1936 when the War Department appropriation included additional funds for the Signal Corps. Early that year Friedman had hired Herrick "Frank" Bearce to replace Lawrence Clark, who moved temporarily to the Navy Department. When Kullback's and

Sinkov's assignment to the field reduced his cryptanalytic personnel by half, Friedman convinced the Corps to reserve some of the new moneys for three new billets in SIS. Over the next few years, as the world slid ever closer to war, additional positions were created, three or four at a time.

Samuel Snyder was part of the first intake. A grocer's son from a tough neighborhood in Washington, Snyder survived the Great Depression by working in a variety of temporary government jobs, including a stint at the Veterans Administration, where he computed pension benefits. Seeking a permanent position, he took every Civil Service examination in sight, including one for an assistant statistical clerk. After this test Snyder heard nothing for months and eventually decided to go into business with his older brother. Then, out of the blue, he received a phone call from a man who introduced himself as William Friedman and invited him to an interview in the Munitions Building on the Mall. The caller was vague about the type of position available, but Snyder, who was having second thoughts about joining his brother's business, decided that he had nothing to lose but some time. In the event he lost little of that.

The interview with Friedman lasted less than fifteen minutes. Friedman asked Snyder a few questions about his background and his education (he was studying chemistry at night at George Washington University), then asked him to take a brief typing test that consisted of copying a page from an old army codebook. Snyder, who learned little about the position except that it involved statistics, was neither impressed nor encouraged by what he considered a rather cursory interview; after several weeks passed without further word, he concluded that the position had been filled by someone else. Then, in August 1936, he received a brief letter from William Friedman offering him a post as assistant cryptographic clerk. Snyder had no idea what the title meant or what the work entailed, but it was permanent employment at a decent salary, and he promptly accepted. His introduction to cryptanalysis was so casual as to be unsettling. On Snyder's first day Friedman welcomed him to SIS, explained briefly the nature of the work and the need for secrecy, introduced him to his colleagues, handed him several pamphlets on cryptology, and then left him to his own devices. For the first day or two the new cryptographic clerk read his pamphlets and waited for opportunities to question his fellow workers, who seemed to spend most of their time scribbling on graph paper. Soon he was helping on various projects and pursuing the on-the-job training that would turn him into a cryptanalyst.[41]

The suite of offices occupied by SIS in the Munitions Building was renovated to accommodate more staff, but space remained at a premium. The corridor door now opened into a small room where William Friedman's longtime secretary, Louise Newkirk Nelson, performed the additional functions of receptionist and security officer. She knew everyone by name and face, and no strangers entered without Friedman's personal authorization. To the right of the entry was a door leading to Friedman's private office, and beyond the secretary was a second door opening into a large room with long tables that served as the work space for the remainder of the staff. Off this workroom was a walk-in vault containing file cabinets, storage shelves, and another worktable. Each afternoon at closing time, the staff returned their classified materials to this secure room, but during the day the vault was the haunt of John Hurt, who preferred this small, private area for his translations and linguistic studies.

The only phone in the office was on Friedman's desk, although Louise Nelson had an extension on hers. Whenever a call came in for one of the staff, Nelson would sound a buzzer in the back room using the Morse code equivalent of the first letter of that person's last name. John Hurt, for example, would be summoned with four short buzzes for *H*. The irrepressible Hurt would invariably jump up and shout "Hitotsu, Futatsu, Mitsu, Yotsu!" (Japanese for "one-two-three-four!").

Down the outside corridor was a small room that contained sorting and tabulating machines. Friedman was among the first to perceive that machinery could perform many of the routine operations traditionally completed by humans working with pencil and paper. He urged his staff to identify hand procedures (counting, sorting) that could be mechanized. When War Department parsimony blocked his efforts to obtain tabulating machines for SIS, Friedman approached a friend at the Bureau of Labor Statistics and received permission for his analysts to experiment with the bureau's tabulating machines at night when the machinery was usually silent. In 1936 SIS finally secured its own machines. Initially, each cryptanalyst performed his own machine operations, but this resulted in such confusion and delay that in 1937 Friedman assigned Sam Snyder to supervise the processing schedule and run the machines for the entire office.[42]

With the return of two experienced codebreakers from the field and the gradual addition of new personnel, SIS expanded its cryptanalytic activities beyond the hitherto exclusive focus on Japan. The specific impetus for expansion came from G-2 in response to developments in the international situation. By the late 1930s the bellicose nationalism of Germany and Italy increasingly preoccupied American policy makers, and disturbed even the normally placid waters of army intelligence. Although prewar G-2 was largely indifferent to signals intelligence (which was, after all, diplomatic rather than military in content), it may have felt a need to broaden the scope of the dozen or so translated intercepts that now arrived at its offices each week. When G-2 asked SIS to extend its cryptanalytic coverage, it encountered no resistance from William Friedman, who was eager to move beyond the Japanese problem.

In the early thirties SIS had focused on Japanese codes and ciphers because they represented the path of least resistance for novice codebreakers. The successes of Yardley's Cipher Bureau marked Japan as the most promising target. Without additional staff, Friedman had subsequently been unable to take on new targets, but the interest was always there. In 1931 he had convinced Charles Mendelsohn, a veteran of the Cipher Bureau who was then teaching history at the City College of New York, to review several bundles of unsolved German diplomatic messages from World War I. Mendelsohn had solved German ciphers during the war, and Friedman hoped to uncover additional technical data concerning German cryptography. Mendelsohn labored only briefly and with little result, but the effort suggests that from the earliest days of SIS Friedman was thinking beyond Japan.

In the late spring of 1938, shortly after the annexation of Austria by Nazi Germany and just as Berlin was opening a political offensive against Czechoslovakia that in September would culminate in the Munich Agreement, Friedman directed Solomon Kullback to open an attack against German communications. While in Hawaii, Kullback had tinkered with German ciphers as a sideline to his main duties, and he was eager to take on the problem. Despite recent additions in personnel, staff remained scarce, and for almost a year Kullback worked alone with only occasional help from one or another colleague. In late 1938 Italy and Mexico became the third and fourth countries on the target list of SIS. Friedman asked Abraham Sinkov to head the effort against Italian codes and ciphers. Sinkov was a natural choice because of his experience and seniority and because, having made a preliminary analysis of Italian traffic while in Panama, he was the only member of the staff who knew anything about Italian cryptography. Friedman chose Frank Bearce to work Mexican systems.

The expansion of cryptanalytic activity was facilitated by improvements in the intercept program. In 1937 Joseph Mauborgne, recently promoted to general, was appointed chief signal officer. A skilled cryptanalyst, who in 1914 had published a solution to the famous PLAYFAIR cipher used by the British army, Mauborgne believed strongly in the value of signals intelligence. For the first time in its young life, SIS had a friend in high places. Perhaps recalling a time, not so distant, when the receiving set in the basement of his quarters at the San Francisco Presidio represented the effective intercept capability of the U.S. Army, General Mauborgne took a special interest in radio monitoring. In 1937, in an effort to enhance the administrative status and independence of intercept elements, the War Department elevated the Provisional Radio Intelligence Detachment at Fort Monmouth to full company status and created Radio Intelligence Detachments in Hawaii, Panama, the Philippines, and the Eighth and Ninth Corps Areas. The creation of separate detachments in the field was an especially important step toward improving operations. Until then, intercept was conducted by spare personnel temporarily detached from general duties by the department signal companies. Now intercept would have designated personnel who could be trained for extended service in a specialized field.

Earlier intercept operations had been unsystematic, with neither fixed monitoring schedules nor specific targets. Operators worked their receivers whenever they found time from other duties, and all too frequently they simply scanned the airwaves for targets of opportunity or followed vague guidelines, such as the injunction to copy Japanese government traffic. Mauborgne brought order and direction to the effort. From Washington, each radio intelligence detachment now received specific targets arranged according to priority. In January 1938, for example, SIS directed the detachment in Panama to attempt around-the-clock coverage of the following traffic: first priority, Japanese and Italian diplomatic from Rome to Tokyo; second priority, Japanese diplomatic from Berlin to Tokyo; third priority, Japanese diplomatic to and from Central and South America. Washington's directive even identified by call sign the Italian and German radio stations that carried the first- and second-priority traffic.[43]

To accommodate shifting priorities and the technical capabilities of particular stations, intercept directives were frequently revised. In early 1938 the detachment in the Eighth Corps Area (Fort Sam Houston) was ordered to monitor Berlin stations communicating with Tokyo and, secondarily, Mexico City stations working Tokyo and Europe. When, after a month of effort, it became evident that Berlin-Tokyo traffic could not be heard at Fort Sam Houston, SIS advised the detachment to drop Berlin stations and add Japanese diplomatic traffic from Tokyo to Rome.[44] Occasionally, assignments were quite specific. A station might be instructed to drop everything in order to intercept all messages to and from a particular Japanese consulate or to search recent traffic for a specific message.[45]

Mauborgne followed the work of the stations closely. He made a point of acknowledging good work but would promptly, though gently, point out deficiencies and suggest remedies. One day a monitoring station would be praised for its zeal and care in completing a difficult intercept assignment; the next day it might be admonished for missing two messages specifically sought by SIS. Faltering stations would receive advice as well as admonition. When Fort Sam Houston experienced difficulty in intercepting traffic, it received from Washington suggestions for the best time to search the airwaves and the number of stations that should receive attention. In forwarding advice, Mauborgne always emphasized that the comments were not criticisms but efforts to share hard-earned experience.[46]

Intercept activities were determined by cryptanalytic and intelligence requirements. Traffic was the raw material of cryptanalysis, and the codebreakers needed all the messages they could get in new or only partially readable cryptosystems. Embassies and consulates routinely reported certain political, economic, and social events, and an intercepted message of a particular date when compared with a newspaper story or speech transcript of the same date might provide clues to a code or cipher. Once readable, messages provided intelligence, and certain circuits were monitored for what they might reveal about international events and issues. Occasionally, intercept facilities were targeted against a specific intelligence problem.

In the late 1930s army intelligence received numerous reports of suspicious activity by Japanese citizens living in Mexico: "road builders" in the port of Vera Cruz who knew nothing about roads but sent coded messages to Tokyo; a Japanese radio station near Chihuahua that exchanged encrypted messages with a mysterious station near Guaymas; a clandestine Japanese radio station broadcasting from an abandoned salt mine on the Mexican penal island of Maria Madre.[47] G-2 turned to SIS to confirm reports of clandestine Japanese stations. SIS accepted the assignments, but the results were invariably negative or inconclusive. In the spring of 1938, for example, the U.S. military attaché in Mexico City heard from a paid informant that a radio station (call sign and frequency unknown) was communicating at night with Tokyo and various Japanese ships at sea from a building on the outskirts of the Pacific port of Mazatlán. The building was allegedly also a rendezvous for Japanese diplomats. Washington ordered the monitoring detachment at Fort Sam Houston to abandon its regular assignments in order to devote its entire effort to intercepting traffic from this station. The detachment searched the airwaves with meager results.

Early one morning an operator briefly heard an unknown station transmitting in what appeared to be a Japanese code, but the signal was so weak and the static so strong that he could not copy the transmission. The next morning, at about the same time and on the same frequency, an unidentified station was heard transmitting in the same code. This transmission was copied and sent to Washington. Although the frequency was monitored on subsequent mornings, nothing further was heard from the elusive station; after several days of futile effort, Fort Sam Houston was directed to abandon the special coverage and return to its normal assignments. Shortly thereafter, the military attaché obtained photos of the alleged Japanese station. The photos showed a small shack with an antenna and a small gas generator. The officer decided that the original report was overblown and that he would not pay his informant for any further information about "Japanese stations."[48]

SIS enhanced its access to foreign diplomatic communications by making an arrangement with commercial cable companies. Such companies had been the principal source of traffic for Herbert Yardley's Cipher Bureau until questions concerning the legality of revealing private communications to unauthorized parties dissuaded the firms from further cooperation with the government. After the creation of SIS, the Signal Corps renewed contacts with the private sector. In 1933 it approached the Radio Corporation of America (RCA) for information about the location and technical characteristics (transmitters, frequencies) of certain radio stations in Mexico. Since these Mexican stations routinely communicated with RCA stations in the United States, the Signal Corps assumed that the company would have such information. Within a week of receiving the request, RCA responded with the desired data. Similar requests were made to other companies. The American Telephone and Telegraph Company, for instance, provided information regarding radio and telephone developments in Japan.[49] In all such cases the companies provided purely technical information about foreign communications facilities and developments. No messages were passed to SIS.

The situation changed in 1938 when RCA agreed to allow SIS secret access to its message files. By then the War Department had contrived a legal rationale for intercept activities specifically prohibited by the Radio

Act of 1927, the Communications Act of 1934, and the International Tele-
communications Convention of 1932. These laws allowed exceptions to the
prohibition in cases involving directives from "lawful authority." In March
1938 the secretary of war, responding to a request from G-2, specifically
authorized the chief signal officer "to maintain and operate in time of
peace under strictest provisions to insure secrecy, such radio intercept and
cryptanalytic services as are necessary for training and for national defense purposes."[50]

General Mauborgne may well have shown this authorization to
David Sarnoff, the head of RCA, and added an appeal to the business-
man's patriotism. Whatever the approach, it worked. SIS was soon receiving copies of diplomatic telegrams passing between various foreign ministries and their embassies in Washington via RCA circuits. Every morning
Lieutenant Earle Cook, an army officer attached to SIS, would stop at the
Washington office of RCA on his way to the Munitions Building. Dressed
in civilian clothes, Cook was indistinguishable from the hundreds of employees and customers who passed in and out of the building each day. At
the manager's office he would pick up a large envelope containing the telegrams filed in the preceding twenty-four hours by the various embassies
in Washington and carry this collection to a small room under the rear
staircase. The room was furnished with a large table, a fixed camera, and a
light stand. After photographing the dozen or so telegrams, Cook would
return the file to the manager and proceed to work with the exposed film.
SIS had converted a closet near the cryptanalytic offices into a darkroom,
and here the film would be immediately processed. The messages were distributed to the codebreakers the morning they were collected.[51]

By 1939 SIS was collecting from its monitoring stations and RCA a
steady stream of foreign messages. With the exception of some Japanese
military communications intercepted in the Philippines, the traffic was entirely diplomatic. Much of this traffic was filed without study because SIS
lacked the staff to process the material. Although William Friedman's
office had grown well beyond the corporal's guard that had launched the
army's cryptanalytic program in 1930, the staff still numbered fewer than
twenty-five men and women in Washington. In response to the Austrian
Anschluss and the Munich crisis, the War Department, in late 1938, had
asked the chief signal officer to outline a program of expansion for SIS,
but the implementation of the proposal would await future crises. In the
meantime, there was sufficient staff to work only a handful of problems.

Japan remained the principal target, followed in priority by Germany, Italy, and Mexico. There was no attempt to study the codes and ciphers of any other countries.

Although William Friedman maintained general supervision of all staff operations, he was less engaged in the details of specific cryptanalytic problems. He now devoted most of his time to questions of general administration and the preparation of texts for Signal Corps courses in cryptology.[52] Friedman had selected Frank Rowlett to direct the effort against Japanese cryptosystems. Rowlett assumed personal responsibility for Tokyo's machine ciphers, monitoring the operation of the RED system and studying traffic for signs of new machines. He was assisted by Robert Ferner. Lawrence Clark and Harold Jones studied Tokyo's hand systems, while John Hurt and Paul Cate worked on translation and codebook recovery. Clark could not devote his full attention to Japanese ciphers, since he had also assumed from Sam Snyder responsibility for coordinating the operation of the tabulating machinery. After the solution of the RED machine, SIS access to high-grade Japanese diplomatic traffic was limited only by the ability of the intercept stations to collect messages. Access to low- and medium-grade traffic was ensured by the solution of a range of secondary ciphers that were read almost as soon as they went into service.

The increasingly comprehensive coverage of Tokyo's diplomatic communications provided a unique window on the evolution of Japanese foreign policy. In the fall of 1937, for example, Japanese messages revealed Tokyo's desire to include Italy in the Anti-Comintern Pact that Japan and Germany had negotiated in November 1936. Friedman's team had caught glimpses of those negotiations in several Japanese radiograms from the fall of 1936, but coverage of the talks had been sporadic, probably due to inadequate intercept. When Japan began conversations with Italy, looking to Rome's adherence to the agreement, improved coverage allowed SIS to follow closely the course of the discussions. On 8 October 1937 Friedman sent G-2 a decrypted message in which the Japanese foreign ministry detailed for its ambassador in Rome the guidelines he was to follow in negotiations with the Italians. Four days later, SIS circulated a message in which the Japanese affirmed that the Anti-Comintern Pact was directed against the Soviet Union ("our chief enemy") and that Tokyo should not allow it to become an instrument for associating Japan with Italian ambitions in the Mediterranean. The same message revealed Tokyo's desire to avoid any impression that Japan had aligned itself with a fascist bloc and its fear that such an impression would encourage Britain, France, China, and the United States to form a counterbloc.[53] Other decrypts in the fall of 1937 revealed that Japan would not attend the so-called Nine Power Conference scheduled to convene in Brussels in November to discuss Far Eastern questions, particularly Japanese aggression in China. These decrypts also exposed Italy's plans to support Japan in its opposition to the conference and its defiance of threatened sanctions.[54]

Results of the effort against other targets were not as impressive. Solomon Kullback attacked the German problem with the assistance of Milton Berkowitz and Frank Lewis, novice cryptanalysts who joined SIS in 1939. Lewis, a short, wiry man with an Adolph Menjou moustache, was typical of the trainees recruited by Friedman at the end of the decade. After drifting during the Great Depression through temporary jobs in several federal agencies, he had been befriended by a sympathetic personnel clerk who arranged an interview with two men from the War Department who said little about their agency but pressed Lewis about his hobbies. Chess? Yes. How about bridge? A little. Did he like puzzles? Of course. Did he know anything about cryptanalysis? No. Would he be willing to speak to a man named Friedman at the Munitions Building? Why not? The interview with Friedman proved uneventful. After a few general questions, the mysterious Friedman handed Lewis some pamphlets on cryptology and asked him to review them and return in a couple of weeks. Lewis found the material fascinating and, to the annoyance of his wife, would often work through the night and into the early morning on the cipher problems. When he returned to the Munitions Building, Friedman congratulated him on completing his "training course" and introduced him to his new supervisor, Solomon Kullback. A "gruff, Russian bear of a man" who wasted little time on pleasantries, Kullback promptly handed his new assistant a stack of German intercepts and told him to work out the encipherment. Lewis, who would eventually become one of the army's best codebreakers, began his cryptanalytic apprenticeship wondering what he had got himself into.[55]

Kullback's team was hindered by the absence of continuity in the German problem. Yardley's Cipher Bureau had had some success against World War I–vintage German diplomatic systems, but work against this target had been largely abandoned after 1921. This early work was of little help when, seventeen years later, Kullback again took up the problem. In early 1939 Charles Mendelsohn, who had solved German ciphers for Yardley and briefly advised SIS in 1931, took another leave of absence from his professorship at the City College of New York to help Kullback, but progress remained slow. Like most foreign ministries, the Wilhelm-strasse employed several cryptosystems. Kullback focused on an unenciphered code, the Deutsches Satzbuch (DESAB), and by mid-1939 this book had been sufficiently reconstructed to allow messages to be read. Unfortunately, the unenciphered DESAB carried only 5 percent of Berlin's diplomatic traffic and then only low-grade messages concerning visas, couriers, and embassy accounts. Kullback made little headway against the systems that carried Berlin's more confidential communications.

Abraham Sinkov directed the attack against Italian ciphers with the assistance of Samuel Snyder. Vernon Dooley joined the effort whenever he could spare time from his work compiling new codes for the U.S. Army. Another new recruit, Arnaldo Berenguer, who joined in 1939, worked half the day on Italian systems and half on Mexican. Progress against Italian systems was retarded by the same lack of continuity that plagued the German problem. A handful of Italian intercepts had received cursory attention from Yardley in 1918. Sinkov had made a preliminary analysis of Rome's ciphers while in Panama in 1937 but had read no messages. In 1939 Sinkov and his team were attacking two systems: a two-part, unenciphered code known to the Americans as "X" and an enciphered, one-part code known as "Trujillo" (or "TR"), since most of the messages in this system were intercepted on the Rome–Ciudad Trujillo (Dominican Republic) circuit. No messages had been read in either system.[56]

Mexico, the last target, was the responsibility of Frank Bearce, who received part-time help from Arnaldo Berenguer. Mexican diplomatic traffic was lighter than Japanese, German, and Italian, but the cryptosystems were less sophisticated and the analysts had the benefit of earlier work on the problem. During World War I, MI-8 had solved several Mexican diplomatic and military ciphers as had, after the war, Yardley's New York Cipher Bureau. Within months of establishing a Mexican desk in the fall of 1938, SIS was reading at least one cipher system.[57]

As SIS's activities increased, so did its visibility in the corridors of American foreign policy. Decrypts were now routinely passed to G-2, which had been so impressed by the cryptanalysts' revelations concerning the Anti-Comintern Pact that it moderated somewhat its supercilious attitude toward signals intelligence. In late 1937 the White House had received its first translations of foreign messages, and since then the president had been at least an occasional recipient of signals intelligence.[58] It could not have been too long after this that the secretary of state began to see selected translations. It would be a mistake, however, to exaggerate the contributions of SIS to American foreign policy at the end of the decade. These contributions were limited by particular characteristics of the service, its operations, and its customers.

In 1939 SIS remained, despite modest increases in staff, a small service, and its operations were limited by the lack of human resources. Progress against the German and Italian targets was particularly retarded by the lack of cryptanalysts. Translators were also in short supply. Although much improved, the intercept program still struggled to provide Washington with traffic. Many intercepts were still sent to SIS by registered mail, although an increasing number were reenciphered at the monitoring stations and radioed to the War Department.[59] Messages were decrypted and translated anywhere from three to twelve days after interception, which meant that often signals intelligence lagged behind other sources of information. On 21 October 1937, for example, SIS translated a Japanese message (transmitted on 13 October) indicating that Japan would not attend the Nine Power Conference scheduled to convene in Brussels on 3 November to discuss the Far Eastern situation, including Tokyo's military activity in China. This would have come as no surprise to American policy makers, since the same information had reached the State Department through routine diplomatic reporting channels a week earlier.[60] Some events (e.g., the important Molotov-Ribbentrop Agreement of 23 August 1939) were reported in the press before they appeared in the SIS Bulletin.[61]

Occasionally SIS was ahead of other sources with important intelligence. Sigint was at its best not in reporting fast-breaking events but in illuminating the early phases of diplomatic developments before they had acquired sufficient momentum or visibility to attract the notice of diplomats and journalists. The exchanges among Japan, Germany, and Italy leading to the latter's adherence to the Anti-Comintern Pact is a case in point. On 28 October 1937, Colonel George Strong, an officer in G-2, warned Maxwell Hamilton, the chief of the State Department's Division of Far Eastern Affairs, that "reliable information" indicated that Italy had agreed to join Germany and Japan in the Anti-Comintern Pact. Hamilton was surprised, since earlier that month the American embassy in Tokyo had assured Washington that neither Japan nor Italy saw any need for a formal agreement to combat communism.[62] Strong's information was based on decrypts that traced Tokyo's successful efforts to secure Rome's adherence to the pact. Indications had appeared as early as March 1937, and by October the evidence was conclusive. On 7 October SIS translated a message (dated 1 October) indicating that the Japanese ambassador in

Rome had been directed to open negotiations; the following day, another translation revealed the guidelines for those discussions. On 26 October a third message (transmitted on the nineteenth) contained the text of the treaty to which Italy agreed to adhere. American diplomats did not report the negotiations until 29 October, the day after Colonel Strong's warning to Hamilton.[63]

In the first quarter of 1939, SIS averaged 150 translations a month. Nearly all (98–99 percent) were Japanese, with the remainder German and Mexican. Few German translations appeared in the Bulletin, since DESAB, the only German system SIS could read, carried low-grade administrative messages, only a handful of which were of any interest. Mexican traffic was always light and its content inconsequential (for Washington), so that only occasional message dealing with oil sales or refugees would be worth translation. Japanese communications were potentially more significant, but even their value was limited. In intelligence a single source tends to encourage tunnel vision. The preponderance of Japanese traffic in the translations created an imbalance that exaggerated a Japanese perspective on events. Sigint revealed an international scene as observed by Japanese diplomats who interpreted that scene in terms of Japanese concerns and interests. While never without interest, these interpretations were potentially problematic in terms of scope, accuracy, and insight. In short, American cryptanalysts eavesdropped on Tokyo's diplomats talking about what mattered to them. Sometimes this also mattered to Americans, sometimes it did not, and sometimes it was difficult to know if it did or not.

Without access to other traffic (German, Italian, French, Russian, Chinese), there was often no opportunity to confirm, challenge, or expand the information contained in Japanese intercepts. Japanese ambassadors, moreover, were generally no more prescient and conscientious than their colleagues in other diplomatic services, and their reports often carried little that could not have been learned from the press or the dispatches of American diplomatic observers. Thus, Tokyo's envoys were as surprised as everyone else by the Nazi-Soviet Nonaggression Pact of 23 August 1939, and they had no special insight into events as Europe slid toward war. In the last week of August 1939, neither President Roosevelt nor Secretary of State Hull would have been surprised to learn from the intercepts that the Japanese ambassador in Paris believed that "Europe is on the eve of war" or that his colleague in Berne had concluded that there was "a considerable possibility of war."[64]

No one can now say how much sigint passed across the desks of President Roosevelt and his diplomatic advisers in the last months of peace. Whatever the amount (and it would have been slight), it probably had little impact on policy making. The problems facing American policy makers at the end of the decade were not so much those of intelligence as of resources and influence. American ambassadors in Berlin, Rome, Tokyo, Paris, and other major capitals conscientiously supplied Washington with a stream of generally accurate (and occasionally insightful) dispatches on political affairs. These reports were supplemented by press coverage of the deteriorating international situation. By 1939 Roosevelt did not need decrypts to conclude that Hitler was a serious threat to peace and democratic values, or that a commonality of interest linked the regimes in Berlin, Rome, and Tokyo. The White House and the State Department knew what was happening in Europe and the Far East; they just could not do anything about it as they struggled in vain against timid isolationism and military weakness at home and intractable nationalism and fascism abroad. In short, signals intelligence was at this time largely irrelevant to American policy makers. On the strategic level it told them little that they did not already know; on the tactical level it was too limited to inform particular diplomatic decisions even if the domestic and international environment had not narrowed the range of those decisions.

The influence of sigint was also undercut by the president's approach toward foreign policy in general and intelligence in particular. In decision making Roosevelt preferred intuition to system. He had great (some would say exaggerated) confidence in his ability to take the measure of any international situation or personality. In a decision-making environment where the president's instincts and hunches counted for more than the briefing books and memorandums passed to the White House by the State and War Departments, intelligence reports tended to become marginalized. When Roosevelt wanted information, he canvassed indiscriminately a variety of official and unofficial sources. He was inclined to credit a conversation with an old school chum just home from a holiday in Germany as much as a report from army intelligence; he often exhibited a preference for the more informal, not to say eccentric, sources of information. Signals intelligence would have been just one among many sources vying for his attention and confidence; indeed, sigint would have been at a distinct disadvantage in the competition.

Roosevelt's approach to intelligence was reminiscent of a schoolboy's. Fascinated by tales of intrigue and adventure (*Kim*, Rudyard Kipling's classic story of espionage, was one of his favorite books), the president, like most other Americans, thought that any intelligence worth the name came from the world of devious agents, purloined documents, and moonlit escapes across frontiers. Radio intercept and codebreaking was a strange and arcane technical field that held little interest for him. On any given day Roosevelt would place more credence on an anecdotal report from a trench-coated Harvard classmate who had just stepped off the Orient Express than on a piece of paper prepared by a group of mathematicians, card punchers, and linguists.[65] It was an attitude shared, with more or less intensity, by most military and diplomatic authorities in Washington.

The Signal Intelligence Service was in transition. It had come a long way from the handful of earnest mathematicians who, nine years earlier, had gathered in Room 3406 of the Munitions Building to hear William Friedman explain the difference between a code and a cipher and to study ten-year-old Japanese cipher messages because no current messages were available. SIS was now a functioning intelligence service with a cadre of experienced codebreakers, a chain of functioning intercept stations, and a record of cryptanalytic success. Yet for all its growth and achievements, SIS remained limited in its operations and its influence. Compared with its foreign counterparts, it was still a small service of modest attainments. No matter how impressive they may have seemed in the American context, its achievements would have been deemed unremarkable in Europe, where during the 1930s the cryptanalytic services of even minor powers, such as Austria and Hungary, routinely read the ciphers of a half dozen governments. Even SIS's greatest prewar achievement, the solution of Japan's RED machine, was duplicated by at least two European services, Britain's Government Code and Cypher School and the cryptanalytic unit of the German foreign ministry.[66]

In the summer of 1939 the Signal Intelligence Service was poised to become a major source of intelligence for American policy makers, but the effort would require changes in the administrative, political, and diplomatic environment in which it operated. Those changes began in September when Adolf Hitler launched his panzer divisions against Poland and precipitated a world war.

Chapter Three

Toward Pearl Harbor

The German invasion of Poland on 1 September 1939 set off alarms in chancelleries and intelligence offices across Europe as political and military leaders sought answers to questions affecting the future of Europe and, perhaps, the world. How long would the war last? Would Hitler seek peace after conquering Poland, or would he extend the war into Western Europe? What were Italy's intentions? Russia's? Did Britain and France have the military might and political will to overcome Germany? The sound of distant tocsins echoed, if only faintly, down the normally somnambulant corridors of U.S. Army intelligence. Five days after the attack, Army Chief of Staff General George Marshall received from a senior officer in the War Plans Division, General George Strong, a recommendation to expand the Signal Intelligence Service. Strong argued: "In the present situation, and in its possible developments, it is of vital importance that we have accurate, timely information as to the plans and intentions of the principal parties concerned. Such information is essential to the State Department for political purposes and to the War and Navy Departments for operations and planning."[1]

General Marshall promptly approved the recommendation and directed the chief signal officer, General Joseph Mauborgne, to outline an expansion program. On 14 September Mauborgne submitted a plan that called for the immediate addition of 26 civilian personnel (7 cryptanalysts, 2 cryptanalytic aides, 4 translators, 3 tabulating machine operators, and 10 clerks) and the recall to active duty of 8 army reserve officers who had completed cryptologic training courses. The new personnel would be assigned to the current efforts against German, Italian, Japanese, and Mexican cryptosystems. The chief signal officer (who almost certainly acted upon the advice of William Friedman) saw no reason to take on additional targets when the old ones presented more than enough challenges. Mauborgne also called for additional support for radio intercept. He proposed to increase the Second Signal Service Company by one officer and 26 enlisted men in order to establish a new monitoring post near Washington. He also recommended the allocation of twenty-six thousand dollars to equip the new station, and an additional seventy-six thousand dollars to purchase new equipment for the existing stations.[2]

General Mauborgne's plan was immediately implemented. Within days the Signal Corps arranged with the National Park Service to occupy an abandoned hospital building at Fort Hunt, a former army post just down the road from George Washington's plantation at Mount Vernon. Personnel from the Second Signal Service Company soon converted the old wards and examination rooms into Monitoring Station 7. Fort Hunt joined an army intercept network that included monitoring stations at Fort Hancock, New Jersey (MS-1); the Presidio, San Francisco, California (MS-2); Fort Sam Houston, Texas (MS-3); Corozal, Panama Canal Zone (MS-4); Fort Shafter, Hawaii (MS-5); and Fort McKinley, Philippines (MS-6).[3]

Meanwhile, at the Munitions Building William Friedman began to fill the twenty-six new slots that would more than double the staff of the Signal Intelligence Service. The problem, as always, was how to identify individuals with the requisite aptitudes. One young man was recruited from the garment industry because Friedman had noticed the solutions he submitted to cipher contests in the *Cryptogram*, the newsletter of the American Cryptographic Association.[4] In general, however, the days were past when Friedman would peruse the statistical clerk and mathematician sections of the Civil Service List for one or two likely candidates to invite to the Munitions Building for a quiet talk. Pressed to hire and train immediately more than two dozen civilian cryptologic personnel, Friedman (through the chief signal officer) convinced the secretary of war to allow SIS, if necessary, to recruit new personnel outside the Civil Service List and the cumbersome civil service regulations.

Cautious feelers were now extended to university language and mathematics departments. Gone, too, were the days when after a few minutes of conversation Friedman would make a judgment about a candidate's suitability. Security was now a more explicit concern, and the Federal Bureau of Investigation was called in to check the backgrounds of candidates. In addition to evaluations of intellectual aptitude and educational qualifications, personnel files now contained notations on loyalty, reputation, and lifestyles: "No leftist tendencies." "Does not make a very favorable appearance and is eccentric." "Reliable, conscientious and loyal." "Not successful in any of his endeavors." "Brilliant linguist."

Along with personnel security came a gesture toward enhanced physical security of the service's premises. Uniformed guards now stood at the door to SIS offices in the Munitions Building, although these officers were not always clear on the requirements of their position. The guard on the day shift, for instance, prided himself on his knowledge of the staff and would drop names ("Oh, you mean Jones in the Mexican section") at the slightest provocation.[5] An inquisitive visitor might have determined the table of organization of the service and its principal operations after a short conversation with this friendly security man.

Although welcome, in the short term the army's increased interest in radio intelligence had only a modest impact on the operations of the Signal Intelligence Service. The targets (Japan, Germany, Italy, and Mexico) remained unchanged from before the war. In the first months of the conflict, intercept operations were amended to increase coverage of German communications, and Monitoring Stations 3 (Fort Sam Houston, Texas) and 4 (Panama Canal Zone) were specifically directed to make German diplomatic traffic to and from Central and South America their immediate priority.[6] As new staff came aboard, many were assigned to the lagging German and Italian problems, but they would require months of training to achieve even a modest level of cryptanalytic skill. Progress against the cryptanalytic problems was frustratingly slow. Fully a year into the European war the American sigint program had advanced only marginally beyond its position in the summer of 1939, and in one area it had actually regressed.

German systems continued to resist all efforts to penetrate their secrets. To be sure, the basic codebook of the German foreign ministry, the DESAB, had been sufficiently reconstructed so that all messages in this code were readable even before July 1940 when American authorities in the Panama Canal Zone found a copy of the codebook in the baggage of a clandestine German courier transiting the Panama Canal on a Japanese steamer. This system, however, carried only low-grade administrative and consular messages. Solomon Kullback's German section had discovered that occasionally DESAB was enciphered with reciprocal bigram tables. Unfortunately, this system (known as *Spalierverfahren*) was observed only on the relatively quiet Berlin-Havana, Berlin–Port-au-Prince (Haiti), and Berlin–Ciudad Trujillo (Dominican Republic) circuits, and the low volume of traffic undermined solution efforts. The section had identified what it believed to be two high-grade diplomatic systems, but it had made no progress against these systems beyond suspecting that one was enciphered by a running string of random additive. A system used by German military attachés in Washington and Tokyo was under study, but the analysts were unsure whether it was a machine or hand cipher.[7]

In the Italian section Abe Sinkov's small team had made significant progress against the unenciphered diplomatic code known to SIS as "X." By the summer of 1940, most of the messages in this code were readable. The system, however, was used by Rome only for low-grade administrative traffic, and the intelligence product was negligible. The section had also identified the encipherment and reconstructed a portion of the codebook for Trujillo (TR), a medium-grade system used by the Italian foreign ministry to communicate with its Caribbean legations. Traffic was light, however, and only a few messages in Trujillo were read. At least two high-grade diplomatic systems had been identified, but although Sinkov's team had made some progress toward identifying the encipherment, they had read no messages.[8]

Ironically, the most successful section was the one that received the least attention. During the first year of the war, the small Mexican desk under Frank Bearce achieved comprehensive coverage of its target. The main Mexican diplomatic codebook was reconstructed, and 90 percent of the traffic between the Mexican foreign ministry and its embassies was read. A polyalphabetic cipher used by the treasury department and, less frequently, by the foreign ministry was also solved. The section also cracked two ciphers used by the president of Mexico to communicate personally with his ambassador in Washington and the consul general in New York City.[9]

Frank Rowlett's Japanese section remained the largest and most active of the cryptanalytic teams, and the exploitation of Tokyo's communications remained SIS's most productive operation. By mid-1940 the section was able to read fifteen Japanese diplomatic systems, including the RED machine. Seven of these systems, however, were obsolete, and few, if any, messages encrypted with them were intercepted. Four others were used only for low-level matters, mainly consular and commercial affairs. Only four systems provided access to high-grade traffic: RED; CA, a special code (occasionally enciphered by machine) for personal communications between the foreign minister and ambassadors; K-2, an enciphered code used by the foreign ministry for directives concerning the use of codes and ciphers; and J-15, a code used at Tokyo's smaller diplomatic missions.[10]

The exploitation of these systems provided important information about Japanese foreign policy and, indirectly, the policies of other governments. Access to Tokyo's high-grade communications was incomplete, however, and in the first twelve months of the war actually decreased. In early 1940 the Japanese foreign ministry introduced a new code for secret communications, and throughout the year SIS struggled to accumulate sufficient traffic in the new system to begin the long process of reconstructing the codebook. At the same time Rowlett and his team confronted an even more serious threat. Late in 1938 RED messages indicated that Tokyo was dispatching communications technicians to its embassies. On 7 January 1939 SIS translated a message from the Berlin embassy that referred to an "improved" cipher machine and mentioned the "B Code [sic]". On 19 February a message indicated that something referred to as "Cipher Machine B" would enter service on 20 February. No one at SIS had ever heard of such a machine. The next day the army's listening posts intercepted three messages from the Japanese legation in Warsaw that should have been readable but were not. Within a week a trickle of unreadable messages became a flood. It was the nightmare that had haunted William Friedman and Frank Rowlett since the solution of RED (the "A machine") in 1934. Japan had introduced a new cipher machine.[11]

It took some time for Tokyo to distribute and install the new machines at its diplomatic posts, and some stations continued to use the old "A machine" (RED) after the outbreak of the war. By early 1940, however, only a handful of RED messages were intercepted each month as most high-grade traffic was entrusted to the new cipher machine that SIS christened PURPLE. As American codebreakers watched their access to Tokyo's most secret communications disappear, the battle to solve the new machine superseded all cryptanalytic problems and operations in the Munitions Building.

The narrow focus of the army's cryptanalytic operations on a handful of targets, the slow progress against German and Italian systems, and the inability to read PURPLE undercut the ability of SIS to produce significant intelligence through most of 1940. The experience in the spring of that year illustrates the limitations of American signals intelligence. As Germany launched successful attacks against Denmark and Norway (April) and France and the Low Countries (May), the White House and

State Department frantically (and futilely) scrambled to contrive a policy that would contain German aggression, stiffen the resolve of the threatened nations, and dissuade Mussolini from joining Hitler. Signals intelligence provided little help in these endeavors. In May, for example, SIS published 440 translations (up from 190 in August 1939, the last month of peace), of which 84.5 percent were Japanese, 7.5 percent Mexican, 7.0 percent German, 0.4 percent Italian, and the remaining fraction unidentified. German, Italian, and Mexican messages provided no significant intelligence. The German messages dealt with consular or low-grade administrative matters: the consulate in Los Angeles requested additional staff; the legation in Guatemala reported the collection of six hundred dollars for the Reich Red Cross; the consulate in São Paulo, Brazil, confirmed that the consul general had departed on vacation.[12] The two Italian translations consisted of a message from the embassy in Washington reporting the establishment of an American consulate in Greenland and a message from Rome informing the Italian diplomatic mission in Cairo of the arrival at Alexandria of a steamship carrying important documents.[13] The Mexican messages were no more exciting. In one the legation in Copenhagen requested instructions for the disposition of the mission's furnishings and archives now that Denmark had been occupied by the Germans. In another the foreign ministry in Mexico City authorized its legation in Brussels to withdraw to Paris in the face of the German invasion of Belgium.[14]

In spring 1940 Japanese messages provided the only useful sigint concerning political events in Europe and elsewhere. One must be careful, however, not to exaggerate the importance of the Japanese decrypts. Messages in the high-grade PURPLE machine remained impenetrable. Most of the readable messages dealt with relatively low-priority matters, such as the defense of Japanese business interests in Mexico or negotiations for Peruvian textiles, providing little assistance to American policy makers preoccupied with political and military developments in Western Europe. Communications dealing specifically with such developments rarely provided information beyond that reported by the international press or American diplomats in Britain, France, Germany, and Italy, although the Japanese messages often supplied confirmation of such reports. Intercepts, for example, provided Washington with no warning of the German offensive against Scandinavia in April 1940, since Tokyo was as surprised by the attack as Copenhagen and Oslo. In the last week in May, SIS decrypted messages from Tokyo's diplomatic representatives in Berlin, Rome, and Vienna warning their foreign ministry that Italy was close to joining Germany in the war. At the time, however, diplomats in every European capital were predicting Italian belligerency, and Washington was receiving similar warnings from its own embassies.[15]

American diplomats in Western Europe drew upon the same sources that their Japanese counterparts used for their reports to Tokyo, and often (as was the case in Paris and London) the Americans' sources were better. Furthermore, Japanese diplomats could be as gullible as anyone. One wonders what American codebreakers (and, for that matter, Tokyo) made of the dramatic reports from Japanese representatives that German victories against Belgium, France, and Holland were the result of a "high-temperature gun" that emitted heat so intense that opposing troops could not leave their trenches.[16] Of more interest were messages that provided a glimpse of Tokyo's espionage and subversion programs, such as a message from Tokyo to Singapore reporting the creation of a special school to prepare agents for work in the South Seas and the Near East and identifying various Japanese firms that would provide commercial cover for these spies.[17]

SIS understood that its reliance on Japanese traffic limited its ability to serve the intelligence requirements of the army and the U.S. government. The service needed to intensify the attack against German and Italian ciphers and open attacks against other targets of potential intelligence value. Through 1940, however, lack of staff prohibited any expansion in operations. The new employees who had joined SIS in the early months of the European war had all been assigned to long-running operations. The situation improved in the fall of that year when the War Department authorized SIS to hire forty-eight additional staff as of 1 January 1941.[18] The new staff allowed the army to expand its cryptanalytic operations to include the diplomatic communications of several new targets, including Brazil, Vichy France, and Spain. There was also an effort to improve coverage of Japanese communications. For all of its success since 1932, the Japanese program at SIS had been limited to diplomatic traffic. No Japanese military systems had been solved, in part because of a lack of intercepts. The Imperial Army in the Home Islands and its garrisons and operational units in China, Korea, and Formosa relied on low-powered transmissions that were difficult for the U.S. Army's intercept stations to monitor. The station at Fort McKinley in the Philippines had been established in large part to capture such transmissions, but operations had been plagued by indifferent leadership, personnel shortages, and inadequate equipment. In late 1940 General Mauborgne, the chief signal officer, ordered a renewed effort against Japanese military traffic. Fort McKinley received additional radio operators and the latest receivers and direction finders.[19] In a further effort to jump-start the Japanese military problem, SIS turned to Herbert Yardley.

After the demise of the New York Cipher Bureau, Yardley did not retire into respectable obscurity. Unemployed and resentful of his treatment by a government that, in his mind, was indifferent to the value of signals intelligence and to his unique contributions to the national security, he resolved to write his memoirs. In the spring of 1931 he astounded the general public and outraged the War Department by publishing in the *Saturday Evening Post* a series of articles that detailed his codebreaking work for the U.S. government. The articles were the basis of a book, *The American Black Chamber,* which appeared in June. At a time when the very existence of signals intelligence operations was a closely held secret, Yardley's exposé caused a sensation. The book sold 18,000 copies in the United States and another 5,500 in Great Britain. There were French, Swedish, Chinese, and Japanese editions, with sales in Japan alone topping 33,000. Yardley's revelations concerning American codebreaking against Germany in World War I were bad enough, but his exposure of the peacetime operations of the Cipher Bureau, particularly the success against Japanese codes and ciphers during the Washington Naval Conference of 1921–1922, was a serious embarrassment to the government. When asked by an excited press to confirm Yardley's sensational charges, the State Department denied that it had had access to Japanese messages during the Washington Conference. Army Chief of Staff General Douglas MacArthur and senior officers in the Military Intelligence Division stated that they knew nothing about the Cipher Bureau.[20]

After the publication of *The American Black Chamber,* Yardley pursued various business ventures, including real estate speculation, screenwriting, and the development of a commercial secret ink. But the Great Depression was not kind to entrepreneurs, and none of the schemes engaged his attention for very long. An attempt to duplicate his earlier success by publishing *Japanese Diplomatic Secrets, 1921–1922,* an account of Tokyo's policy at the Washington Naval Conference based on his personal collection of decrypted Japanese messages, collapsed when he reluctantly acquiesced in the government's decision to impound the manuscript on national security grounds.

By 1938 Yardley was unemployed and casting about for a reliable source of income. He retained an interest in codes and ciphers and, though inclined to embellish his cryptanalytic achievements, his abilities were real. But after *The American Black Chamber* there could be no place for him in the cryptanalytic service of the U.S. government. Fortunately, there were other services. In the summer of 1938 Yardley, then living in Queens, New York, was visited by an official of the Chinese embassy in Washington. Major Xiao Bo was nominally an attaché at the embassy, but his real job was to serve as Washington station chief for General Tai Li, Chiang Kai-shek's shadowy intelligence director. Xiao Bo invited Yardley to China to organize and direct a Chinese Black Chamber. While in the service of Tai Li, Yardley would receive an annual salary of ten thousand dollars, along with various perquisites befitting his professional stature. Eager for fame, adventure, and a steady income, Yardley accepted the offer. Traveling under the cover name "Herbert Osborne," he reached Chungking, China's wartime capital, in November 1938.

Adopting a cover identity as an exporter of hides, Yardley moved into the villa of a former mayor of Chungking, a rat-infested twenty-room mansion whose amenities did not include bathrooms. The professional arrangements were no less problematic. Tai Li's cipher unit occupied dank caves in the hills outside Chungking. Work was often interrupted by Japanese bombing raids, one of which destroyed Yardley's villa. Yardley spoke no Chinese, and to his surprise he discovered that his staff were neophytes in the art of codebreaking. Although Yardley would later brag that he had solved nineteen different Japanese cryptosystems while in China, the famous American codebreaker spent most of his time teaching Tai Li's men the general principles of cryptanalysis. This was useful but unexciting work, and increasingly Yardley sought diversion in women, drink, and gambling. After twenty months he admitted that there was nothing for him in China, and he returned quietly to the United States in the summer of 1940.[21] Within weeks another visitor came knocking on his door.

At the Munitions Building the effort to accelerate the attack against Japanese military ciphers was retarded not only by a lack of intercepts but also by the lack of continuity in the problem. Until the summer of 1940, no one in SIS had studied the problem, and there was little knowledge of Japanese army cryptographic practices. In September a desperate William Friedman turned to Herbert Yardley, the one American with recent experience in this subject. It was not an easy decision. In the years since Yardley had tried to find a place for Friedman in the postwar Cipher Bureau, a growing animosity had poisoned relations between America's two greatest cryptanalysts. The ill will was especially strong on Friedman's part, fueled by a distaste for Yardley's flamboyant personality and lifestyle, professional jealousy, and a revulsion at Yardley's betrayal of national secrets for personal profit.

Friedman was prepared to put the interest of the Signal Intelligence Service before his personal feelings, but he could not bring himself to deal directly with his onetime friend. He sent Frank Rowlett to ask the famous codebreaker for help. Negotiating through Rowlett, Friedman and Yardley agreed, in October 1940, that the latter would receive four thousand dollars for a report on his cryptanalytic work in China. The affair was to be strictly secret, and Yardley would prepare this report at home. His only contact with SIS would be Rowlett, the chief of the Japanese section, who would visit Yardley at his current residence near the Munitions Building to receive progress reports and to pass on questions from the cryptanalysts.

Gratified by this testimony of professional respect and eager to return to the good graces of the American government, Yardley, at least at the beginning, threw himself into the assignment. Like so many of his endeavors, however, this project fell short of its promise. The preparation of the report proved a tiresome burden. The sessions with Rowlett became little more than monologues in which Yardley would regale his restless listener with highly embellished stories of life in China. Yardley eventually submitted several papers under the general title "Japanese Military Codes and Ciphers in Occupied China, Period 1938–1940," but Rowlett considered them useless and dismissed the whole relationship with Yardley as a waste of time and money. Japanese army messages remained unread, and Yardley would never again work for American signals intelligence.[22]

In the months following the French armistice, as British and German pilots fought to control the skies over the British Isles and Hitler consolidated his mastery over the European continent and pondered further conquests, the U.S. government moved slowly to improve its intelligence posture. Early efforts focused on improving coordination among the various agencies involved in intelligence and counterintelligence and encouraging a more efficient division of labor. In the summer of 1940, for example, President Franklin Roosevelt approved a directive that gave the army's Military Intelligence Division and the Office of Naval Intelligence responsibility for all foreign intelligence except in the Western Hemisphere, where the FBI would collect intelligence and conduct counterintelligence operations. The presidential directive said nothing about signals intelli-

gence, but the new emphasis on coordination forced army and navy cryptanalysts to consider their relationship.

The navy entered the signals intelligence field in 1924 when it added
a Research Desk to its Code and Signal Section. Composed of an officer in
charge, a cryptanalyst, and two cryptographic clerks (a Japanese-language
translator was later added), the Research Desk studied various cipher systems submitted to the Navy Department for possible adoption, tested the
security of systems compiled by the Code and Signal Section for use by
American naval forces, and attacked foreign cipher systems for intelligence purposes. To facilitate the latter effort, in 1926 the navy began to
develop a string of intercept stations. From the start the naval sigint program focused on Japan and by 1931, in addition to notable success against
Japanese naval codes and ciphers, the Research Desk had solved several
Japanese diplomatic systems.[23] Before 1930 no serious attempt was made
against other foreign systems, although two ciphers used by the Chinese
Kuomintang party to communicate with its representatives in California
were solved at the request of the Office of Naval Intelligence.[24]

For the first six years of its operation, the Research Desk worked in
secrecy and isolation. It had no contact with its counterpart, the joint
army/State Department Cipher Bureau in New York City, although after
the bureau's closure Herbert Yardley unsuccessfully offered his services
to the desk as an instructor in cryptanalysis. In 1930, however, the naval
codebreakers sought help from the fledgling Signal Intelligence Service
that had been established that same year in the Army Signal Corps.
As part of a congressional investigation into communist subversion in
the United States, the Research Desk had been studying without success several thousand encrypted messages of Amtorg, the Soviet trade
agency in New York. For several months the army and navy codebreakers
collaborated on the Amtorg problem, but the Russian ciphers proved impenetrable.[25]

Although army-navy collaboration on the Amtorg messages had
been cordial, the appearance of a new cryptanalytic actor on the intelligence stage was unsettling and vaguely threatening to the navy. While
there was no likelihood that William Friedman and his novice codebreakers would turn their attention to foreign naval messages, diplomatic communications were another matter. The army's new unit might well focus on
diplomatic sigint, since military communications, the only other possible
target, were notoriously difficult to intercept in peacetime because foreign

armies communicated along landlines or with low-powered radio. Any interest by the army in diplomatic cryptanalysis might impinge upon the navy's operations. Since its creation, the Research Desk had focused its energies on Japanese naval and diplomatic cryptosystems, with a pause in 1930 to attack the Russian Amtorg messages. In 1930–1931 Japanese diplomatic became, at least for a time, its only productive cryptanalytic operation, since the Amtorg messages remained unsolved and a decision by the Imperial Navy to revamp its codes and ciphers resulted in a temporary blackout in the U.S. Navy's ability to read Japanese naval communications. From the navy's perspective, a decision by the army to work Tokyo's diplomatic traffic would be not only a wasteful duplication of effort and an inefficient use of America's scarce cryptanalytic resources but also a potential challenge to the navy's monopoly over an important source of intelligence. It was in the navy's interest to secure quickly an agreement delimiting the two services' respective fields of operation before the Signal Intelligence Service had a chance to establish itself.

In October 1931 the director of naval communications proposed to the chief of naval operations an allocation of signals intelligence responsibilities between the army and the navy. The navy would assume responsibility for all naval sigint and for diplomatic sigint relating to the four major naval powers: Britain, France, Italy, and Japan. The army would be responsible for all military sigint and for diplomatic sigint relating to all countries except the four major naval powers. To facilitate the performance of their respective tasks, the services would freely and promptly exchange relevant intercepts and cryptanalytic materials. The free exchange of information, however, would be limited to the services. The navy had no intention of sharing signals intelligence with civilians, including those in the White House and the State Department. The proposal specified: "There should be, however, a fixed and well-understood agreement that no information obtained through this source be disclosed to any other departments of the government or to any individual within or outside the Army and Navy except the highest ranking responsible officers of the two military services."[26]

If adopted, the proposal would ensure the navy's preeminent position in signals intelligence. It protected its monopoly over Japanese cryptanalysis, the only currently productive source of signals intelligence, and established a preemptive claim over the diplomatic traffic of all the major powers of the day except the Soviet Union.[27] Of course, in 1931 the Research Desk had neither the resources nor the appetite to work anything but

Japanese traffic, but it wanted to be well positioned for the future. In return for these privileges, the navy graciously allowed the army to assume responsibility for the impenetrable Russian ciphers, the diplomatic traffic of dozens of secondary powers in which the navy had absolutely no interest, and all military sigint, which, at the time, amounted to nothing. In short, without surrendering anything to the army, the proposal protected established naval sigint operations and assured naval control over future operations of significance.

The proposal by the director of naval communications had little impact except as a stimulus to a series of fruitless meetings between senior communications officers of the two services. The army balked at a formal agreement. The chief signal officer saw no harm in a general agreement so long as it was purely verbal and both parties understood that it could be changed whenever one party wished, a live-and-let-live position that effectively negated the very purpose of the agreement. Major D. M. Crawford, the officer in charge of SIS, who considered his unit primarily a code compilation service for the army, saw no need to allocate responsibility for diplomatic cryptanalysis, since he believed that State Department policy prohibited this practice by any agency. An effort by the army to seek guidelines from the State Department drew a stern rebuke from the navy, which considered the approach to the diplomats nothing less than a security breach. In reaction to this outrage, a naval intelligence officer complained, "If the Army can not be trusted to use a semblance of discretion in disclosing these matters outside the military services then we will lose everything by our efforts to cooperate."[28]

Although the army and navy could not agree on a formal allocation of signals intelligence responsibilities, they cooperated informally on a number of specific issues. In the summer of 1935, for example, army and navy communications specialists worked jointly to impede the visit to the United States of a Japanese delegation that was touring several countries to study cryptology and communications security. Two companies involved in the production of communications equipment, American Telephone and Telegraph and International Business Machines, were asked to withhold information from the Japanese. The services also arranged to feed the delegation information attesting to the security of the Kryha cipher machine, which both the army and navy had solved.[29] There was also occasional cooperation on the working level. On one occasion the navy passed to SIS Japanese messages intercepted by the naval monitoring station in China. On another occasion SIS asked the navy to intercept a week's worth of Mexican diplomatic traffic that was transmitted by a specific Mexican station whose frequency, for technical reasons, army stations had trouble fixing.[30]

Following Germany's invasion of Poland, General Mauborgne and Admiral Leigh Noyes, director of naval communications, discussed the more efficient application of American signals intelligence resources. At the end of these discussions, the navy had the impression that the army was content to focus on German diplomatic communications while leaving Japanese communications to the naval cryptanalysts. This was almost certainly a misunderstanding (or wishful thinking) on the navy's part, since Mauborgne, who took a special interest in the work of SIS, would hardly have agreed to abandon the army's only productive source of signals intelligence. SIS continued to work the Japanese diplomatic problem. When the navy complained, it merely replied that the Army General Staff had ordered it to study Japanese, German, and Italian diplomatic systems, and this directive superseded any alleged agreements.[31] When, in the spring of 1940, the collapse of France and the extension of German control over much of Western Europe again raised questions in Washington about intelligence coordination and cooperation, SIS and its navy counterpart, now renamed OP-20-G, reopened the matter of allocating targets. The issue, however, was now complicated by the presence of other actors on the sigint stage.

The Coast Guard became involved in signals intelligence in the 1920s when its responsibility for enforcing Prohibition led it to intercept and solve the codes used by rumrunners seeking to smuggle illicit liquor into the country by sea. With the end of Prohibition in 1933, the Coast Guard shifted its sigint effort to the detection of traditional smuggling activities. The outbreak of war offered new opportunities. By 1940 the Coast Guard was monitoring the traffic of merchant ships in order to enforce American neutrality laws and searching the ether for the transmissions of clandestine stations in the United States and South America. These clandestine transmitters serviced German, Italian, and Soviet secret agents in the Western Hemisphere. Where possible, the Coast Guard decrypted this traffic and passed the translations to the FBI, which, under the terms of a presidential directive of 24 June 1940, was responsible for intelligence and counterintelligence in the Western Hemisphere. When it became apparent that the bureau was not sharing this information with other agencies, the Treasury department, then the peacetime authority over the Coast Guard, directed the Guard to pass the information also to the State, Navy, and War Departments.[32]

For its part, the FBI had taken the first steps toward an independent cryptanalytic capability by forming a codebreaking unit in October 1939. In return for instruction from bureau technicians in "document examination," SIS instructed a handful of agents in cryptanalysis. Initially, the FBI codebreakers focused on German espionage traffic in the Western Hemisphere, but J. Edgar Hoover, the bureau's ambitious director, could not resist an opportunity to expand his agency's role in the increasingly important realm of foreign intelligence. Within a year, FBI cryptanalysts were working German, Japanese, and Vichy French diplomatic traffic. To accelerate this effort, the FBI initiated a program of clandestine entries into foreign embassies and consulates in search of cryptographic materials. It also profited from close relations with British Security Coordination (BSC), the New York City headquarters of Britain's Secret Intelligence Service (MI-6). BSC shared with the FBI information on certain cipher systems that it had collected through its own clandestine operations in New York and Washington.[33]

The increasingly crowded field of signals intelligence received another entrant in the summer of 1940 when the Federal Communications Commission (FCC) established the National Defense Organization (soon renamed the Radio Intelligence Division) to monitor clandestine espionage stations. Charged with licensing radio stations and enforcing broadcast regulations, the FCC controlled several monitoring stations in the continental United States and in Alaska, Hawaii, and Puerto Rico. Under the direction of George Sterling, a commission supervisor who had worked in signals intelligence during the First World War, these stations began to search the airwaves for German and Italian clandestine broadcasts. After intercepting such broadcasts, FCC agents would attempt to pinpoint the location of the transmitter. Once fixed, the location, along with any intercepts, would be shared with the counterespionage division of the FBI. One operation located an unlicensed station on Long Island (call sign, TEST) communicating with a station in Hamburg, Germany (AOR). Suspecting domestic espionage, the FCC notified the FBI and indicated that, if the bureau took no action, commission agents would raid the station. At the last minute J. Edgar Hoover revealed that station TEST was indeed a German spy radio, but one under the control of the FBI. During a visit to his family in Germany, William Sebold, a naturalized American citizen, had been blackmailed into working for German intelligence as a radio operator servicing several agents in the United States and Mexico. Sebold revealed his espionage mission to American authorities and agreed to cooperate with the FBI, which used station TEST to identify Nazi agents in North America and control their reports to Germany. Their hand forced by the FCC, Hoover's agents closed down Sebold's operation and arrested several members of the German network. Unfortunately, the ensuing judicial proceedings revealed sensitive information about American signals intelligence operations. The TEST-AOR case also strained the FBI's relations with the Coast Guard, which already were frayed by disagreement over the distribution of clandestine intercepts. The Coast Guard (whose monitors had also identified radio TEST as a German clandestine station) accused the bureau of allowing TEST to transmit information to Hamburg, particularly news of ship movements, that actually assisted German U-boat operations.[34]

The army and navy dealt with these interlopers on the signals intelligence stage by ignoring them. When, in July 1940, SIS and OP-20-G reopened the question of dividing intercept and cryptanalysis responsibilities, there was no question of including other agencies in the discussions. If the services could agree on nothing else, they agreed on the need to defend their control of signals intelligence. The common front was apparent when, at the instigation of the White House, General Sherman Miles, assistant chief of staff for intelligence, chaired an interdepartmental meeting to improve intelligence coordination and exchange. The participants included General Joseph Mauborgne, the army's chief signal officer; Admiral Leigh Noyes, director of naval communications; Admiral Walter Anderson, director of naval intelligence; and Edward Tamm, associate director of the FBI. In what was clearly an orchestrated performance for the record, Miles and Anderson informed Tamm that the services were operating monitoring stations to intercept international radio communications and were obtaining additional messages through special arrangements with commercial cable companies. Neither the general nor the admiral provided any details about targets, procedures, or results.

This news probably came as no surprise to Tamm. The FBI representative noted that his agency was not receiving any information from these operations even though items of interest to the bureau surely appeared, if only occasionally, in the intercepted traffic. Admiral Anderson blandly assured Tamm that, pursuant to the recent presidential directive assigning intelligence responsibilities, the Office of Naval Intelligence (ONI) passed to the bureau intelligence relating to the Western Hemisphere. The director of ONI, however, said nothing specific about information gleaned from radio and cable intercept. General Miles said nothing at all. The army and navy representatives did promise to search their records to ensure that the FBI had received everything necessary for its work.[35]

The armed services had little interest in giving the FBI a place at the signals intelligence table. Before Pearl Harbor the bureau received almost no communications intelligence material from the army or the navy, although in the spring of 1941 the navy passed a German diplomatic codebook (probably the DESAB) and a Japanese naval codebook to J. Edgar Hoover in return for information on the bureau's progress against Vichy French systems.[36] For its part, the army kept Hoover at arm's length and rebuffed his forays into signals intelligence. In December 1940, for example, Hoover informed military intelligence that the FBI had information that a certain "Radio Station Chapultepec" in Mexico was communicating daily with Germany; he requested that army monitoring posts place the mysterious station under around-the-clock surveillance and pass any intercepts to the bureau. SIS's dismissive reply merely noted that the Chapultepec station was a legitimate transmitter that had been passing private and governmental messages between Mexico City and Berlin since 1914, and that it appeared on publicly available lists of registered transmitters. On another occasion, in the summer of 1941, Hoover proudly announced to military intelligence that his bureau was in a position to decipher certain Vichy codes, and he graciously offered to read any Vichy messages of interest to the army. SIS did not deign to respond to this approach.[37]

If the services could ignore outsiders, they could not ignore each other. Discussions in July 1940 looking toward a division of signals intelligence activities deadlocked over intercept and decryption assignments. Once again, diplomatic traffic was the issue. The navy maintained its long-held position that intercept and cryptanalytic assignments should be divided along national lines. In the area of diplomatic signals intelligence, it now wanted responsibility only for Japan and the Soviet Union, while leaving Germany, Italy, Mexico, and Latin America to the army.[38] Since the only diplomatic traffic OP-20-G was successfully working was Japanese (although it maintained a token watch on German and Vichy communications), this plan complemented current operations, required the navy to relinquish no important programs, and ensured its monopoly on the most productive sigint problem.

Still loath to abandon the Japanese problem, which, even during the struggle against PURPLE, remained its most successful sigint operation, the army preferred a division of responsibility according to circuits. Each service would intercept all diplomatic traffic on assigned circuits (e.g., army: Tokyo–Mexico City; navy: Tokyo-Moscow), and the services would then divide the traffic equally and pursue independent cryptanalysis. While dividing responsibility for intercept, this arrangement maintained the duplication of cryptanalytic effort. The shrewd proposal served the army's interests, however, by shifting some of the burden for diplomatic intercept to the navy without shifting opportunities of cryptanalysis. In the summer of 1940, OP-20-G had neither the appetite nor the resources to study any diplomatic systems but Japanese, so in practice the army conceded nothing by agreeing to share German, Italian, and Mexican cryptanalysis. Furthermore, since the navy was already working Tokyo's traffic, SIS simply affirmed the status quo by dividing responsibility in this area.

Discussions continued for several weeks and resulted, on 3 October 1940, in a compromise that dealt mainly with intercept. Particular international circuits were to be assigned exclusively to either the army or the navy, although a few circuits would be monitored jointly. In the area of cryptanalysis, the army assumed sole responsibility for Mexican traffic and the navy for Russian. The agreement said nothing about cryptanalysis of Japanese, German, Italian, or any other diplomatic traffic, leaving (by implication) both services to work these targets.[39] The agreement was little more than a stopgap measure that postponed hard decisions about dividing sigint operations to avoid duplication of effort, but in the fall of 1940, both services were preoccupied by questions concerning a different kind of cooperation.

On 5 September 1940, the War Department received a startling message from General George Strong, the army's representative on the American Military Observer Mission then in London for staff conferences with senior British officers. The general cabled: "Are you prepared to exchange full information on all German, Italian, and Japanese code [sic] and cryptographic information therewith? Are you prepared to agree to a continuous exchange of important intercept in connection with the above? Please expedite reply."[40] At a meeting with the British chiefs of staff on 31 August, Strong, who seems to have had a flair for the dramatic, had astonished his hosts (as well as his colleagues on the observer mission) by announcing that the U.S. Army was working on Japanese and Italian codes and ciphers, and proposing that London and Washington exchange information on their cryptanalytic operations. The British were particularly surprised by the proposal, since the Royal Navy had been rebuffed by the U.S. Navy in October 1939 when it suggested exchanging information on Japanese codes and ciphers.[41] Within days the British accepted the proposal, prompting Strong's message asking the War Department if it was prepared to share with a foreign power the secrets of its most sensitive intelligence operation.

Since the fall of France, the Roosevelt administration, realizing that the United States was linked to Britain's destiny by a web of culture, history, language, and political interest, had been seeking ways to support the British within the limits set by a public opposed to armed intervention and a military establishment ill equipped to ensure American security. Staff conversations and technical exchanges were a promising area for mutual assistance, but both countries were cautious about revealing secrets. In July 1940 President Roosevelt, in consultation with Secretary of the Navy Frank Knox and Secretary of War Henry Stimson, overrode objections from army and navy specialists and accepted a proposal from London that the two governments hold a joint staff conference in Britain.[42] Apparently the arrangement included the exchange of information on certain technical matters. In late August a British mission under Henry Tizard arrived in Washington to begin several weeks of discussions on a range of technical topics, including submarine detection devices (asdic) and air defense radar. As the Tizard mission met with its American counterparts, senior officials in the War Department considered dispatching civilian scientists and qualified army officers to Britain to exchange information on a range of military, scientific, and technological subjects. Cryptanalysis, however, was not one of those subjects.

The conversations and exchanges were conducted discreetly in order to maintain the pretense of American neutrality and to protect the Roosevelt administration from the political ire of American isolationists in an election year. The American Military Observer Mission traveled to Britain to discuss "standardization of arms," a suitably vague formulation that hid its real purpose, which was to discuss cooperation between the armed services of the two countries. The evidence suggests that the mission had no instructions to raise cryptanalytic questions and that General Strong seized the initiative in proposing cryptanalytic collaboration. No signals intelligence specialists (nor, for that matter, intelligence officers of any sort) were included in the mission, a serious omission if the delegation was expected to discuss a highly technical field that was poorly understood by outsiders. General Strong's fellow observers, Admiral Robert Ghormley and Army Air Corps General Delos Emmons, were completely surprised by Strong's proposal; indeed, Emmons was probably unaware that the army even had a signals intelligence program. Strong was committed to collaboration with the British and before his departure from Washington had expressed to the army chief of staff his understanding that the United States should henceforth "give all information possible to the British to aid them in their present struggle and furnish them such material assistance as will not interfere seriously with our own defense preparations."[43] He was also convinced that collaboration would greatly assist the United States in strengthening its military defenses, a conviction reinforced upon his arrival in London by his discovery that Britain was a gold mine of technical information. Finally, Strong's cable of 5 September and the reaction to it in Washington suggest that American authorities had not prepared a policy concerning cryptanalytic cooperation with London, an inexplicable lapse if Strong had been directed to propose such cooperation.

When Strong's cable reached Washington on 5 September, General Sherman Miles, chief of army intelligence, immediately directed Colonel Spencer Akin, the officer then commanding the Signal Intelligence Service, to solicit the navy's opinion. In a meeting with Admiral Anderson, director of naval intelligence, and Admiral Noyes, director of naval communications and the officer responsible for naval signals intelligence, Akin learned that the navy's "off-hand" response to the inquiry from London was an emphatic no, although Anderson promised to submit a more considered, if no more positive, response later. General Miles then sought the advice of General Mauborgne, the chief signal officer, who was on an inspection visit to Fort Monmouth, New Jersey. With his request Miles enclosed a copy of a memorandum, "Proposed Exchange Basis with the British," prepared "several days ago" by Colonel Akin and William Friedman.[44] This informal study suggests that, like other elements in the army, SIS had been giving thought to the possibility of collaboration with Britain. In the area of cryptanalysis, Akin and Friedman recommended an exchange of "any and all material that we have on a basis of complete reciprocity," but only if the navy acted jointly with the army in the exchange and only if the material included information about specific foreign cryptosystems. The exchange would also extend to training manuals and information about mechanical codebreaking techniques. Akin and Friedman also proposed a swap of intercepted traffic to ensure the widest coverage of targets. Their only reservations concerned the sharing of information about American codes and ciphers. The navy, however, had more concerns. When asked for his comments on the memorandum, Commander Laurance Safford, officer in charge of OP-20-G, agreed that information concerning American high-grade ciphers should be withheld from the British, and he flatly rejected any collaboration in the areas of intercept and cryptanalysis.

On 7 September General Mauborgne, who was already familiar with Akin and Friedman's memorandum, strongly endorsed, "as a matter of utmost importance to National Defense," the idea of cryptanalytic cooperation with Britain, although he believed that for the moment each country should rely on its own intercept facilities. Two days later, General Miles passed this endorsement, along with his own, to Army Chief of Staff General George Marshall. Marshall secured the approval of the secretary of war and on 11 September signed an order stipulating that "information to be given to authorities of the British Empire will include . . . cryptanalytic information."[45]

It is easy to understand the army's enthusiasm for cooperation with the British. When General Marshall authorized the exchange of cryptanalytic information, Japanese traffic was still the only productive source of intelligence for the Signal Intelligence Service, although this source had significantly declined in value after Tokyo's introduction of the yet unsolved PURPLE cipher machine. German and Italian traffic produced negligible intelligence and would continue to do so as long as Berlin's and Rome's high-grade ciphers remained impenetrable. American codebreakers knew nothing about the work of the Government Code and Cypher School (GCCS), their British counterparts, but they were vaguely aware of Britain's cryptanalytical achievements during the First World War and assumed that GCCS was working hard to repeat those successes in the present war. Perhaps the British were already reading high-grade German and Italian ciphers. An exchange of "any and all material" might well result in information crucial to an American entry into Nazi and fascist communications. With luck an exchange might even help the effort against PURPLE.

Unfortunately, SIS had little to offer in return. Britain was not at war with Japan, and the Americans had no information about the status of Britain's work against Japanese communications. What if GCCS did not need or value information on Japanese diplomatic ciphers, the principal product that SIS would bring to the exchange? In the midst of a life-and-death struggle with the Nazis, would the British share the secrets of German cryptography in return for a copy of the cipher used by the Mexican treasury? SIS stood to benefit significantly from an active exchange, but it needed something important to bring to the table. Within days it had something big.

For eighteen months the battle to solve the PURPLE machine had consumed SIS. Although a handful of Japanese diplomatic missions (mainly in Asia) continued to use the old RED machine, the embassies in the major capitals, including Berlin, London, Moscow, Rome, and Washington, used exclusively the new cipher for their most sensitive communications. The inability to read PURPLE resulted in a virtual blackout in Washington's access to Tokyo's high-grade diplomatic traffic. SIS needed a solution, but the problem seemed intractable. PURPLE divided the Latin alphabet into two groups, one with six letters and one with twenty. The letters forming "the 6's" and "the 20's" varied from day to day, and the machine enciphered each group separately. Within weeks of the appearance of the new machine, Rowlett's team had ascertained how the 6's were enciphered, and Leo Rosen, a recent graduate of the electrical engineering program at the Massachusetts Institute of Technology, had devised an electromechanical apparatus to speed the process of recovering the plaintext equivalents of the 6's in a particular message. This produced a skeleton of a message in which, occasionally, the meaning of individual words might be guessed. The process, however, was complicated by the apparent absence of any relationship between the plaintext and shifting values of the letters constituting the group of 20's.[46] If the team could identify a relationship, perhaps by determining that PURPLE enciphered plaintext letters in a predictable, cyclical manner, they would be able to duplicate the process and break into the system.

In the Japanese section, Frank Rowlett worked fourteen-hour days with a small team that included Robert Ferner, Genevieve Grotjan, Leo Rosen, and Albert Small, names that would become legendary in American signals intelligence. Observations and results were regularly exchanged with OP-20-G, where naval cryptanalysts were separately attacking the Japanese machine. The pressure was intense. At the request of his old friend, the chief signal officer, General Joseph Mauborgne, William Friedman put aside the administrative work that increasingly monopolized his attention to conduct special studies into the cryptographic principles underlying the machine. For his part, Mauborgne, no stranger to cryptanalysis, took a personal interest in the problem and visited the Japanese section almost daily to discuss the work and encourage the staff. The liaison officer from MID who each day collected the translations of Tokyo's diplomatic correspondence anxiously pressed Rowlett for progress reports. Finally, in September 1940, the perseverance and hard work paid off.

On the afternoon of 20 September, a hot, humid Friday in Washington, Genevieve Grotjan, a studious young statistician who had come to SIS from the Railroad Retirement Board in 1939, quietly approached the table in the crowded Japanese section where Rowlett, Ferner, and Small were reviewing current efforts and commiserating over the prospects for cracking PURPLE. Politely interrupting the senior officers, she asked if they could come to her desk in the next room to look at what she had found. As the men leaned over the battered wooden desk, which was covered with worksheets, Grotjan pointed to a line on one sheet, then a line on another sheet. She then stepped back from the desk and waited silently. Al Small saw it immediately. He yelled, "Whoopee!" and ran around the small room, clasping his hands above his head like a victorious prizefighter. Bob Ferner, normally quiet and reserved, clapped his hands like an excited child and shouted "Hooray, hooray!" Rowlett jumped up and down and shouted, "That's it! That's it!" at Grotjan, whose eyes had filled with tears. People rushed into the room from other sections. Friedman pushed his way in to ask what the commotion was about. Rowlett pointed to the worksheets: "Look what Gene has just discovered." Friedman, the old master, examined the sheets and immediately understood. His thin frame seemed to sag from fatigue. It was one of the great moments in cryptanalytic history. Working with six messages, transmitted on the same day and partially reconstructed by SIS after the identification of the 6's, Genevieve Grotjan had noticed the presence of repeated sequences in some of the cipher texts, a discovery that provided the crucial entry into what had seemed an impregnable cipher machine.

One week later, on 27 September, Rowlett handed Friedman two decrypted PURPLE messages. These solutions, however, involved messages that had shared a common setting on the cipher machine (which was capable of multiple settings), and it would be several weeks before Rowlett's team had determined a method for establishing the settings of enough messages to produce a steady flow of translations. Progress accelerated when navy Lieutenant Frank Raven discovered a pattern to the daily settings. To capitalize fully on their success, Rowlett's team (with assistance from the navy) constructed two fully automated analogs of the PURPLE machine. Soon additional copies of the machine were constructed, with at least two going to OP-20-G, where naval cryptanalysts took up some of the burden of decrypting and translating the flood of secret messages that soon began flowing into Washington.[47]

The solution of PURPLE reopened access to Tokyo's high-grade diplomatic communications and significantly improved America's bargaining position in any exchanges with Britain. Even if the British had no immediate need for the fruits of American cryptanalytic efforts, they would understand that the solution of PURPLE was an impressive feat that established the United States as a potentially valuable partner in the signals war. However, the navy, suspicious of British intentions and concerned that any cryptologic exchanges would reveal secrets crucial to the national defense and, perhaps, assist the British in reading American codes and ciphers, had no intention of sharing information about PURPLE or any other codebreaking success. When proposing guidelines for collaboration with the British, Colonel Spencer Akin and William Friedman had advised that the army and navy act jointly. Naval opposition, especially from the codebreakers in OP-20-G, probably explains why no action was taken after General Marshall authorized cryptanalytic exchanges with London. General Sherman Miles, assistant chief of staff for intelligence, worried that the United States would lose a golden opportunity. On 4 October, almost four weeks after Marshall's authorization, Miles wrote to Lieutenant Colonel W. Regnier, military aide to Secretary of War Henry Stimson, to reiterate the importance of an immediate cryptanalytic exchange with the British. Emphasizing the practical benefits that would accrue to the United States as a result of such an exchange, he noted that army codebreakers would obtain information about hitherto impenetrable foreign cryptosystems, particularly those used by secret agents. The resulting intelligence might expose German and Italian espionage in the United States and provide Washington with insight into Axis designs on the Panama Canal and Latin America.

As the general surely intended, these arguments reached the secretary of war. On 23 October, Miles, General Joseph Mauborgne, and Assistant Secretary of War John McCloy met with Stimson to review the status of the army's signals intelligence program and discuss cooperation with Britain. The secretary of war, who seems to have been only vaguely aware of the program, was amazed at the "wonderful progress" of his codebreakers. It took no time to convince him that the exchange project should go forward. Stimson then led his colleagues to the Navy Department, where the secretary of the navy, Frank Knox, was, by prearrangement, waiting with Admiral Leigh Noyes and Admiral Walter Anderson. The case for exchange was made once again, and the army's representatives sought to assuage the navy's security concerns. The scales tipped when Admiral Harold Stark, the chief of naval operations, was called in for his advice and strongly supported the idea of sharing codebreaking information with Britain. In the name of the two services, the meeting proceeded to endorse the proposed cryptanalytic exchanges. The next day Stimson secured the agreement of Secretary of State Cordell Hull and notified President Roosevelt, who responded (through his military aide, General Watson) that he was happy to accept the judgment of his secretaries of war and navy in this matter and approved the proposed exchange.[48]

The president's approval removed all administrative obstacles to an arrangement with the British, although as late as December, Stimson and Knox had to quash a rearguard effort by oppositionists in OP-20-G whom the secretary of war considered nothing less than insubordinate. That month American and British representatives apparently initialed in Washington a one-page agreement outlining terms of cooperation that included the exchange of information relating to the diplomatic, military, and naval cryptographic systems of Germany, Italy, and Japan.[49]

To implement the agreement, the army and navy dispatched a joint mission to England. Originally, the army expected William Friedman to lead this delegation, but in December Friedman had been hospitalized after a nervous collapse brought on, in part, by the long struggle against PURPLE. To replace him, SIS selected Abraham Sinkov, one of the original analysts recruited by Friedman in 1930 and currently head of the Italian section, and Leo Rosen, an electrical engineering graduate of MIT who had contributed significantly to the solution of PURPLE. Both were selected, in part, because they were single and thus would not leave behind spouses and children as they ventured into a war zone subject to air attack by the Luftwaffe.[50] Sinkov and Rosen were given temporary army commissions as, respectively, captain and lieutenant. To fill its places in the delegation, the navy selected Lieutenant Prescott Currier, a specialist in Japanese diplomatic and naval attaché ciphers whose experience in naval signals intelligence extended back to the mid-1930s, and Ensign Robert Weeks, a young officer with only limited experience in cryptanalysis.

At least one author, noting the "lack of stars and eagles" on the uniforms of the Americans, has suggested that the seemingly junior status of the delegation "was unlikely to make British officialdom sit up and take notice."[51] This view does the mission an injustice. The delegation was deliberately conceived as a low-key, specialist mission to engage in technical discussions with their British counterparts. In the course of the mission its members were more likely to meet (mainly civilian) cryptanalysts than encounter the chief of the Imperial General Staff. The assignment required individuals experienced in and knowledgeable about cryptanalysis. In the army at least, these individuals were all civilians, since SIS employed no uniformed cryptanalysts. It would have been expecting too much to ask the army to commission as colonels or generals civilians who had never held any military rank in the regular army or reserve forces. The situation was different in the navy, where regular officers served as cryptanalysts in OP-20-G, but even there the most senior officer, Laurance Safford, was only a commander, and his vocal opposition to any cooperation with Britain precluded his selection for the delegation. It is also useful to recall that by American standards Sinkov and Currier were senior cryptanalysts. Except for Friedman, nobody in SIS had served longer than Sinkov, who had joined Frank Rowlett and Solomon Kullback in the founding class of SIS entrants.[52] In OP-20-G, where uniformed officers were required to serve periodically at sea, few except Safford had worked at cryptanalysis longer than Currier. Admittedly, Leo Rosen and Robert Weeks were junior, but Rosen, at least, had played a central role in a major cryptanalytic problem, and his background in electrical engineering prepared him well for technical discussions.

Although the delegation was supposedly a joint service mission, the army and navy did not collaborate in its organization and preparation. There were no joint consultations on the goals of the mission and no effort to agree on a common presentation to the British. The army and navy representatives met each other for the first time on the day of departure, although Currier and Sinkov knew each other slightly from previous interservice consultations on minor cryptologic problems during which they discovered a mutual interest in the famous Voynich manuscript.[53] Each service determined for itself what it would share with the British. The army decided to empty its cupboards. Sinkov's and Rosen's baggage apparently included a copy of the RED machine, a copy of the PURPLE machine, several additional Japanese diplomatic codes and ciphers solved by the army, the German diplomatic code (DESAB3) in its complete form as confiscated by the army from a clandestine German courier in Panama, the Italian diplomatic systems "X" and "TR" with their relevant encipherments as partially reconstructed by SIS, and from the Mexican desk a diplomatic code and three diplomatic ciphers. In return for these treasures, the army representatives were instructed in general terms to seek information on British work against German, Italian, Japanese, and Russian cryptosystems.

These instructions were a model of clarity and detail when compared with those given the naval delegates. Currier and Weeks were briefed by neither OP-20-G nor naval intelligence, and they received no directives beyond an offhand injunction "to get whatever you think we should get and have a look around."[54] Their baggage included all the navy's work on the latest version of the Japanese navy's fleet code, known to OP-20-G as JN-25B, some direction-finding manuals, and possibly other Japanese naval and diplomatic systems solved by naval codebreakers. The JN-25B materials were by far the most important of these items, but the system had been in service less than two months, and American codebreakers had recovered so few encipherment and code values that the codebook Currier and Weeks packed for the voyage to England was "almost empty."[55]

The mission began with a security lapse. Information concerning the mission was closely held, and only a handful of senior officers in the War and Navy Departments knew that the four officers would sail to England on HMS *George V*, a battleship that was bringing the new British ambassador, Lord Halifax, to the United States. Secrecy was so tight that the team had been ordered to reveal the destination and the purpose of the trip to no one, not even their wives. When, on 24 January 1941, Prescott Currier stepped into a chauffeured dark sedan and sped off into the half-light of early morning, his wife had no idea where he was going or when he would return. Within a few hours, however, she received a phone call from her friend Mary Wenger, the wife of Commander Joseph Wenger, another officer in the close-knit naval sigint community. Mary Wenger had just received a call from a friend in Annapolis who said that she had driven past the harbor and seen Prescott Currier and Bob Weeks boarding a launch with some other men and a lot of baggage and wooden crates. Fortunately, Axis intelligence services were not as vigilant as navy spouses.[56]

The small group and its baggage set out in two motor launches to meet the *George V*, which was anchored in the roads about two miles from shore. For reasons of protocol and security, they could not board the battleship until Lord Halifax and his party debarked, so the American delegates spent an unpleasant half hour circling in rough seas while trying to protect themselves and their precious wooden crates from the rain that pelted the open boats.

Once aboard the British warship, the Americans were shown every courtesy. The voyage across the Atlantic was uneventful but long. Leaving the American coast behind, the *George V* sailed south to join the escort of a convoy bound for the British Isles. The convoy, mainly ships carrying Argentine beef, was slow, and the battleship could proceed no faster than the slowest merchantman. After two weeks at sea, the battleship sailed into the large British naval base at Scapa Flow, Scotland.

The American passengers were met at the dock by an assistant naval attaché from the U.S. embassy in London, who had arranged for them to continue their journey south by flying boat. Unfortunately, the young officer had been told nothing about the group and its baggage, and the Americans discovered that their crates would not fit through the door of the plane. The captain of the *George V* promptly came to their assistance by arranging for them to board HMS *Newcastle,* a cruiser sailing immediately for the south of England. Although shipboard space was so scarce that their crates had to be lashed to the top deck, the impressionable Americans were delighted by the trim *Newcastle* and its veteran captain, an old seadog who paced his bridge in thigh-high seaboots and a bright red foul-weather jacket.

The travelers, however, were soon reminded that they were in a war zone. While enjoying the fellowship and hot soup of the cruiser's wardroom, the Americans heard a terrific crash followed by what they thought was the sound of heavy chains being dragged along the steel deck above their heads. Clanging claxons and shouting officers soon revealed the truth. A marauding Stuka dive-bomber had pounced on the cruiser, dropping one bomb and strafing the upper decks. As he rushed from the wardroom, Lieutenant Currier tried to recall from his sea duty how long a human could survive in icy, northern waters, but the sound of machine guns, as the German plane returned for another pass, quickly turned his thoughts to the precious crates of cryptologic equipment stacked on the exposed deck. The attack was brief, but when the Americans came on deck they fully expected to see their crates splintered and their contents destroyed. To their surprise, the hardwood boxes had weathered the air attack as well as the cruiser's armored plate; their only damage, several pockmarks from spent bullets.

The *Newcastle* made port on the evening of 7 February. The Americans were met by two cars and driven through the night to Bletchley Park, the wartime headquarters of GCCS, Britain's cryptanalytic organization. Without any time to compose or refresh themselves, they were taken straight to a darkened building, guided through two sets of heavy blackout curtains, and led into a small room furnished with a single desk, behind which stood three men. Without ceremony the Americans were introduced to their hosts, Commander Alistair Denniston, the operational director of GCCS, Commander Edward Travis, his deputy, and Lieutenant Colonel John Tiltman, the chief of the military section, who welcomed them to Bletchley Park and expressed their hope that the visit would be productive. The formalities completed, the visitors were ushered from the building and chauffeured to the nearby estate of the head of the Anglo-Persian Oil Company, who had placed his elegant home and its staff at the disposal of GCCS. As the weary Americans settled into their rooms in the large mansion, they were probably glad that their introductory call at Bletchley Park had been mercifully brief. They had no way of knowing that the simple meeting, the first encounter between American and British cryptanalysts during the Second World War, marked the start of a relationship that would significantly affect the course of the war.

For the next several weeks, the Americans toured GCCS facilities, visited intercept stations, examined equipment, observed processing operations, and generally talked shop with their British counterparts. After pledging to reveal the information only to the directors of their respective cryptanalytic and intelligence services, the army and navy delegates were briefed on Bletchley Park's most secret operation, the attack against "Enigma," the high-grade cipher machine used by the German armed forces. They also observed the operation of the "bombe," the mechanical device used to crack the Enigma ciphers.[57] The army and navy teams each had their own car and driver and generally went their separate ways, but in the evenings they sat together to compare notes and review the events of the day. All were impressed by the spirit of goodwill and cooperation that was evident in all visits and conversations. They agreed that all their questions were answered without prevarication and that everything was open to them. Whatever personal reservations about cooperation with the British the four Americans may have harbored before their mission were largely assuaged by the time the delegation boarded the battleship HMS *Revenge* for the return voyage, first to Halifax, Nova Scotia, and then by American destroyer to the Washington Navy Yard.

Although some in the navy, particularly Commander Safford in OP-20-G, the most vocal critic of Anglo-American collaboration, believed that the Americans received little in return for the precious secrets of the PURPLE machine, the army's SIS considered the Sinkov mission an unqualified success. The army delegates returned from GCCS with important information on German, Italian, Japanese, and Russian cryptographic systems, the very subjects of most concern to the army codebreakers. Some of this information, especially that dealing with Axis military and air force systems, provided an introduction to cryptologic territory hitherto unexplored at SIS. There were also unexpected treats: a new Mexican cipher, a complete Brazilian codebook, partially reconstructed Chilean and Argentine codes, and descriptions of German, Italian, and Russian meteorological codes (crucial for planning air and sea operations). Reviewing the results of their mission, Sinkov and Rosen concluded, "The material . . . will result in a saving of several years of labor on the part of a fairly large staff."[58]

Much of the material could not be exploited at the time because SIS lacked the necessary staff or could not intercept the traffic, but some, particularly the information on diplomatic systems, was immediately useful. Although GCCS had not cracked the high-grade German diplomatic ciphers, the British cryptanalysts had determined the nature of these ciphers. They confirmed that the Reich foreign ministry used four different systems to communicate with its embassies and consulates, and that all four used the same codebook, each differing only in the type of encipherment applied to that code. Solomon Kullback's German section had recovered the basic codebook, DESAB, which, unenciphered, served the foreign ministry for routine consular and administrative communications. For lack of traffic the Americans were struggling with the next most secure system, the *Spalierverfehren*. GCCS also lacked sufficient traffic to make much progress against *Spalierverfehren*, but the British corroborated Kullback's belief that the system was enciphered with reciprocal bigram tables, and they donated a set of tables recovered from the German consulate in Reykjavik, Iceland, during the British occupation of the island. As for the Wilhelmstrasse's remaining two systems, Sinkov and Rosen learned from their hosts that the most secret was a one-time-pad (OTP) system, while the next system in importance (dubbed FLORADORA by GCCS) used a long additive.[59] GCCS admitted that it had, for the time being, abandoned work on these two formidable ciphers, but at least the Americans now knew what they were facing.

While British insights into German cryptography were most welcome, information concerning Italian cryptosystems proved the most immediately useful. As head of the Italian section in SIS, Sinkov was especially interested in British success against Rome's codes and ciphers, and

he returned from Bletchley Park with information that significantly accelerated his section's work. When Sinkov departed on his mission, SIS was
reading two Italian diplomatic systems, neither of which produced significant intelligence. At Bletchley, Sinkov acquired information (including
partially reconstructed codebooks) concerning two additional diplomatic
systems hitherto unknown to the Americans, as well as details concerning
a new version of Trujillo, one of the systems already under study at SIS.
This information accelerated the work against Rome's communications to
such an extent that in order to exploit the opportunity six additional analysts were added to the four already committed to the effort. By the summer of 1941 they were decrypting messages in "IMPERO," the first high-
grade Italian diplomatic cipher read by SIS.[60]

As both London and Washington intended, the Sinkov mission
launched a program of cryptanalytic exchanges. The War Department
wasted little time in capitalizing on the new relationship. Sinkov and
Rosen had hardly unpacked their bags before SIS was seeking from its new
British contacts material on French diplomatic systems, especially those
used between Vichy and the French territories in the Western Hemisphere.
In return, SIS began sending to Bletchley Park cryptanalytic findings relating to German, Italian, and Japanese communications.[61]

In August, Commander Alistair Denniston crossed the Atlantic to review American cryptanalytic operations and discuss further collaboration. While willing to share information about its work against the ciphers
of Germany, Italy, and a range of secondary powers, GCCS hoped that
each partner in the nascent relationship would play to its strengths. In
terms of intercept and processing, the Americans were better situated
than the British to exploit their successes against Japan, and Denniston's
mission was, in part, intended to encourage his hosts to keep their eye on
the ball. He first visited OP-20-G, where he judged the personnel "keenly
alive, enthusiastic about their work and anxious to develop it," but found
the offices so cramped that he compared his meetings there to "conferences in a telephone exchange to which the general public was freely admitted." He noted with approval that the navy's sigint operations focused
on Japan but worried that in its eagerness to share with the army credit
for the continuing success against Japanese diplomatic communications
OP-20-G was neglecting naval work. He also believed that the small sections devoted to German and Italian naval ciphers received too little
traffic to make any significant contribution to the evolving joint effort despite receiving "a lot" of material from GCCS, and suspected that the ana-

lysts working these problems might be more profitably employed against Japan.[62]

Denniston then spent a week at SIS, outlining for the senior officers the status of current operations at GCCS, devising a secure channel for passing material between Bletchley Park and the Munitions Building, arranging for the assignment to SIS of a British liaison officer, and visiting the various sections to observe operations against Japanese, German, Italian, French, and Latin American communications. In Kullback's German section he noted that collaboration was already producing promising results in solving a problem that had seemed intractable. He was less sanguine about SIS's emerging interest in Vichy French and Latin American communications, areas in which GCCS was helping with material and technical observations. Here again, Denniston feared that the lack of traffic seriously undercut the prospects for success and worried that these operations would interfere with SIS's main effort against Japan. His concern about distractions was partially assuaged when the Americans undertook to cooperate with Britain's codebreaking unit in the Pacific, the Far East Combined Bureau (FECB), on the Japanese army problem, an undertaking he considered "one of the best results of my visit." As mentioned earlier, SIS's work against the ciphers of the Imperial Japanese Army had faltered for lack of traffic and continuity, problems that Herbert Yardley's temporary rehabilitation in the fall of 1940 did little to resolve. Collaboration with FECB resuscitated the effort by providing American codebreakers access to traffic and the experience of cryptanalysts more familiar with Japanese army communications practices.[63]

Another important result of the British mission was the friendship Denniston forged with William Friedman. The two seemed to have hit it off from the first, and the senior American cryptanalyst made a strong impression on the British visitor. Convinced that Friedman's experience and skill made SIS cryptanalytically superior to OP-20-G, Denniston concluded that "he alone of those I met is competent to deal with all major problems of cypher breaking and of cypher security." This confidence in the abilities of SIS's senior cryptanalyst was a useful counterweight to certain reservations Denniston had concerning American sigint operations. An important figure in British signals intelligence since 1914 and head of GCCS since 1919, Denniston remained faithful to time-tested methods. He dutifully admired the machine sections in SIS and OP-20-G but upon his return to Bletchley advised his colleagues that he was "not convinced that these mechanical devices lead to success. Close personal effort makes one intimate with the problems which, when served up mechanically, fails to appeal." He also recorded his doubts about the American practice of recruiting mathematicians, statisticians, and engineers, and then moving them from problem to problem as operations required:

> Our success in reconstruction of diplomatic books is founded on continuity of contact with the subject and the drafters of the telegrams. A first class linguistic knowledge and a study of the political situation are the qualities of our best book-builders and these are lacking in the U.S.A.
>
> The staff there is interested in the solution of a cryptanalytical problem and the contents of the results do not concern them. Even in the Japanese work the finished document based on the translation of the cypher telegram is not always of the standard we aim to maintain. It might nearly be said that they wish to find mathematical formulae or mechanical methods to solve their problems while we aim to provide the various intelligence services with a clear and accurate text.

Although its potential contribution to the American signals intelligence program far exceeded that of any other nation, Britain was not the only country with which SIS established relations in the winter of 1940–1941. In October 1940, as the War and Navy Departments debated sharing cryptanalytic information with London, General Joseph Mauborgne offered China a shipment of obsolete but serviceable Signal Corps equipment for the nominal sum of two hundred dollars and "other valuable considerations, which valuable considerations need not be set down on paper at any time." The "considerations" Mauborgne had in mind included access to Chinese information about Japanese army codes and ciphers. The Chinese promptly provided an obsolete Imperial Army field code and suggested a collaboration in which Chungking would exchange intercepts for a share in any intelligence resulting from the solution of Japanese traffic relating to China. For reasons that remain unclear but probably concerned Washington's distrust of Chinese security, SIS did not pursue this suggestion, but it did provide Chungking with textbooks and pamphlets for teaching cryptanalysis.[64] In the late fall of 1940, cryptanalytic training materials were also shared with the governments of Canada and the Union of South Africa.[65] The Canadian connection proved especially significant.

A loyal dominion of the British Empire, Canada had rushed to Britain's defense in September 1939. War measures included the establishment of army and navy radio monitoring stations, but, untrained in the skills of signals intelligence, the Canadians initially acceded to British advice to focus on intercept while leaving the more ambitious tasks of codebreaking and traffic analysis to GCCS. Within the year, however, notable intercept successes, in particular the identification of the Spanish army's order of battle entirely from plain-language broadcasts, encouraged the Canadians to consider establishing a full-fledged signal intelligence service. Since the British had already made it clear that they considered such a service beyond the needs and capacities of their dominion partner, the Canadians looked south.[66]

On 19 November 1940 Captain E. M. Drake, Canadian Corps of Signals, accompanied by Colonel H. P. G. Letson, the military attaché at Ottawa's legation in Washington, called at the War Department office of General Joseph Mauborgne. Captain Drake commanded the Canadian army's listening post at Rockcliffe Airport, Ottowa, and he had come to the U.S. Army's chief signal officer for advice on organizing a cryptanalytic organization in the Canadian army. Specifically, he requested information about American cryptanalytic organizations and procedures and proposed a visit to the Signal Corps' monitoring stations. Mauborgne, who was not in the habit of discussing his service's most secret operations with just any foreign officer who walked through his door, was taken aback by this forthright approach. He curtly explained that the War Department had not yet determined a policy for sharing cryptanalytic information with foreign governments, even friendly ones. A tour of intercept stations was out of the question until Washington had settled on a policy that would consider the position of other parties, such as Great Britain, as well as Canada. When the general (curious, perhaps, about the potential fruits of the collaboration with Britain then under discussion in Washington) asked if London had furnished Canada with much material on German, Italian, Japanese, and Russian systems, Drake readily admitted that the British had so far provided nothing. Mauborgne, who now realized that the Canadians really were starting from scratch and had nothing to trade, suggested that if Ottawa was serious about a signals intelligence service and cryptanalytic cooperation with other powers, it might make the acquisition of such material its first order of business. As a consolation prize he sent the Canadians home with some instructional pamphlets on cryptanalysis.[67]

Mauborgne was only slightly more forthcoming the following spring when, on 2 May 1941, he received another Canadian delegation composed of two mathematicians from the National Research Council, Gilbert de B. Robinson and H. S. M. Coxeter. Once again he declined to provide details about the organization and techniques of the U.S. Army's SIS, although he alarmed his visitors by warning that a professional service required at the minimum 50, and ideally 250, personnel, each with a year of training. Insisting that he had no people to spare, he deflected a request that the War Department detach an officer to advise Ottawa but allowed that he did know of an individual experienced in the business who might be interested in helping the Canadians: Herbert Yardley. Acknowledging that Yardley was in some disfavor in "certain circles in the United States Government," Mauborgne assured his guests that the former director of the American and Chinese cryptanalytic services was highly qualified and, as fortune would have it, was at that moment living in Washington.[68]

Robinson and Coxeter wasted no time in pursuing Mauborgne's lead. They returned to the Canadian legation and immediately phoned their superior, C. J. Mackenzie, the acting president of the National Research Council, who authorized them to approach Yardley. That very afternoon, Yardley called at the legation by invitation and impressed the young Canadians with his experience and confidence. He certainly did not weaken his position when, in contrast to Mauborgne's position, he blandly assured his listeners that an office of ten to fifteen people could serve very nicely and that he could easily train such a group in six weeks' time. Within a week, Yardley was in Ottawa, where he convinced (not without some effort) a committee representing Canada's army, navy, and foreign office to allow him to organize and direct a small cryptanalytic service to investigate, initially, Axis clandestine and Japanese diplomatic traffic.[69] The new service, known as the Examination Unit, began operations in June 1941 in a small room in the National Research Council buildings in Ottawa. Assuming his old alias, "Herbert Osborne," Yardley threw himself into the work, thankful for another chance to return to what had always been his first love and true métier. Within two weeks he confirmed his patrons' confidence in him by solving a cipher used by German agents in Brazil to report the movements of merchant ships. By September, Yardley was routinely reading German clandestine traffic out of South America and had cracked ciphers used by the governments of Vichy France and Colombia. By October he had solved a medium-grade Japanese system. By December he had been dismissed.[70]

Yardley assumed that the controversies surrounding the publication of *The American Black Chamber* and the abortive effort to publish *Japanese Diplomatic Secrets* were a thing of the past. He was wrong. In Washington, his exposure of American signals intelligence successes in the 1920s still rankled army and navy officers, many of whom believed that he was an untrustworthy opportunist who would do anything for money. By engineering Yardley's dismissal from the Examination Unit, these officers would remove a perceived threat to the security of American, British, and Canadian signals intelligence and wreak revenge on someone who was little better than a traitor in their eyes. The Examination Unit's director had been the subject of conversations during Commander Denniston's visit to SIS in August. The British were already unsettled by the presence in Ottawa of "one Colonel Yardley who also had worked in Chungking and who had written a book entitled *The Black Chamber* which was very harmful to [the] United States cryptographic organization."[71] London's reservations were apparently confirmed during Denniston's conversations with American sigint authorities. Calling at Ottawa before his return to GCCS, Denniston informed the Canadians that they could expect no sigint cooperation from either the Americans or the British so long as Yardley was anywhere in the picture. When the Canadians reminded their visitor that the American cryptanalyst had been recommended by no one less than the chief signal officer of the U.S. Army, Denniston bluntly replied that General Mauborgne (who had retired in July) had been speaking for himself, and his attitude did not represent the views of other American intelligence officers. He added that GCCS would be happy to detach for service in Ottawa an experienced cryptanalyst to replace Yardley.[72]

Denniston's ultimatum did not go down well, but Ottawa believed that London's and Washington's cooperation was crucial to the future of Canadian signals intelligence. On November 22 Yardley was informed that his services were no longer required. The following week he received a reprieve when the interdepartmental committee that supervised the Examination Unit decided to send a delegation to Washington to determine the extent of American opposition to Yardley.

In Washington the delegation, Lieutenant C. H. Little from naval intelligence and Lester Pearson from External Affairs, first interviewed Captain Edward Hastings, RN, the representative in the American capital of Brigadier Stewart Menzies, chief of Britain's secret service. Hastings informed Little and Pearson that American signals intelligence circles considered Yardley a shameless self-promoter and a mercenary whose cryptanalytic abilities were no more than ordinary. He assured his listeners that both London and Washington were eager to collaborate with the Examination Unit, but he repeated Denniston's warning that neither the British nor the Americans could work with someone they so disliked and distrusted.

The Canadians heard the same story from the Americans. Admiral Noyes, director of naval communications, bluntly asserted that Yardley should be in prison and that the navy would "not touch [him] with a ten foot pole." General Dawson Olmstead, Mauborgne's replacement as chief signal officer, said that the Signal Corps considered Yardley untrustworthy. When asked about Yardley's technical competence, Olmstead replied by asking the Canadians whether, if they were hiring a chef and one applied who was a known criminal, they would be interested in his ability to make an omelet. General Olmstead's views were seconded by General Sherman Miles, director of military intelligence. When asked point-blank if Canada could expect cooperation from the United States if Ottawa retained Yardley, the army officers replied no.

Surprisingly, the only American to defend Yardley was William Friedman, who tried to be fair. Friedman acknowledged that the publication of *The American Black Chamber* had seriously damaged the interests of the United States, and that army and navy officers would never again trust its author. He also confirmed that Yardley was a self-promoter preoccupied with making money. On the other hand, Friedman pointed out that Yardley was a hard worker, an administrator who was capable of inspiring loyalty in his staff, and a good codebreaker, although he had little knowledge of machine ciphers, and his methods were becoming increasingly outdated. In the end, however, the army's senior cryptanalyst admitted that there could be no cooperation so long as Yardley remained in the Examination Unit.[73] Yardley's fate was sealed. If Yardley was the price Ottawa had to pay for cooperation, then it would pay the price. On 6 December 1941 Pearson informed the American that the decision to end his services stood. Two weeks later, Yardley returned to the United States. The founder of American signals intelligence would never again work in cryptanalysis.

While senior army and navy officers pursued their vendetta against Herbert Yardley, SIS continued its work against an expanding list of targets. In the late fall of 1941, the service was organized into four sections under the command of Lieutenant Colonel Rex Minckler, who in June had replaced Spencer Akin upon the latter's promotion to signal officer for the Philippine Department. With the title "civilian assistant," William Friedman continued as the senior technical adviser to the military commander. Major Harold Hayes was the executive officer and the chief of

A Section (Administration), which, in addition to handling matters of budget and personnel, supervised the machine unit. Major Harold Doud was chief of B Section (Cryptanalysis), which now included subsections for Japan, Germany, Italy, France, and South America, as well as a traffic desk and a clerical pool. Under Captain Earle Cook, C Section (Cryptography) tested and produced codes and ciphers for use by the army. D Section (Laboratory) was essentially a one-person operation as Major A. McGrail developed secret inks and tested suspicious letters for invisible writing.[74]

The cryptanalytic element remained the backbone of the organization. In the fall of 1941 Solomon Kullback's German desk solved a Kryha cipher machine used by the commercial representatives of the German foreign ministry, although the traffic in this system (designated KW by the Americans) was relatively low-grade.[75] Abraham Sinkov's Italian desk was regularly decrypting messages in three systems, including the high-grade IMPERO, and the number of Italian translations in the SIS *Bulletin* had increased from two or three a month in the spring of 1940 to twenty-five or thirty a month by the fall of 1941. The old Mexican unit had been renamed the South American desk to acknowledge SIS's growing interest in the governments to the south of the United States. While maintaining its mastery over Mexico City's cryptosystems, the renamed unit had scored successes against several new targets. It had begun studying Brazil's communications in December 1940 and by the late spring of 1941 had recovered enough values in the low-grade "A Code" to produce its first Brazilian translation. That spring the unit began reconstructing a second Brazilian code with the help of a list of identifications from GCCS and traffic from a monitoring station established secretly inside the American embassy in Rio de Janeiro.[76] At the same time, the codebreakers solved a polyalphabetic cipher used by the Colombian foreign ministry to communicate with Bogotá's diplomatic representatives in Europe.

By the end of the year, the South American desk was beginning investigations of Portuguese and Spanish ciphers. The creation of the French desk, the newest cryptanalytic unit in the organization, reflected growing concern in Washington about pro-German tendencies in Vichy. American policy makers worried that, under pressure from Berlin, Vichy would allow Germany to extend its influence into the French empire, particularly France's territories in the Western Hemisphere. In such an eventuality, the status of French naval units based in the Caribbean at Fort-de-France (Martinique) would become a pressing question. In the early fall of 1941 the French desk registered its first success when it began reading the so-called Colonial Code used by Vichy to communicate with French territories in the Western Hemisphere. This success provided Washington with a potentially important window on Vichy's intentions.[77]

With the solution of PURPLE, the Japanese section had reacquired access to Tokyo's most secret communications. Exploitation of this success was shared with OP-20-G. The navy claimed a role in the operations, since naval cryptanalysts had joined their army counterparts in the attack against PURPLE and had contributed to the final solution. Naval personnel also provided necessary reinforcement to army analysts and translators who, if left to their own resources, would have been overwhelmed by the demands of processing forty to fifty Japanese messages a day. Naval authorities, moreover, were not about to let the army claim credit for the single most important source of intelligence concerning Japan. On its own, OP-20-G had scored important victories against Japanese maritime communications, but peacetime reports on the movement of a fleet oiler or the deployment of a destroyer flotilla lacked the drama and immediacy of intercepted instructions to the Japanese ambassador in Washington or reports from the imperial embassy in Berlin. In a bureaucratic environment where visibility in the corridors of power meant influence, these authorities wanted naval personnel to be directly associated with cryptanalytic success. This desire only intensified after December 1940 when, after the introduction of JN-25B, a new version of the main fleet cipher, OP-20-G lost access to the more important messages of the Imperial Japanese Navy.

Soon after the solution of PURPLE, the two services reached an agreement on processing Japanese diplomatic messages.[78] The army would decrypt and translate messages originating on even-numbered days, while the navy handled messages transmitted on odd-numbered days. SIS sent copies of its translations to the army chief of staff, MID, the secretary of war, the secretary of state, ONI, and ("in exceptional cases only") the military aide to the president. All copies except those sent to MID and ONI were to be returned to MID for destruction. Messages translated by OP-20-G went to the chief of naval operations, ONI, the secretary of the navy, the secretary of state, the naval aide to the president, and ("in exceptional cases only, when directed") MID. In January 1941 the services agreed to accept responsibility for delivery of signals intelligence to the White House on alternate months, with the army beginning in January.[79]

The army withdrew from this agreement in the spring when an incident raised questions about the handling of "special material" in the

White House. In May a crumpled translation was discovered in the waste-basket of the president's military aide, General Edwin Watson. On 6 May SIS had intercepted a message from the Japanese embassy in Berlin informing Tokyo that "an absolutely reliable source" reported that the United States had broken Japan's diplomatic cipher. On 20 May Ambassador Nomura reported from Washington that "I have discovered that the United States is reading some of our codes though I do not know which ones." American cryptanalysts waited anxiously until it became apparent that, whatever their suspicions, the Japanese maintained their faith in the security of PURPLE. It was a close call, but so long as the source of the security leak remained unknown, SIS was not about to entrust Magic (as the decrypts were now code-named) to a White House aide who could not distinguish top secret intelligence from that day's page torn from his appointment calendar. Also, MID had concluded that since the content of Magic was exclusively diplomatic, the State Department was the more appropriate vehicle for passing the material to the president.[80]

The army's withdrawal from the dissemination agreement seriously disrupted the distribution of signals intelligence. In July and September, President Roosevelt saw no Magic documents, although his naval aide, Captain John Beardall, briefed him on the contents of the latest decrypts, and Secretary of State Hull also discussed the contents with him. At the end of September the president told Beardall that he wanted to see the decrypts, but the naval aide explained it was impossible, since September was an army month and only the army could deliver the documents. Roosevelt's request has usually been interpreted as an implicit criticism of the army, but it was directed at the navy as well. For security purposes the navy had always insisted that Magic not be distributed in the form of straight translations. It preferred to distribute "memos" summarizing the contents of one or more translations, and on at least one occasion it attacked the army for distributing the actual translations to the State Department and within the War Department. Roosevelt's request to see translations rather than memos required both the army and the navy to change their practices. During October (a navy month) the White House continued to receive only memos, a sign that the navy was as resistant as the army to changing established procedures. Roosevelt finally put an end to the farce in early November by insisting that he receive the translated decrypts. At a hurriedly summoned conference on 10 November, the services agreed that henceforth the navy would deliver Magic (in decrypt form) to the White House, while the army would deliver it to the secretary of state.[81]

The question of who actually saw Magic remains vexing. The various dissemination agreements are uncertain guides. At the White House the president read Magic, but at least one of his assistants, General Watson, had access to the intercept material, and perhaps others did also. The secretary of state appears on every distribution list, but it seems that Magic circulated well beyond the desk of Cordell Hull. Sumner Welles, the undersecretary of state, saw it, as did at least one assistant secretary, Adolph Berle, and the chief of the Division of Far Eastern Affairs, Maxwell Hamilton. Stanley Hornbeck, the special adviser on Far Eastern affairs, may also have been privy to the secrets. Two of Hull's personal assistants shared responsibility for receiving the materials each day from the army courier. Time pressures often required the messenger to leave the locked pouch containing the material with one of the assistants, from whom it would be retrieved the next day in exchange for that day's pouch. Furthermore, it is not clear that all the recipients saw all or even the same translations from day to day. On any given day, did Hull decide which, if any, of the decrypts would be shown to Maxwell Hamilton? Did the personal assistants have any role in determining which decrypts received the attention of the secretary of state? At this distance in time it is impossible to answer these questions with certainty.

Ambiguities concerning the distribution of Magic complicate the already difficult effort to determine the influence of signals intelligence on American diplomacy in 1941. As mentioned earlier, various factors, including the loss for eighteen months of high-grade Japanese traffic when Tokyo introduced the PURPLE cipher machine, the inability of SIS to read any European traffic at a time when Washington was preoccupied with events in Berlin, London, Moscow, Paris, and Rome, and Franklin Roosevelt's rather cavalier attitude toward signals intelligence conspired to limit the influence of codebreaking on American policy in the first year of the war. As late as January 1941, Secretary of War Henry Stimson still had to admonish Roosevelt for not reading the decrypts sent to the White House. That year, however, other problems had been at least partially resolved.[82] With the solution of PURPLE in September 1940, Washington regained access to Tokyo's most secret communications and thereby recovered a window on events and attitudes in various capitals, the most important being Berlin and Rome. For instance, in the spring of 1941 the reports of Japan's ambassadors in Berlin and Rome provided indications of Hitler's intention to turn on the Soviet Union. SIS translated several of these reports and passed at least some to the State Department, where (along with information from other sources) they served as the basis for a warning by Undersecretary Sumner Welles to the Soviet ambassador about the threat to the Soviet Union.[83] Welles's action is of special interest because it represents the first documented case of sigint influencing American diplomacy since the birth of SIS in 1930.

Signals intelligence also became more visible on the horizon of American policy makers as their immediate preoccupations shifted from Europe to the Far East. As the central question changed from "What will Berlin (or Rome) do?" to "What will Tokyo do?" the dependency on Japanese messages became a strength rather than a weakness. The Magic background to Pearl Harbor has been examined and reexamined in hundreds of books and articles, and there is little point in detailing once again the futile negotiations in the summer and fall of 1941 that were the prelude to war in the Pacific. It is easy to exaggerate the importance of signals intelligence in the diplomacy of those months. In the matter of sigint the question is not so much "What did Washington know?" (the answer being "Whatever Tokyo chose to tell its embassies"—information that did not include the intention to attack Pearl Harbor on 7 December 1941), but "What difference did it make?" The answer to the latter question is "Very little." Events in the final months of 1941 would have played out pretty much the same even if Washington had had no access to Japanese diplomatic communications.

Signals intelligence gave the United States a tactical advantage in the negotiations by providing advance notice of what the Japanese representatives, ambassadors Nomura and Kurusu, would say; by allowing Washington to confirm that the diplomats were accurately reporting the American position to their government; and by revealing Tokyo's negotiating strategy. Thus, on 7 November, when Nomura presented to the secretary of state Japan's so-called Proposal A, a statement of Tokyo's terms for a settlement in the Far East, Hull not only was already aware of the content of this proposal but also knew that the ambassador had in his pocket a less-stringent fallback position, "Proposal B," in the event that A failed.[84] Such information would have been of inestimable value to the United States if Washington and Tokyo had been engaged in real give-and-take negotiations. Unfortunately, they were not.

In 1941 Japan and the United States were on a collision course that could be avoided only if one or the other forsook long-established policies and deeply cherished beliefs about themselves and others. Neither country was prepared to take such a step. The Japanese were determined to pursue their imperial ambitions in the Pacific, and the Americans were determined to stop them. On the strategic level Washington wanted to restrain Japanese militarism, distance Tokyo from Berlin and Rome, assert the Open Door in the Far East, ensure an independent China, and buttress (at least during the war) the position in the region of Britain, France, and the Netherlands. American policy makers did not need signals intelligence to identify these objectives (some of which predated the creation of SIS), nor did they need signals intelligence to tell them that the Japanese would challenge them, since Japan's position was evident in its public words and deeds and in the reports of American diplomats in Tokyo, Berlin, and Rome. Neither did signals intelligence guide American policy makers in charting a course to reach their objectives. The decisions to embargo scrap iron and oil are cases in point. When diplomatic firmness failed to divert Japan from the paths of militarism and expansion, Washington turned to economic sanctions. It persisted with these sanctions even when intercepts clearly revealed that such punishments were aggravating the very behavior they were intended to restrain. Similarly, Washington continued to insist on Japan's military withdrawal from Chinese territory long after sigint indicated that Tokyo had no intention of liquidating its China venture.

When diplomats are committed by choice or necessity to a particular policy, signals intelligence plays little role beyond monitoring the course of that policy. In the final weeks of 1941, Magic merely confirmed what American policy makers already believed: that Japan was bent on military expansion, and that short of surrendering fundamental interests, there was nothing the United States could do to deter war in the Pacific. While Washington struggled to maintain the charade of negotiations in order to gain precious time to prepare its Pacific defenses, signals intelligence was reduced to watching the clock tick off the last few seconds of peace.

Chapter Four

Marching to War

War fell upon Monitoring Station 6 (Fort McKinley, Philippines) from the sky. When news of the Japanese attack against Hawaii reached Manila on the morning of December 8, the station commander, Major Joseph Scherr, assembled his small detachment of the Second Signal Service Company, issued sidearms, and set the men to digging trenches for an expected attack. Throughout the day, as the men completed their defenses and checked their equipment, they seemed insulated from the air attacks that pummeled air bases and military installations on Luzon and Mindanao. To everyone's surprise, no Japanese aircraft appeared over the station, and exploding bombs and sputtering machine guns did not interrupt the clang of picks and shovels and the static of radio receivers. The illusion of security was shattered the next morning when several "Betties" (medium bombers) peeled away from a flight of Japanese bombers heading for nearby Nichols Field and made a run against the station. Officers and enlisted men ran for their newly dug trenches as, for the first time, personnel of the Signal Intelligence Service came under fire. No one was hurt in the attack, and the intercept facilities were undamaged; less than half a mile down the road, however, a Pan-American Airways transmitting tower was demolished.

The detachment prepared for the worst. Major Scherr ordered files destroyed, radio equipment moved into bunkers at Fort McKinley, and the station wired for demolition. Before Pearl Harbor, MS-6 had been intercepting Japanese diplomatic traffic, but with the attack against the Philippines the unit abandoned this target and concentrated on Japanese tactical circuits, especially those carrying air-ground communications. The intercept operators were soon able to predict the direction and timing of Japanese air attacks on the islands, although initially U.S. Army Air Corps commanders, who had no experience with this kind of intercept work, were inclined to ignore the predictions. Lieutenant Harold Brown assumed command of the monitoring station when Scherr was promoted and assigned to the staff of General Douglas MacArthur's signal officer, General Spencer Akin, himself a former commander of the Signal Intelligence Service. On Christmas Eve, MS 6 was dissolved as an SIS unit and moved to Corregidor Island, where most of the personnel were assigned to general communications duties.

Most radio intelligence work ceased, although in the new year a few of the specialists were detached from general duties to resume monitoring Japanese army and air force communications as the enemy advanced against the remnants of American and Filipino resistance. From the dank tunnels of the island fortress, the operators faithfully radioed to Washington information about Japanese communications. On 24 March General MacArthur, who had departed the Philippines for Australia earlier that month in a party that included General Akin and Lieutenant Colonel Scherr, ordered Lieutenant Brown and the sigint personnel to evacuate to Australia. Brown and most of his men escaped, but a handful remained on Corregidor until the fortress fell on 6 May. One or two somehow eluded capture and joined guerrilla units in the jungle. The rest went into Japanese prisoner-of-war camps.[1]

In Washington, war came to the headquarters of the Signal Intelligence Service with less drama but no less impact. The shipboard fires at Pearl Harbor had hardly cooled before winds of change began to circulate in the corridors of the Munitions Building, and the currents were especially strong in the offices of SIS. The events of 7 December catapulted SIS into an administrative and operational maelstrom. In the last months of peace the codebreakers had been hard-pressed to keep up with the intercepts, but in the weeks after the Japanese attack those months now seemed positively tranquil. Suddenly SIS had to find, train, and assimilate the additional staff required by mobilization, while responding to frantic demands from diplomatic and military authorities for information about the intentions of Japan, its European allies (German and Italy declared war on the United States on 11 December), and a range of other potentially hostile or ambivalently neutral powers. These demands would affect not only the size and operations of the Signal Intelligence Service but also its very identity.

Pearl Harbor convinced Secretary of War Stimson that something had to be done about the army's signal intelligence program. Even before the debacle in Hawaii, the deficiencies of the program were increasingly apparent. SIS decrypted only a small percentage of the total number of diplomatic messages it intercepted each day, and only a small number of the decrypted messages were deemed worthy of translation.[2] In its selection of messages for translation—indeed, in its selection of targets to monitor and cryptanalytic problems to attack—SIS was left largely to its own devices, receiving from MID little more than general directives to intercept Japanese, German, and Italian communications. Rarely, if ever, before Pearl Harbor did the codebreakers receive guidance from military or diplomatic authorities regarding the types of information desired.[3] Translations were passed, without comment or analysis, to MID, where they were read by a handful of officers, who then selected a small number of these translations for circulation, again without commentary or analysis, to the army's Magic distribution list. In the parlance of the intelligence profession, Magic translations were "raw" intelligence, untreated by the application of informed analysis by specialists with access to other sources of information. Those on the distribution list read the translations, made of them what they could, and then returned them to the courier. Prohibited from retaining translations, the readers could not refresh their memory of earlier messages or place that day's messages in a larger context.

The secretary of war believed that signals intelligence required more system and direction if it was to be an effective instrument for the prosecution of the war. In the weeks after Pearl Harbor, as Washington absorbed the bitter reports of defeat or retreat at Guam, Wake, and the Philippines, the case for reform became increasingly compelling. On 19 January 1942, four days after leaders in London and Washington were shaken by the surrender of Singapore, Britain's bastion in the Far East, Stimson asked Alfred McCormack, a respected New York attorney who had been recommended by Assistant Secretary of War John McCloy, to study the problem and recommend reforms for improving the operational effectiveness of army sigint. McCormack, whose appetite for work was exceeded only by his disdain for mediocrity and received wisdom, set to work with a vengeance. He demanded and received full access to SIS records. Military assistants, whose assignment to his staff often depended more on seniority and professional patronage than on personal abilities, were summarily dismissed when their energy or intelligence fell short of their boss's high expectations. Secure in the support of the secretary of war, McCormack cared nothing for rank, reputation, or any of the other prerogatives that normally preoccupied the denizens of the War Department.

After two months of study, McCormack returned to Stimson with his report. He recommended a major expansion in the operations of SIS: more intercept and more cryptanalysis. Expanded operations, however, would prove useless unless there was a concurrent effort to improve the processing of the product of these operations. In particular, there should be a system for evaluating the raw translations, comparing them with other sources of information, and reporting the resulting intelligence to policy makers in a manner that brought out the significant features and placed events in context. Finally, McCormack called for a redefinition of the army's sigint mission. Traditionally, SIS had defined its mission in narrow terms. It would attack a handful of targets, selected because they seemed immediately relevant to American military or diplomatic concerns or, less frequently, because an opportunity, such as access to a foreign codebook, suddenly presented itself. This approach to signals intelligence reflected, in part, the scarcity of resources available to SIS in the prewar period, but it also reflected an organizational conservatism that permeated all aspects of American intelligence before Pearl Harbor.

McCormack wanted army signals intelligence to think big. He believed that all government activities were now ancillary to fighting the war, and that organizations as diverse as the Agriculture Department, the Commerce Department, the State Department, and the Treasury Department had to contribute to the common goal. It was the responsibility of the War Department not only to direct the military effort but also to ensure that the efforts of other agencies and departments were directed intelligently to the pursuit of victory. To fulfill this responsibility, the War Department had to collect and disseminate information on a range of political, economic, and social topics, hitherto considered beyond the interest of army intelligence. To fulfill its own leading role, the War Department "must know as much as possible about the objectives, the psychology and the methods of our enemies and potential enemies (and of our Allies as well) in order to make the right decisions in military matters." In short, total war required total intelligence. The pursuit of total intelligence, in turn, required an activist and expansionist SIS that would take the communications of the entire world, not just four or five governments, as its purview.[4]

McCormack's recommendations were well received by Stimson, who had independently reached similar conclusions. On 15 January 1942, four days before the New York lawyer joined his department, the secretary of war had personally directed that a special section be established in the Far Eastern section of MID to index, classify, evaluate, and disseminate material produced by SIS. In late March, shortly after McCormack submitted his recommendations, this section was designated the Special Service Branch and elevated to a separate office functioning under the assistant chief of staff for intelligence. Colonel Carter Clarke, a career officer with extensive experience in intelligence, was appointed its director and became "the authorized representative of the assistant chief of staff, G-2, for the purpose of supervising all signal intelligence activities of the War Department."[5] Clarke had assisted McCormack in his evaluation of army signals intelligence, and he shared the New Yorker's commitment to a large and comprehensive sigint program. Describing his view of the role of SIS, Clarke noted: "Our primary task is to paint for our superiors as completely a realistic picture as possible of the activities 'behind the arras' of all those associated with and against us."[6] McCormack recognized a soul mate when he saw one; accepting a wartime commission as colonel, he agreed to serve as Clarke's deputy.

Soon renamed the Special Branch, Clarke's command was assigned responsibility for analyzing sigint received from SIS and disseminating that sigint within the War Department and to other agencies. Toward these ends, Clarke initiated the Magic Diplomatic Summary. Previously, signals intelligence had circulated within the War Department and to outside parties, such as the State Department, in the form of verbatim translations of decrypted messages. These translations went to the customers without any commentary or analysis. The Magic Diplomatic Summary was an instrument for making the signals intelligence product more user-friendly. Each day Special Branch received (via teleprinter or courier) several sets of all messages translated by SIS in the previous twenty-four hours. These messages would be distributed to Clarke, the editors of the summary, the desks responsible for following events in particular countries or regions, and the top secret library.

In consultation with the geographic desks, the editors selected those messages that illuminated the more important events and issues of the day. These items (only a tiny proportion of the total number translated that day by SIS) would be summarized, collateral information from other sources (including non-sigint sources) would be incorporated, and the resulting intelligence would be printed in narrative form and distributed to top diplomatic and military decision makers. As the Magic Diplomatic Summary evolved, the coverage would be divided into four main headings: military, political, economic, and psychological warfare/subversion. Messages from different sources but dealing with the same topic would be interwoven into a single narrative. For example, traffic from the Japanese embassies in Lima, Quito, and Santiago might be incorporated into a single report in the summary's economic section dealing with Japanese efforts to control shipping along the west coast of Latin America. Ongoing stories could be tracked over several days or even weeks, and breaking events could be placed in context or related to previous events.

The first Magic Diplomatic Summary appeared on 20 March 1942. Its four pages included items concerning Japanese infiltration into Madagascar and Argentina's intention to purchase French vessels (Vichy traffic); German-Japanese trade and Russian influence in Iran (Japanese traffic); Rome's concern over the sinking of a Chilean merchant ship, the SS *Tolten,* by a fascist submarine (Italian traffic); and German agent reports on American naval construction programs (clandestine traffic). The second summary (21 March) was only one and a half pages long and carried only two items (both from Japanese traffic): one dealing with Russian influence in Iran, and the other with the *Tolten.* The four pages of the third summary (22 March) addressed four topics. Japanese traffic was the source for reports on Russian troop movements, Italian economic conditions, and Chilean-Japanese relations. Italian traffic revealed the reply of the Italian foreign ministry to the inquiries of the Chilean ambassador in Rome in the matter of the *Tolten* (a tiresome affair that would haunt the pages of the Magic Diplomatic Summary through the end of March).[7] By the last year of the war, the daily summary was routinely twelve to twenty pages long and reported a range of diplomatic, military, and economic topics. The summary for 5 November 1944, for example, included items on German difficulties in Hungary and the Carpatho-Ukraine region; Finland's military and economic problems; Italy's policy toward Argentina; Chilean-Russian relations; Czechoslovakia's postwar economic plans; and Japanese appeals to Filipino students. The next day the summary reported the views of neutral diplomats in Berlin; figures on Japanese military expenditures; bomb damage to the Tientsin-Pukow railway; Latin American reactions to Argentina's proposal for a hemispheric conference; gasoline shortages in Thailand; and diplomatic reports from Chungking on Sino-American tensions.[8]

The Magic summaries got off to a slow start in part because Special Branch required time to assemble a team of analysts and editors. McCormack assumed responsibility for recruiting staff for the new office, bringing to the task the same energy and purpose that had swept aside all obstacles during his special research for Stimson. He was convinced that the work of Special Branch required personnel who were inquisitive and skeptical, able to pursue a line of investigation, and prepared by training and experience to evaluate evidence. McCormack, never one to hide a prejudice, did not think for a moment that he could find such people in the U.S. Army, and he constantly protested the War Department's effort to foist on him deserving officers who had been judged unfit for field duty. Not surprisingly, the New York attorney believed that individuals with the necessary qualifications were most likely to be found in the legal profession, especially that part of the profession housed, fed, and employed in New York City. Under McCormack's supervision, Special Branch recruited so many attorneys that War Department wags referred to it as "the best law office in Washington."[9]

In packing his office with corporate attorneys, McCormack constantly tangled with the Civil Service Commission, which did not see why the war should interfere with its time-tested practice of compiling examinations for every conceivable government position and requiring agencies to fill their vacancies from lists of those who had scored highest on the particular exam. Civil Service examiners could not understand (and for security reasons could not be told) what Special Branch was doing; consequently, they could not grasp its unique needs and saw no reason to treat it any differently than the National Park Service. When it wanted to recruit someone to work on signals intelligence, Special Branch had to convince the Civil Service that the job position was really necessary and that a particular candidate was qualified for a particular job. McCormack once labored for five months to secure approval for the employment of an especially able attorney because the Civil Service Commission could not understand why he wanted an attorney for a post that performed no legal work. On another occasion the commission rejected one of McCormack's candidates for a position as research analyst on the grounds that the individual, a Rhodes scholar and senior executive in a major corporation who agreed to take an 85 percent reduction in salary to join the war effort, had never done any research. Not surprisingly, recruitment was slow, and by August 1942 Special Branch had a staff of only thirty-nine officers and civilians.[10]

While McCormack wrestled with his natural enemies in the Civil

Service Commission, Carter Clarke supervised the expansion of the Signal Intelligence Service. In April 1942 SIS received from the newly created Military Intelligence Service (MIS) new directives, which reflected the ambitious vision of Clarke and McCormack.[11] SIS was directed to establish new intercept stations and to attack vigorously the codes and ciphers of not only America's enemies, but also "all major neutral and allied powers."[12] SIS now had the whole world as its stage. Unfortunately, other actors were crowding the footlights.

In the spring of 1942 the Radio Intelligence Division (RID) of the Federal Communications Commission reopened the discussion of collaboration among the various services and agencies involved in signals intelligence. To improve coverage and avoid costly duplication of effort, RID proposed consolidating all clandestine intercept. With the exception of a statement from the navy that it would be happy to centralize clandestine intercept and processing in OP-20-G, the proposal achieved little beyond serving as a pretext for a meeting of the Interdepartmental Intelligence Conference (IIC), a consultative body composed of representatives from the army, navy, FBI, and State Department. IIC appointed a subcommittee representing the army, navy, and FBI to consider whether signals intelligence could be handled in its entirety by those three agencies or whether other agencies should be encouraged to contribute.

To no one's surprise, the subcommittee decided at its first meeting (21 April 1942) to recommend that only the army, navy, and FBI be authorized to conduct signals intelligence operations and that the IIC create a standing subcommittee on communications intelligence to allocate signals intelligence assignments among the three agencies. No action was taken on these recommendations, apparently because the navy was working behind the scenes to exclude the FBI from signals intelligence. Scandalized by the bureau's position that sigint was no different than any other form of evidence and that it should be revealed in an open court of law if necessary to secure a criminal conviction, the navy concluded that the FBI should be excluded on security grounds from any sigint role except in cases of criminal communications (e.g., gambling cases).[13] While discussions over who should belong to the signals intelligence community continued, in May the subcommittee managed to agree on a formula for distributing signals intelligence that would send diplomatic sigint to the White House, the State Department, and the Navy and War Departments. Clandestine traffic would go to State, Navy, and War, while Navy and War would retain, respectively, naval and military translations.

By June the navy had abandoned its campaign against the FBI, and the IIC could stop arguing about who should sit at the sigint table and start arguing about how large each diner's portion should be. On 17 June the IIC created a new subcommittee, again composed of representatives of the army, navy and FBI, to allocate cryptanalytic tasks. The following week, in an act that broke all bureaucratic precedent, the navy agreed to abandon its claim on diplomatic traffic. For some time the only diplomatic traffic under systematic attack by naval cryptanalysts had been Japanese, although, at least until Pearl Harbor, OP-20-G had small sections assigned to German and Vichy French diplomatic communications. Although the navy piously announced that neither operational efficiency nor the larger national interest was well served by current arrangements that divided diplomatic intercept and processing between the armed services, its gesture was not entirely disinterested.

Six months into the war and only two weeks after the navy achieved its first decisive victory against Japan at the Battle of Midway, OP-20-G had more Japanese naval traffic than it could handle, to say nothing of German and Italian naval traffic. The requirements of combat operations pushed other matters aside. Now more interested in the intentions and movements of Japanese carrier groups and German submarine wolf packs than in the musings of the Japanese ambassador in Rome, OP-20-G was eager to reassign its diplomatic section of thirty-eight people to more pressing naval problems. The navy would, however, reserve the right to reclaim a role in diplomatic sigint in the future; in the meantime, it would expect to receive from the army all diplomatic translations, which the navy would continue to distribute to the White House. The army readily agreed to assume responsibility for all diplomatic communications and accepted the navy's conditions. For its part, the FBI could only acquiesce, hoping that it would receive a small piece of the sigint pie.

On 30 June the allocation committee agreed on a division of codebreaking responsibilities that assigned all diplomatic and military cryptanalysis to the army and all naval and non–Western Hemisphere clandestine cryptanalysis to the navy. The FBI retained control over domestic criminal communications and shared with the Coast Guard cryptanalytic unit now attached to OP-20-G responsibility for clandestine communications in the Western Hemisphere. The Joint Chiefs of Staff endorsed this allocation and passed it to the White House, along with a recommendation that the president issue a directive limiting cryptanalytic operations to the army, navy, and FBI. Roosevelt accepted the recommendation and on 8 July issued orders prohibiting agencies such as RID, the Office of Censorship, and the Office of Strategic Services from engaging in crypt-analysis.[14]

While interagency committees bickered over jurisdiction, the Signal Intelligence Service went to war. Intercept received immediate attention. In the early spring of 1942, SIS received traffic from twelve major sources (the number of receivers in operation at each intercept station appears in parenthesis):[15]

MS-1. Fort Hancock (15): Japanese, German, Italian, Spanish, Mexican, French, Argentine, and Chilean diplomatic.

MS-2. San Francisco Presidio (8): Same as above, plus Japanese army.

MS-3. Fort Sam Houston (9): Same as MS-1.

MS-4. Corozal, Panama (16): Same as MS-1.

MS-5. Fort Shafter, Hawaii (12): Same as MS-1.

MS-6. Corregidor, P.I. (12): Japanese military.

MS-7. Fort Hunt (19): Same as MS-1.

MS-8. RCA, Washington: French, Mexican, Swedish, Spanish, and Latin American diplomatic in and out of Washington.

MS-9. U.S. embassy, Rio de Janeiro: Same as MS-1.

MS-10. Traffic received from GCCS: Various diplomatic and military.

MS-11. Western Union, Washington: All foreign government traffic in and out of Washington.

MS-12. RCA, New York: All traffic on Berlin-Tokyo circuit.

In addition, signal radio intelligence (SRI) companies attached to major army commands to collect tactical intelligence contributed traffic in the early months of the war. In April 1942, for example, the 122nd SRI at Fort Sam Houston and the 123rd SRI at Fort Jupiter, Florida, collected Mexican army communications and the diplomatic traffic of assorted foreign governments, while the 125th SRI at Fort Lewis, Washington, searched for Japanese army traffic.

The intercept network, while much improved from its prewar condition, was still inadequate to meet the demands of belligerency, especially in view of the ambitious mission envisioned for SIS by Carter Clarke and Alfred McCormack. The number of receivers in service was woefully low, many targets (e.g., Japanese military communications) were poorly covered, and some targets (e.g., German army and air force traffic) were not covered at all. SIS moved quickly to improve intercept. The Second Signal Service Company was elevated to battalion status to provide the command and administrative structure for an increase in radio intercept personnel. In March the army decided to establish four new listening posts. Two large stations, one on each coast, would provide general diplomatic coverage, while two smaller stations would be positioned to capture Japanese military communications.

For its West Coast facility the army purchased Two Rock Ranch, a cattle farm outside the agricultural community of Petaluma, California, about forty miles north of San Francisco. Plans called for the facility to begin operations with twenty-five antennae and eighty intercept positions. Vint Hill Farms, part of a large private estate that straddled the line dividing Prince William and Fauquier Counties in rural Virginia, was selected for the main East Coast station. On 1 July the stations at Fort Hunt and Fort Hancock ceased operations, and their personnel relocated permanently to Vint Hill to begin intercept operations in barns that only a month before had sheltered livestock. Until the establishment of a large station at Asmara, Eritrea, in the summer of 1943, Two Rock and Vint Hill would be the army's principal sources of diplomatic traffic.

For the smaller stations, the army initially identified sites in Iceland and Alaska. The Iceland site was never developed, but the Alaska facility, established eventually at Fairbanks, aimed thirteen directional antennae at the Far East in a search for Japanese and other traffic. To supplement the work of the fixed stations, SIS sought alternative sources of traffic. In May 1942, for example, military attachés in Latin America were directed to covertly obtain from local cable and radio offices copies of government traffic, especially that of Spain and the Axis powers.[16]

As army engineers and communications specialists surveyed sites for new intercept stations, SIS searched for a new home. Even before Pearl Harbor, it had become increasingly apparent that the quarters in the Munitions Building were inadequate, so no one believed that the warren of cramped offices and closets could absorb the expansion in personnel and operations envisioned by Clarke and McCormack. SIS officers began searching for a site with one or two large buildings, preferably on a tract of land large enough to allow for future growth and sufficiently isolated from downtown Washington to enhance security, but not so distant as to strain connections with the War Department. They found what they were looking for across the Potomac River at Arlington Hall Junior College, a small finishing school for young women. The War Department could move quickly when it wished. With the wartime powers of the federal government behind it, the army simply informed the somewhat startled owners that they would receive a fair market price of $650,000 for their school. The army proposed to take possession immediately; to avoid delays while the owners removed furniture and equipment, it threw in another $40,000 to purchase all furnishings. Events moved so quickly that when a lieutenant and six enlisted men appeared to take possession of the property, several students were still in the dormitory. The young women needed little prompting to pack their bags and vacate the premises. The college gardener and telephone switchboard operator, who were as surprised by the appearance of the army as the fleeing students, agreed to continue under the new management.[17]

The movement of a top secret military unit with its files and equipment across the Potomac and into a facility designed for receiving the public at afternoon teas and lectures on nineteenth-century French poetry proved a logistical nightmare. Security was the first priority, and the advance party immediately set to erecting a double, eight-foot fence around the property and constructing a gatehouse. As soon as the perimeter was secure, the safes began to arrive. Each stood eight feet high and six feet wide and weighed almost a ton. Over a dozen had to be moved, and they posed no end of difficulty. Two fell to the driveway while being maneuvered off trucks; they remained undamaged, but pavers had to be summoned to repair the roadway. When an especially large safe was rolled into position in the former college dining room, the staff stood back and waited to see if the floor would give way and send the behemoth crashing into the basement (it didn't).

With the vaults in place, personnel began to arrive with their precious files. Arlington Hall had been designed to serve the needs of a residential college, but this configuration did not always complement the operational requirements of a cryptanalytic service. The first group to arrive was Al Small's Japanese army section, which moved into the former dormitory, under the eaves of the main building. It was the hottest summer in years, and clerks and analysts sweltered in tiny rooms crowded with work tables and file cabinets. There were bathrooms between every two dormitory rooms, but cool towels and refreshing baths existed only in the fantasies of the sweating staff, since water to the upper floors had been turned off. Secretaries used the bathtubs as filing cabinets.

While the Japanese army section worked surrounded by bathrooms, lavatory facilities were at a premium in other parts of the same building. The second floor, for example, had only one bathroom. Unfortunately, it was in the so-called Purple Room, where each shift a small crew of men and women operated the PURPLE analog that SIS used to decrypt messages in Tokyo's high-grade machine cipher. PURPLE remained the service's most precious secret, and details of the operation were closely held even within the organization. Once every hour, the Purple Room crew had to cover the machine and other materials with blankets while staff from other offices on the second floor were allowed to use the bathroom.[18] Working conditions improved slightly when the operational sections moved into two large wooden structures that were thrown up in record time on the lawns behind the main building.

Expansion meant new people as well as new facilities as SIS sought additional staff to handle expanding operations. Discrete job announcements were distributed to Civil Service offices and, for the first time, recruiters spread out across the country. Ann Caracristi was recruited while still a history student at Russell Sage College. In her last semester of study she was approached by the dean, who asked if she was interested in working in Washington for the Signal Corps doing something called cryptography. Caracristi was not sure what cryptography was, but she wanted to contribute to the war effort, and Washington promised to be at the center of things, so she completed several forms and within a week or two received a letter accepting her application. She was neither tested nor interviewed for the position, although she received several packets containing simple problems in cryptanalysis that she was to study. After graduation Caracristi reported to the Munitions Building and was immediately directed to a classroom at George Washington University, a few blocks away. The new recruit spent the following five weeks with several young men and women reviewing William Friedman's *Elements of Cryptanalysis* under the supervision of Evelyn Ackley, a former professor of mathematics at Skidmore College. During this training, government agents checked Caracristi's background by interviewing friends and former teachers. She reported to Arlington Hall just as it opened and was assigned to the Japanese army section, where she started her new work as a cryptanalyst by sorting traffic by date of intercept.[19]

Katharine Swift, a young schoolteacher from Michigan, followed a similar path to the Signal Intelligence Service. In the summer of 1942 she was attending the French school at Middlebury College and heard a classmate talking about her new job with the Signal Corps in Washington. Swift's best friend in Michigan had already gone to Washington to work and regaled Swift with letters describing the capital's exciting social life. Single and living at home, Swift saw the Signal Corps as her ticket to a new life in Washington. She abandoned summer school, teaching, and Michigan and sent in her application. "The temptation was irresistible," she would later recall. "Of course they were looking for any warm body at the time." She reported to the Munitions Building the week after the move to Arlington Hall. She and two other female recruits were taken to the Hall by bus. The new headquarters of the Signal Intelligence Service was a mess— crates and packing boxes blocked the corridors; people rushed about waving papers and looking for offices; staff cars, transport trucks, and dispatch motorcycles roared in and out of the main gate. The bewildered recruits were hastily interviewed by a distracted officer and then returned to the bus, which carried them to George Washington University to join Professor Ackley's current training class. The class proved only an interlude. After just two weeks of instruction, Swift was ordered to Arlington Hall and assigned to the section working the meteorological ciphers of various countries.[20]

A year later, recruitment and training were no more methodical. In the spring of 1943 Juanita Moody was a first-year student at Western Carolina College when, hoping to contribute to the war effort, she wrote a letter to the army recruiting office in Charlotte, North Carolina, inquiring about positions in military intelligence. Invited for an interview, she spoke to an officer about a clerical position in something called cryptology. She was hired on the spot and the next day found herself on a train for Washington. Upon her arrival she went immediately into a training group of new recruits at Arlington Hall while investigators checked her background. The process was facilitated by the fact that the investigator assigned Moody's case knew her family and vouched for her personally. After three weeks of training she was assigned to the German section. Without any indoctrination into the work of the section, she was taken to a large room by an officer who announced, "This is the German section," then abandoned her. For several minutes she stood alone in the doorway wondering what she was supposed to do. Then a man walked up, handed her a sheet of paper containing rows of printed numbers and a stack of numbered cards, and told her to compare the paper with the cards and note the numbers that appeared on both. She was launched on a career in cryptanalysis.[21]

While SIS hastened to recruit new staff, it often had to fight to retain the staff it had. The armed services were putting into uniform every male who could walk, talk, and see his reflection in a mirror. The military draft threatened to suck civilian codebreakers, translators, and cryptanalytic clerks into an army, which seemingly trained and assigned personnel without considering their aptitudes, experience, or present contributions to the war effort. SIS lived in fear that its precious cryptanalysts, today one from the Japanese section, tomorrow one from the German problem, would be plucked from their desks by the army, trained as medical corpsmen or air traffic controllers, and sent to Ascension Island or New Zealand.

Fairly quickly, SIS worked out special arrangements with the manpower authorities to protect its people. William Lutwiniak's experience was typical. A natural codebreaker who had never gone to college but had been winning cryptanalytic contests in magazines such as *Cryptogram* and *Detective Fiction Weekly* since his early teens, Lutwiniak joined SIS in February 1941 and worked mainly on German ciphers. After Pearl Harbor he and his superiors worried that he would be drafted and sent away from his true métier to become an infantryman. He discussed the problem with Captain Harold Hayes, the executive officer, who advised him to visit the recruiting office then established inside the bus terminal on the corner of New York and Pennsylvania Avenues and voluntarily enlist. When Lutwiniak arrived at the office, the recruiting sergeant seemed to be expecting him. In a matter of minutes he was given a cursory physical examination, sworn into the army as a private, and ordered to report to Captain Harold Hayes at the Munitions Building. There, Hayes told Lutwiniak to return to his normal work and for the moment not worry about things like basic training and drill. The captain also promoted him to sergeant on the spot, although he had been a private for only an hour. A couple of days later, Lutwiniak was driven to Fort Meyer, Virginia, to pick up his uniforms. He never received any military training. Norman Willis, a technician in the machine section of SIS, enlisted and spent three uneventful days at the army's Camp Lee training facility before returning to his old job. His military training consisted of a few hours of close-order drill on the old tennis courts at Arlington Hall.[22]

Perhaps inevitably, the transition from peace to war created strains in the administration of army signals intelligence. Beginning in June, the Signal Intelligence Service underwent three name changes in less than twelve months, a sure sign of unsettled conditions.[23] Internally, tasks were reassigned among the various offices, and the cryptanalytic branch underwent a significant reorganization. In the spring of 1942 the cryptanalytic branch retained the organizational arrangement originally established in the 1930s. There were now five country desks (Japan, Germany, Italy, France, Latin America), which were responsible for all the cryptosystems (codes and ciphers) of their respective targets. They were assisted by several support sections (Stenography, Traffic, Tabulating Machinery, etc.). With the move to Arlington Hall, the geographic desks were abandoned in favor of a new organization based on the type of system under study. Believing that the solution of a cipher in one language (French) was more closely related to the solution of a cipher in a second language (Spanish) than to the solution of a code in the first language, authorities decided to place all cipher solution in one group (under Frank Rowlett) and all code recovery in another (under Solomon Kullback).[24]

Administrative reorganization symbolized an important shift in the culture of SIS. Expansion had upset long-established patterns of work and authority in a service that had seen its staff increase from 19 to 331 between September 1939 and December 1941. The egalitarian atmosphere of a craft shop where everyone worked in the same room, all interaction was face-to-face, and supervisors were personally involved in cryptanalytic operations had been replaced by an increasingly bureaucratic environment characterized by hierarchy, written procedures, and impersonal communication. In a sense, SIS was experiencing an industrial revolution, and the change most affected those who remembered the early days. Some adjusted to the new regimen. Frank Rowlett, who discovered political and managerial gifts as sharp as his cryptanalytic skills, flourished in the new environment where requisitions, budgets, and personnel evaluations were now more likely to appear on his desk than intercepts and cipher work sheets. Abraham Sinkov, always the perfect gentleman, accepted with grace orders to proceed to Australia to establish a signals intelligence unit in the new command of General Douglas MacArthur. Others found it difficult to accept change. Solomon Kullback was slow to delegate responsibility, and his insistence on supervising closely every aspect of his burgeoning unit, just as he had before the war when his entire staff sat across the table from him, drove his subordinates (and British observers) to distraction.[25]

The veteran most affected by the changes was William Friedman, the father of the Signal Intelligence Service. His modest titles, "senior technical advisor," "civilian assistant," obscured the fact that he *was* the Signal Intelligence Service for most of its first ten years. He personally recruited the staff, taught them the principles of cryptanalysis, supervised their work as codebreakers, and dealt with the colonels and generals in the Signal Corps and MID. The Signal Corps officers who nominally commanded the service in the 1930s invariably deferred to his expertise and reputation.

He gloried in the role of paterfamilias, respected and emulated by the young staff, whom he considered disciples as much as subordinates.

Friedman's position began to change, however, after the outbreak of war in Europe. As additional staff joined the office and administration consumed more of his time, Friedman became more detached from day-to-day operations. His visits to the worktables became less frequent, and his involvement in cryptanalytic problems decreased significantly. His disciples, Rowlett, Kullback, Sinkov, now directed sections as large as the entire service in 1930, and they became the mentors and authority figures for a new generation for whom the founding father was an increasingly distant figure. A nervous collapse in December 1940, shortly before Friedman was to head the first cryptanalytic mission to Britain, required hospitalization and, subsequently, a long convalescence during which he necessarily reduced his professional activities. When he returned, he found a regime for which he could summon little enthusiasm.

In June 1941 Lieutenant Colonel Rex Minckler assumed command of SIS from the highly regarded Colonel Spencer Akin. Minckler knew nothing about signals intelligence, but he believed strongly in the efficacy of organization, procedures, rank, and official channels. Friedman clashed with Minckler and ridiculed his new commander's preoccupation with organizational matters. Relations with Minckler's successor, Colonel Frank Bullock, were only slightly better.[26]

It was Friedman, however, who had lost touch with the service. He could not acknowledge that with expansion SIS was evolving into a military bureaucracy in which there was no room for a paterfamilias. He became increasingly marginalized. By the summer of 1942 he had been elevated to the role of elder statesman, an icon who received ritual, though perfunctory, homage. His advice on cipher security was occasionally solicited, he worked on the design of new cipher machines, he expanded his classic textbook on military cryptanalysis, and in the spring of 1943, as an acknowledgment of his seniority (and his friendship with Alistair Denniston), he joined another special mission to GCCS, but he would never again return to the central position he had once occupied in American signals intelligence.

Adjustment was also difficult for the junior staff who arrived at Arlington Hall in increasing numbers until, by the summer of 1945, almost eight thousand employees would pass through the gatehouses each day. Until their employment by the army, most had never been to Washington and many had never been away from home. The majority were young women, drawn from small towns across the eastern seaboard by the promise of important war work and the prospect of living amid the glamour and excitement of a capital at war. They rented rooms in private houses, pooled their meager salaries to rent apartments downtown, or competed for vacancies at Arlington Farms, dormitories constructed at Eleanor Roosevelt's instigation near Arlington Hall to house (in much-sought-after private rooms) the single women who flooded wartime Washington.

For the small number of African Americans who found themselves at Arlington Hall, the problems of adjusting to new work in a new place were compounded by racial discrimination. African Americans were no more welcome in the U.S. Army than they were in any other institution in America. Black soldiers were usually assigned to service formations (quartermaster, transport, engineering), where they served in segregated units under white officers. When SIS occupied Arlington Hall, the only African American on the staff was William Coffee, a messenger who carried classified documents among the offices. As SIS expanded into its new facilities, blacks were hired to serve in the cafeteria and clean the offices, but none were recruited for administrative or operational work until the White House intervened.

One morning in 1943 (the date remains uncertain), Colonel Preston Corderman, the chief of the (now renamed) Signal Security Service, summoned Major Earle Cook, director of the communications security (cryptography) section, and informed him that, as a result of a campaign by Eleanor Roosevelt to convince the army to employ more blacks in capacities other than the purely menial, the Signal Corps had directed Arlington Hall to recruit suitable candidates for operational assignments. Corderman, a conscientious officer whose racial attitudes were no more progressive than those of most career military officers, had decided to satisfy the requirement by hiring a handful of blacks and segregating them in communications security, an important unit but one considered a backwater by the cryptanalysts. Cook, whose professional contact with blacks was limited largely to the attendants who cleared the tables in the cafeteria, was at a loss for how to implement Corderman's decision. In desperation, he turned to William Coffee. Working as Cook's delegate to the African American community in the District of Columbia and Virginia, Coffee recruited a number of blacks who were put to work testing the security of ciphers used by some of America's allies in the war. By early 1944, a second group of African Americans was assigned to cryptanalytic duties in the commercial codes section at Arlington Hall. William Coffee, the onetime messenger, was appointed chief of this section. Both groups were segregated from the white cryptanalysts in the offices and the cafeteria.[27]

Relations among both men and women and blacks and whites were often strained. The problem was partly the nature of the work. In the rush to expand, recruiters were inclined to exaggerate the excitement of the work and the glamour of Washington. They showed prospective recruits photos of prewar Arlington Hall, complete with ivy-covered buildings, tennis courts, and riding stables.[28] Recruits, who expected to stroll along shaded walkways to cozy offices where they would spend their days exposing Nazi spy rings or eavesdropping on the conversations of Hitler and Mussolini, soon discovered that cryptanalytic clerks spent their time in dreary, vermin-infested buildings performing routine and excruciatingly tedious tasks with little time for a quick set of doubles or a canter around the paddock. Since security considerations prevented any but the most senior officers from seeing "the big picture," junior staff were often left to wonder how their mundane work fit into the whole and whether the endless (and mind-numbing) sorting of traffic and recording of code groups made any contribution to the war effort.

The nature of the organization also often undermined morale. Arlington Hall was a hybrid organization in which military and civilian personnel mixed promiscuously and in which the normally stabilizing hierarchies of pay, rank, and function were uncertain guides to authority and status. In a typical cryptanalytic section an army captain, a lieutenant, and a civilian might perform the same tasks on the same project, but each would receive different pay. To complicate matters, the lieutenant, because of skill and experience, might assume leadership of the team, though formally outranked by the captain. Not surprisingly, status conflicts and professional jealousies often surfaced. Earnest young officers, fresh from officer training courses, often assumed an "ultramilitary" approach to management and office relationships that irritated civilian employees, especially the women, who resented being ordered about by uniformed martinets who clearly knew less about their work than the employees they supervised. This resentment was not assuaged by the knowledge that though women represented a majority of the staff at Arlington Hall, they held only a tiny proportion of the midlevel supervisory positions and none at all of the senior management posts.[29]

Many of the civilians were highly educated and actively rebelled against military culture. On one occasion a brilliant cryptanalyst in the

Japanese army section, who for form's sake had been inducted into the army and given the rank of sergeant, was summoned to his commanding officer's room and informed that he was being sent to officer training school. The analyst, who had absolutely no interest in becoming an officer and saw no reason that he should waste three months of his time at officer's school, politely refused, noting that he would be no more useful in the Japanese section as a lieutenant than he already was as a sergeant. When the commander made it clear that this was an order, not a request, the sergeant simply replied, "No, thank you," saluted, and returned to his worktable.[30]

Supervisors, both uniformed and civilian, were often frustrated not only by the irrelevance of traditional notions of rank and discipline but also by the presence of free spirits whose eccentricities often tested the patience of colleagues. When Juanita Moody reported for her first day of work, she was somewhat disconcerted to observe one of her coworkers in the German section sitting at his desk in his underwear while his wet pants dried on a nearby radiator. At the next table, a woman worked busily with a large ice pack strapped to her head. A third colleague insisted on putting on a sun visor whenever he entered the section's work spaces.[31] Every section had its own characters. In the French section, one of Katharine Swift's coworkers worried obsessively about the health dangers of drafty offices and insisted on working with his feet in a wastebasket. A supervisor in the Japanese section was infamous for exploding into profanity at the slightest provocation and cowing all his staff except one imperturbable analyst who, with his pinstripe suits, high collars, and straw boater attached to his collar by a cord, seemed to have wandered into Arlington Hall from a dress rehearsal for *The Importance of Being Earnest*.[32]

Working conditions created special problems. British liaison officers, fresh from the privations of Britain, where everything was rationed, marveled at Arlington Hall's seemingly endless supply of paper, pencils, desks, and office supplies of every sort; American employees were often frustrated by government parsimony. In the Japanese army section, arguably one of the most important units in the organization, there were not enough file cabinets for the intercepts that poured in each day from monitoring stations on the West Coast and in the Pacific. The staff resorted to stuffing the messages into cardboard boxes, which were then stored on makeshift wooden shelves along the walls. In the evenings, when most of the section shut down, mice emerged from the walls and floors to nibble through the boxes and eat the paper inside. To prevent the destruction of important materials, the staff resigned itself to bringing food from the cafeteria each day to feed the mice.[33]

Weather, too, could be a problem. Everyone dreaded the onset of summer, when the notorious heat and humidity of Washington turned the offices and work bays into steam rooms. There was, of course, no air conditioning, and the only relief came from huge fans that generated breezes strong enough to scatter papers from the tables but not strong enough to cool perspiring faces. On the worst days an anonymous functionary would appear with a mysterious contrivance of string, glass, and metal tubing that purported to measure both temperature and humidity. He would twirl this apparatus about his head for half a minute and then examine the readings. Everyone held their breath, for if temperature and humidity both registered above ninety, the staff would be dismissed for the remainder of the shift. On such days some of the young men and women would head for the tennis courts; others ran errands or sat under the shade trees much as they might have done when the army's top secret site was an elegant college campus. One analyst in the French section regularly sought out the coolest place she knew in Washington—the ladies lounge in Hecht's department store, where she sat and read a book.[34]

Security considerations required the most immediate and dramatic adjustment in behavior. Few, if any, of Arlington Hall's recruits had been part of an institution where security was an obsession, where employees were required to take oaths of secrecy buttressed by promises of draconian punishment for any violation, where offices sheltered behind rows of high fences rigged with alarms, and where color-coded badges designating clearance to enter various facilities were as much a part of the day's wardrobe as shoes. Because information was strictly compartmentalized on a "need to know" basis, employees were constrained from speaking about their work and had little or no knowledge of what was going on in other areas of the post. Occasionally the security program took on aspects of a comic opera. For several months after the move to Arlington Hall, the regular guard force was reinforced by staff selected from the cryptanalytic sections who, every fourth or fifth night, would be issued weapons and assigned to guard posts. These young cryptanalysts were often highly educated, but they knew nothing about firearms or guard duty, and they received no training. Until the practice of borrowing operational staff for guard duty ended, the nighttime peace of Arlington Hall frequently was shattered by the sound of gunshots as an inattentive linguist on duty at the gatehouse dropped his pistol or a recent engineering graduate walking the

fence line confused the engaged and disengaged positions of his subma-
chine gun's safety lever.[35]

Tests suggested that the security provided by guards, gates, and
guns was illusory. On one occasion security officers directed two WACs
(Women's Army Corps), who had been working at Vint Hill Farm intercept station and were unfamiliar with the routines and personnel of Arlington Hall, to register as civilians at a Washington hotel and to seek ad-
mission to the Hall with no information but the name of an officer in the
personnel section. The next morning the two women appeared, in civilian
clothes, at the main gate, where they explained to the guard that they were
seeking employment and mentioned the name of the personnel officer.
They were given visitors' badges and admitted to the facility, but instead
of going to the personnel office, they entered the headquarters building,
stole two staff badges to replace their visitors' badges, and proceeded to
mix with personnel in the cafeteria and post exchange. From these conversations the impostors learned that the badges they had purloined were not
good for entry into the operations buildings, since they lacked the requisite yellow bands along their tops.

The enterprising pair then left the post, bought colored paper and
glue at a nearby store, and crudely reconfigured their badges. The ruse
worked, and they were admitted without question to the post and the
operations buildings. In the operations buildings they wandered about
various cryptanalytic sections without being challenged, even when they
picked up and walked off with various materials. They had such an easy
time on the day shift that they returned with their homemade badges to
successfully repeat the experiment on the swing and graveyard shifts. At
the end of a very busy day (and night), the two WACs handed in an arm-
load of stolen documents, each marked "Top Secret." None of the material
they stole was reported missing by the offices they victimized. Army commanders were not amused by the results of this exercise. At a meeting of
section heads, the documents were returned to their erstwhile owners. The
nature of what must have been an unpleasant discussion is barely suggested by the dry bureaucratese of the minutes: "As a result of this check,
it was decided that measures should be taken to make all employees more
security conscious."[36]

For all the upheavals of expansion, relocation, and reorganization,
SIS could not be distracted from its operational responsibilities. The war
did not stop while senior officers redrew organizational charts, staffers
moved furniture into new offices, and recruits adapted to their new work.

Messages in readable cryptosystems had to be intercepted, decrypted, and translated, while unsolved codes and ciphers had to be attacked. Thought also had to be given to liaison arrangements with allied services. In 1942 SIS opened relations with Canada's Examination Unit, which began to pass to Washington intercepts and decrypts of Vichy French diplomatic traffic.[37] In the spring, SIS dispatched Abraham Sinkov and a small party of cryptanalytic personnel to Australia to establish a signals intelligence capability in General Douglas MacArthur's command. The American contingent joined Australian sigint personnel to form the so-called Central Bureau, which attacked Japanese army communications.[38] About the same time, the seeds of Sino-American cryptanalytic cooperation planted in 1940 by (now retired) General Joseph Mauborgne bore fruit; in response to a request from SIS for information about Japanese army codes and copies of any captured Japanese cryptographic materials, China sent Washington nineteen "exhibits," including several Imperial Army codes.[39]

Britain remained by far the most important cryptanalytic ally. Since the Sinkov and Denniston missions of the previous year, cooperation between SIS and GCCS had continued in several areas. Collaboration on Japanese diplomatic systems was especially close, with the two partners regularly exchanging intercepts and cryptanalytic observations. By the spring of 1942, the two organizations were also routinely sharing the results of their respective efforts against the formidable German diplomatic ciphers, exchanges that allowed both sides to make progress against FLORADORA and SPALIER. Collaboration was equally close on the Italian diplomatic problem. Against this target the British had the edge in experience, and they generously passed to the War Department all results from their work against the numerous systems employed by Mussolini's diplomats. GCCS also provided the War Department copies of all Vichy codebooks available at Bletchley Park, and British and American codebreakers exchanged observations and results concerning other French diplomatic and colonial systems. SIS's nascent effort against Spain's diplomatic ciphers received a significant boost when GCCS provided a copy of Madrid's basic codebook and samples of the additive tapes used to encipher that code at Spanish embassies in Ankara, Bucharest, Buenos Aires, and Stockholm.[40]

SIS and GCCS further solidified their increasingly productive collaboration by again exchanging cryptanalytic missions. On 26 March 1942 Lieutenant Colonel John Tiltman, chief of the military section at Bletchley Park and an accomplished cryptanalyst who had been breaking codes since 1920, arrived in Washington for a four-week visit. Tiltman's instructions were to visit the army and navy cryptanalytic services with a view to effecting a "complete interchange of all technical knowledge available and in particular to hand over to them all our technical documents."[41] Toward these ends, the GCCS representative brought "a considerable quantity" of material from the various sections at Bletchley Park, including three Vichy French colonial codebooks with cryptanalytic notes and observations by Bletchley's French section; microfilms of FLORADORA materials with inquiries from the British about the methods used by SIS against this German diplomatic cipher; and "descriptions of the methods used for the solution of 3 or 4 different complex ciphers by our Research Section." Concerning the latter, the methods were unknown to the Americans, who were especially appreciative of the new insights. He also informed his army hosts that if they were interested, GCCS could provide some Brazilian and Portuguese diplomatic codebooks.[42]

GCCS hoped that, with the benefits of Anglo-American collaboration increasingly apparent, Tiltman might persuade the army and navy to improve their own collaboration, perhaps by pooling their resources in a joint "research party" to investigate particular cryptanalytic problems. At the working levels interservice cooperation was not uncommon, but at the higher levels service rivalries and institutional inertia militated against any move toward consolidation of resources and joint direction of operations. Although puzzled by the tribal politics of the American services, Tiltman perceived that there was little an outsider could do to influence the situation, and he pragmatically abandoned the effort. "It was immediately obvious," Tiltman informed GCCS, "that any attempt to induce the two services to fuse their cryptographic sections (or even to form a joint section for general research) would be unsuccessful."

Tiltman had also been instructed to reiterate the long-standing British position that SIS and OP-20-G should concentrate on Japanese communications and leave German and Italian to GCCS. SIS, however, exhibited little interest in a formal division of labor, although the scarcity of resources effectively limited its attack against the European Axis powers. The British could impose their view (at least in the short run) by limiting Washington's access to German and Italian traffic and cryptanalytic materials, but Tiltman understood that such a policy would prove counterproductive. For one thing, GCCS *needed* American involvement in some European operations, in particular the intractable German diplomatic problem. Furthermore, collaboration with the United States was simply too important to risk, at least on this particular issue. The common war effort would be better served by the strongest possible American sigint program. Tiltman's pragmatism was again apparent in his reaction to the War Department's newfound interest in German military cryptosystems. He noted that SIS was "singularly badly equipped" to deal with even the lowest-grade army and air force ciphers; indeed, it was only then beginning to form the rudiments of an air section. Still, he advised GCCS to provide assistance on these projects, arguing that it was in Britain's interest that the Americans profit by British experience and not waste time and resources struggling with problems GCCS had already surmounted.

The issue of allocating responsibilities reappeared at a joint British-American-Canadian conference on radio intelligence that convened in Washington during Tiltman's visit. Alistair Denniston, the operational director of GCCS, had first floated the idea of a joint conference of radio intelligence officers and technicians during his visit to Washington the previous summer. Denniston believed that American and British cryptanalysts would benefit from a general exchange of ideas and experiences. He also undoubtedly hoped that the discussions would lay the groundwork for a more systematic division of labor. Early in 1942, the British formally proposed a meeting, and both the Americans and the Canadians accepted the proposal with alacrity. Developments in the Atlantic, where shipping losses were mounting, lent the invitation a certain urgency. In February, German U-boats had switched from a three- to a four-rotor Enigma for their communications, and the result was a blackout in Bletchley Park's ability to read U-boat messages. Without signals intelligence, the war against the underseas killers faltered.[43] What better time to pool information and experiences. The conference was intended as a meeting of experts who would discuss technical matters; consequently, the delegations were composed of specialists from the various radio intelligence elements of each country's armed services. The British delegation included a representative from the Foreign Office. The American delegation included officers from SIS and OP-20-G, but not the FBI. SIS was represented by its commander, Lieutenant Colonel Rex Minckler; his principal civilian adviser, William Friedman; the chief of the cryptanalytic section, Major Harold Doud; the director of intercept, Major Robert Schukraft; and several cryptanalysts, including Frank Rowlett.[44]

The conference opened on 6 April with welcoming remarks by Commander John Redman, the director of OP-20-G and the chair of the meeting. Captain Humphrey Sandwith, RN, the head of the Admiralty's intercept service, then provided an overview of British intercept and radio intelligence organizations and noted some of the more successful operations, including sigint contributions to the sinking of the German battleship *Bismarck*. American and Canadian speakers followed with descriptions of their respective organizations. The conference then adopted a British suggestion to divide into subcommittees to examine various topics, including radio interception, methods (including direction finding) of extracting intelligence from intercepted traffic, antenna systems, radio telephony, radio and radar countermeasures, and special facilities for exchanging intercepted traffic. Two weeks later, the delegates reconvened to hear the reports of the subcommittees.

Not surprisingly, given the critical situation in the Atlantic, many of the reports were more immediately applicable to naval sigint, but recommendations concerning the exchange of raw traffic were relevant to SIS. These recommendations implicitly endorsed the British position that the United States should focus on the Japanese cryptanalytic problem and concede Britain primacy over European problems. Japanese diplomatic and military attaché traffic would go to Washington and to London as required, but the British would receive Japanese army traffic only if specifically requested. The conference delegates agreed that both Britain and the United States should receive and process German diplomatic traffic, but they denied SIS's request for German army and air force traffic by recommending that such traffic go only to London, although some might be mailed to Washington for training purposes. In the matter of the Italian problem, the conferees recommended that Italy's diplomatic, military, and air force traffic should go in the first instance to London by cable or other rapid means and then by mail to SIS. Vichy French traffic would be handled similarly, although only army and air force communications were included on the list of Vichy traffic to be shared with SIS. Spanish intercepts would be exchanged, but each service would independently handle Latin American traffic. Secondary targets, such as China, Portugal, Saudi Arabia, and Turkey, would be left entirely to the British.

The Washington conference was a useful instrument for advancing Allied sigint cooperation, especially in areas, such as naval direction finding, that were crucial to the U-boat war, but it would be easy to exaggerate the conference's impact on SIS. Aside from an important decision to establish independent submarine plotting centers in Washington and Ottawa, it is unclear which, if any, of the recommendations were actually implemented.[45] Even if all the recommendations were implemented, they would have done little but affirm the status quo with regard to SIS operations.

The denial of access to German military traffic except for training purposes would have been disappointing, but currently SIS was not receiving *any* German military traffic from the British. Aside from German and Japanese military communications, the army codebreakers were receiving all the traffic they needed for current operations.[46] The condition that certain traffic (Italian, Vichy French, Spanish) must go from London to Washington by mail rather than by more rapid means such as cable was not a serious constraint, since SIS already used the mails for most of the traffic from its own intercept stations. British primacy over secondary targets was already established, since SIS was not working most of these problems in the spring of 1942. The arrangements for the secondary targets it was working (Latin America) were unaffected by the conference recommendations.

In expanding its operations, army signals intelligence was more immediately affected by direct liaison with GCCS. The Tiltman mission, for example, brought direct payoffs in the form of codebooks, cipher tables, and professional observations on a range of cryptanalytic problems. SIS promptly reciprocated by sending another mission across the Atlantic. In May, Major Solomon Kullback (senior SIS civilians had been given military ranks for the duration) and Captain Harold Brown, another SIS officer, arrived in Britain for a visit that would extend into July.

The Americans spent most of their time at Bletchley Park, but they also visited the center for diplomatic cryptanalysis recently established by GCCS on Berkeley Street in London, the intercept station at Cheadle, and the cryptologic school at Bedford.[47] At Berkeley Street, Kullback and Brown visited the sections dealing with German, Japanese, Italian, French, Spanish, Chinese, Swedish, Near Eastern, and Latin American diplomatic traffic. At Bletchley they visited every office and unit, including the sections working German military Enigma, German *Geheimschreiber* (enciphered teleprinter), German agents' hand ciphers, Italian and Vichy French military and naval communications, and Japanese military attaché ciphers. They were invited into the bombe hut to observe the machines recovering Enigma keys. Even rather obscure operations, such as the attacks against Spanish air force systems and the systems used by the German police, received the visitors' attention. Upon his return to Washington, Kullback reported, "I found the British most helpful and cooperative and was permitted access to every section at Bletchley and London. They were completely frank, open and aboveboard with me and kept no detail of their operation, procedures, techniques, or results from me."[48]

Kullback returned with more than fond memories and good impressions. His baggage included a trove of precious gifts from the British, including a German military Enigma machine and a paper version (schematic of wiring) of the Enigma used by the German clandestine services. There were keys for the *Geheimschreiber,* a Japanese army codebook, a code used by Japanese forces for air-ground communications, a Japanese military attaché codebook (partially reconstructed), and two French codes. Some of the material, such as a Spanish air force code, was positively exotic by SIS standards. All this material was of inestimable value to SIS in advancing its cryptanalytic operations. Indeed, the Kullback mission demonstrated (if further demonstration was necessary) that close collaboration with the British was central to the successful expansion of the War Department's signals intelligence program. To further facilitate that collaboration, SIS sent Captain Roy Johnson to Britain in late 1942 as the army's first resident liaison officer at Bletchley Park.

It is clear that, at least in the diplomatic area, the British withheld little from their ally. In October 1942, GCCS reviewed its contacts with SIS and concluded that in the area of Japanese, German, Italian, Spanish, Portuguese, and French diplomatic communications the "War Department should be able to read everything we read."[49] The Americans were not reading some traffic available to the British (e.g., Balkan and Near Eastern diplomatic), but this was because SIS had not yet decided to attack this traffic. Given this record of cooperation, it is difficult to escape the conclusion that, at least initially, SIS benefited disproportionately from the partnership with GCCS.

Along with the dramatic increase in staff, the British connection was one of the principal factors behind SIS's increasingly impressive performance after Pearl Harbor. With the exception of the Japanese problem (and that is an important exception), the American contribution to the common cryptanalytic effort remained relatively modest through 1942. In July 1941, for instance, SIS had forwarded to GCCS several technical papers, but most dealt with German cryptographic systems in the First World War.[50] Several days after Japan's attack on Pearl Harbor, American and British sigint authorities reaffirmed the importance of collaboration on the German keyword diplomatic system (FLORADORA), and SIS provided a list of recovered keys for this system from 1939. In October 1942 Arlington Hall sent GCCS 1,139 recovered values for a Chilean diplomatic code and offered descriptions and values for Argentine, Ecuadorian, and Venezuelan codes.

While useful, such contributions were somewhat peripheral to the central preoccupations of Allied signals intelligence in 1942. Against most of the significant targets—Germany, Italy, Vichy France, the more important neutrals—the British took the lead. Wherever American codebreakers went, their British counterparts had gone before. It is perhaps suggestive of the true state of cooperation that Lieutenant Colonel Tiltman carried several cryptanalytic gifts with him when he visited SIS, but he seems to have returned to Britain empty-handed.[51] Of course Tiltman (and Denniston before him) certainly obtained from the Americans, through discussion and observation, useful insights into particular problems (for instance, the German diplomatic problem), and these "invisible" contributions could easily have escaped notice in formal reports and appraisals. On at least one occasion GCCS acknowledged that liaison on German diplomatic ciphers had been especially fruitful, particularly in the attack against FLORADORA.[52] Still, the British may have felt that they were giving to the relationship more than they were getting, especially since it often was not apparent to GCCS that their partners actually made use of the gifts from across the Atlantic. At one point Alistair Denniston, director of diplomatic cryptanalysis at Berkeley Street, queried his liaison officer in Washington: "Strictly between ourselves, are the Americans making a massive library of foreign government systems for filing purposes, or do they actually work on the stuff which we send them? We hear so little about Spanish and even French results that sometimes we wonder if they are actually deeply interested."[53]

Frustration over the extent of reciprocity would explain the otherwise curious complaint by Prime Minister Winston Churchill to President Roosevelt in the summer of 1942 that the collaboration between American and British army cryptologists was not as intimate as that between their naval counterparts. Asked by the president to look into this matter, Army Chief of Staff General George Marshall turned to his intelligence chief, General George Strong, for an appraisal of the army's cryptanalytic exchanges with the British. Strong, whose initiative at joint staff conferences in London in August 1940 had been the stimulus to cryptanalytic cooperation between Washington and London, assured Marshall that the "intimate" exchange of information "appears to be quite satisfactory to both sides" and that efforts were in hand to further improve contacts between the two allies. Marshall confidently passed these assurances to the White House.[54] Within months, events would conspire to undermine both Strong's and Marshall's confidence.

In November 1942 the army prohibited Alan Turing, a GCCS cryptanalyst then in the United States on a technical mission, from inspecting a scrambler device undergoing testing at Bell Laboratories. On 2 December Field Marshall John Dill, in Washington as the representative of the British chiefs of staff, wrote General Marshall asking that this prohibition be lifted. Turing, after all, was a senior cryptanalyst and a brilliant mathematician whose ideas about machine cryptanalysis were instrumental in Bletchley Park's successes against the German ENIGMA machine. At the War Department, Dill's letter set off a round of exchanges involving Marshall, his deputy, General McNarney, General Strong, and Colonel Clarke. From these discussions, the chief of staff gained the impression that, irrespective of General Strong's earlier assurances, army intelligence was not pleased with the state of Anglo-American signals intelligence cooperation and that the prohibition against Turing visiting Bell Laboratories was, in large part, retaliation for Bletchley Park's refusal to share its own secrets with the Americans. Colonel Clarke was especially critical, insisting that the British were withholding important material, including German military and clandestine traffic, cryptanalytic material relating to "Slavic" governments (i.e., Russia), and details of Bletchley's "high-speed analyses."[55]

When informed by Marshall of these complaints, Field Marshall Dill (after consulting London) hastened to calm the Americans. He acknowledged that German clandestine traffic might have been withheld before the Allied landings in North Africa but indicated that this issue had now been resolved. In the matter of "Slavic" (Russian) traffic, Dill reminded Marshall that the Sinkov mission had received an overview of British work on Russian communications during its visit to Bletchley Park in the spring of 1941, and that further details could be provided if required. GCCS, however, had stopped intercepting Moscow's traffic after the German invasion of the Soviet Union in June 1941 brought that country into the war as an ally of Britain. As for German military traffic and "high-speed analyses," the field marshal noted that Solomon Kullback had been fully briefed on Bletchley's work in this area and had observed the operation of the British bombes. Furthermore, one American officer and one enlisted man were at Bletchley Park working on Germany army traffic.[56] The Americans were not mollified.

The central issue was access to high-grade German army and air force communications enciphered by Enigma machines. Since G-2 considered the Germany army its principal intelligence target, access to German military communications was a high priority. This priority required a frontal assault on the Enigma cipher machine. Arlington Hall was preparing to place in service its own "E solving machines," American versions of Bletchley's bombes, but exploitation of German military communications required access to traffic, trained personnel, and insights into the technical means of penetrating Enigma. In turn, these requirements depended on British cooperation. The War Department wanted GCCS to provide sufficient traffic and expertise to allow SIS to exploit the German Enigma. The Americans argued that their separate effort would allow greater exploitation of the mass of German military traffic now intercepted, prepare the United States in the event that Japan decided to adopt Enigma for its diplomatic or military communications, and better position the Allies should Berlin introduce new and improved models of their high-grade cipher machine. Since the British were already collaborating with the U.S. Navy against German naval Enigma, there could be no question of principle.[57]

For their part, the British feared that moving part of the Enigma operation across the Atlantic would jeopardize the security of the program by increasing the number of people privy to it and by requiring transatlantic communications that might be compromised by German intelligence. They did not consider collaboration with the U.S. Navy a precedent, arguing (through Field Marshall Dill) that GCCS had "allowed" OP-20-G to exploit naval Enigma traffic because it was vitally important to the navy.[58] Left unspoken was London's reluctance to allow the brash Americans further into the cryptanalytic tent. Like their counterparts in the Foreign Office, the Treasury, the Colonial Office, and the service departments, senior officers in GCCS worried that American ambition coupled with American resources would soon challenge and displace British claims on a leading role in the wartime alliance. Once the Americans started throwing bombes and cryptanalysts at Enigma, Bletchley Park might find itself reduced to a supporting role. By retaining control over Enigma operations, GCCS hoped to keep the center of Allied signals intelligence from shifting irreversibly across the Atlantic. The British were prepared to show the Americans everything in Britain, but they reserved the right to veto exploitation of Enigma traffic by Arlington Hall.

By February everyone had forgotten the Turing affair (in January the British cryptanalyst had received his clearance to visit Bell Laboratories) as instructions, demands, and rejoinders flew across the Atlantic. In early March the British chiefs of staff proposed a formal agreement in which GCCS would retain control over the exploitation of all German Enigma ciphers, as well as German teleprinter traffic (TUNNEY) and Italian machine ciphers, while Japanese PURPLE and military attaché ciphers would be mutually exploited by Arlington Hall and GCCS. The resulting "special intelligence" would be distributed to American and British commanders as required by operations. The Americans considered this position so unacceptable that by mid-March the War Department began to consider the impact of severing existing exchange agreements with GCCS.[59]

Fortunately, cooler heads prevailed. Colonel W. Preston Corderman, who had replaced Colonel Frank Bullock as commander of SIS in February, and Lieutenant Colonel Telford Taylor, one of Alfred McCormack's bright young lawyers in MIS, argued convincingly that Arlington Hall could live with an arrangement that recognized British primacy in the attack against German machine ciphers so long as GCCS acknowledged American primacy in Japanese operations and explicitly accepted the principle of full and complete exchange of raw material, technical observations, and methods concerning all German and Japanese systems.[60] Relations also benefited from the visit to Bletchley Park in late April of yet another American mission, this one composed of Alfred McCormack, Telford Taylor, and William Friedman. The British seized the opportunity to demonstrate their willingness to share information with their ally, and during their seven-week sojourn the Americans daily reported to Washington their impressions of British operations against military and diplomatic targets.

The delegation soon acknowledged that the War Department's ambitions concerning German machine ciphers had to be tempered by a dose of reality. On 14 May McCormack warned his superior, Colonel Clarke, against the facile judgment that Arlington Hall could simply step into the Enigma problem. "The guts of this operation is the intelligence side," McCormack noted, "and at this late date it cannot be duplicated at Arlington." Affirming that the United States "must get in on this really tremendous show," he suggested "turning to the possibility of an American operation here, working in close conjunction with the Park and taking advantage of its intelligence resources."[61]

While the American delegation rediscovered the practicality of collaboration, Commander Edward Travis, the operational director of Bletchley Park, traveled to Washington for talks with General Strong and Colonels Clarke and Corderman. The result was the Agreement Between the British Government Code and Cipher School and U.S. War Department, the so-called BRUSA Agreement (Britain-USA), which apportioned responsibility for Axis military communications. Under this agreement the British retained primary responsibility for German and Italian army and air force traffic, while the United States retained primary responsibility for Japanese army and air force traffic. There would be a complete exchange of technical data through liaison officers in Washington and London, and these officers would have access to all decrypts. With regard to the exploitation of Enigma, Arlington Hall's liaison at GCCS would have access to all Enigma decrypts and could select any number for transmission to the War Department. American personnel would be assigned to the Enigma problem at Bletchley in order to gain experience. The Americans would be allowed to pursue independent solutions of German cipher messages, but had to coordinate their work with British operations in order to avoid duplication of effort. Research into improved methods of exploitation would be conducted in Washington on American processing machines.[62] By the end of the summer, the first of several detachments of American cryptanalysts and intercept operators had arrived in Britain and, in cooperation with GCCS, had begun working German military traffic under the code designation BEECHNUT.

The "Enigma crisis" of 1943 represented a disagreement over control of German military cryptanalysis. While a serious irritant to Anglo-American sigint relations, the problem was localized. The controversy had little impact on collaboration on diplomatic operations; indeed, in January 1943, the very time that London and Washington were exchanging recriminations over Turing and their access (or nonaccess) to each other's secrets, a conference of American and British specialists reaffirmed the now routine procedures for cooperating against diplomatic targets. This understanding was updated again in December 1943.[63] By that time Arlington Hall and Berkeley Street were swapping thousands of intercepted diplomatic messages each month.[64] The exchange of cryptanalytic information was so taken for granted that on at least one occasion Arlington Hall simply asked its operational sections to submit lists of what they wanted from Berkeley Street.

By 1944 cooperation had become so close and mutually beneficial that the two allies began to share (with, perhaps, one or two exceptions) material each had previously declined to disclose to the other. As late as May 1943, for example, Arlington Hall prohibited the Friedman-McCormack-Taylor mission then in Britain from revealing to its hosts any information about American cryptanalytic operations against the communications of governments allied with Britain and the United States. By the fall of that year, this prohibition had been lifted. For their part, the British began to share with their ally the so-called Reserved Series, which previously had been deliberately withheld from the Americans. This series included such politically sensitive items as the traffic of the Vatican and the Jewish Agency for Palestine.[65] In 1944 Arlington Hall began sending to Berkeley Street a "Monthly Information Letter" detailing current operations and enclosing pertinent material. The newsletter for December 1944, for example, was divided into four sections: Machines, General Diplomatic, Japanese Diplomatic, and Japanese Military and Attaché. Among the items covered were descriptions of Arlington Hall's current progress against Czech and Free French diplomatic ciphers, a narrative history of American work against Portuguese systems, a list of newly recovered additives used by Thailand to encipher its main diplomatic code, and a report that American stations monitoring the Berlin-Tokyo circuit had recently intercepted German diplomatic messages in a new letter system.[66]

Occasionally, bumps appeared on the path of collaboration, especially toward the end of the war when both Washington and London began to think more about their place in the postwar world. In late 1944, for example, the Foreign Office was increasingly skittish about Berkeley Street sharing cryptanalytic information concerning certain Middle Eastern countries, particularly Egypt, over which Britain had long exerted influence. For its part, the War Department preferred that Arlington Hall refrain from providing any information about Latin American systems unless specifically requested by the British. Usually, patience, common sense, and goodwill combined to smooth over such bumps, which were never allowed to jeopardize the commitment to full collaboration.

In the diplomatic area, the American signals intelligence had little cause to complain of collaborative arrangements with the British. This may explain the otherwise curious omission from the BRUSA agreement of any reference to diplomatic traffic. The Signal Intelligence Service clearly benefited from its connection with GCCS, and there were no major controversies over diplomatic sigint. Carter Clarke's criticisms at the time of the Enigma crisis, such as his charge that the British were dragging their feet in providing cryptanalytic material relating to "Slavic" governments, were made in ignorance of the true state of affairs on the working level. The fact that the Enigma crisis played out with scarcely a reference to diplomatic ciphers and traffic is testimony to the level of mutual satisfaction in this area of operations.

The U.S. Army's Signal Intelligence Service posed in front of their vault, 1935. *Standing left to right:* H. Frank Bearce, Solomon Kullback, Army Captain Harrod Miller (trainee), William Friedman, Abraham Sinkov, Coast Guard Lieutenant L. D. Jones (trainee), Frank Rowlett. Sitting: Louise Newkirk Nelson. Absent: John B. Hurt. (National Security Agency)

Alfred McCormack, who was selected by Secretary of War Henry Stimson to reform the army's signal intelligence effort after Pearl Harbor. (National Security Agency)

Genevieve Grotjan, who contributed significantly to the solution of the Japanese PURPLE cipher machine, receiving an award. (National Archives)

General Joseph Mauborgne, chief signal officer, 1937–1941, and an advocate for signals intelligence. (National Security Agency)

Abraham Sinkov, senior member of the first American delegation to visit Bletchley Park, the wartime headquarters of Britain's codebreakers. (National Security Agency)

W. Preston Corderman, commander of Arlington Hall Station.
(National Security Agency).

142

The operations buildings at Arlington Hall Station.
(National Security Agency)

Facing page. Top: Arlington Hall, the women's college that served as the wartime headquarters of the Signal Intelligence Service. Bottom: Aerial view of Arlington Hall Station. The original college building is at the upper center. The two multiwinged operations buildings were constructed during the war. (National Security Agency)

Codebreaking at Arlington Hall Station. Note the predominance of women.
(National Security Agency)

The "PURPLE Room" at Arlington Hall Station. The woman on the right is
typing the ciphertext into an analog of the PURPLE cipher machine. The
analog converts the ciphertext into plaintext. (National Security Agency)

The barn at Vint Hill Farm as it appeared in 1942 when the U.S. Army purchased the property for use as an intercept station. (National Archives)

The barn at Vint Hill Farm after renovation. Note the double fence and guard tower. (National Security Agency)

Inside the barn at Vint Hill Farm. The high-speed monitoring room, 1944.
(National Security Agency)

Monitoring Station 4, Asmara (Eritrea). Top: Intercepting low-speed (manual) transmissions. Bottom: Intercept positions. (National Archives)

Nos. 7–9 Berkeley Street, London, the wartime home of the diplomatic section of Britain's Government Code and Cypher School. (National Archives)

Chapter Five

Targets

When, in April 1942, the Military Intelligence Service directed the Signal Intelligence Service to expand its intercept and cryptanalytic operations, it also provided the service with a list of priorities. Struggling to reestablish its credibility after the debacle at Pearl Harbor and a string of Japanese victories in the Far East, army intelligence looked to SIS for help. For the moment at least, signals intelligence was the army's best source of information on Axis intentions. General Hayes Kroncr, the chief of MIS, directed the codebreakers to make Axis army and air force traffic their first priority with an emphasis on German, then (in order) Japanese and Italian military communications. Axis military attaché traffic was the second priority, with Japanese military attaché communications taking precedence over German and Italian. Next in interest were inter-Axis diplomatic communications passing between (in rank order) Berlin and Rome, Berlin and Tokyo, and Rome and Tokyo. German administrative radio nets were next on the agenda, followed by all Vichy French traffic. In sixth position on the list were diplomatic messages passing between Tokyo and Buenos Aires, Lima, Rio de Janeiro, Santiago, Mexico City, Stockholm, Vichy, Bangkok, Lisbon, Madrid, and Moscow. The seventh priority was diplomatic traffic between Berlin and Lisbon, Madrid, and various Latin American capitals. The communications of the Vatican, home of the pope and headquarters of the Catholic Church, completed the list.[1] This catalog of targets represented the first time in its history that the Signal Intelligence Service received such specific instructions concerning the traffic desired by the War Department. SIS had no intention of following these instructions.

The codebreakers' recalcitrance did not reflect willful disobedience so much as the pressure of technical and bureaucratic imperatives. General Kroner's directive, which was composed without consulting SIS, was a "wish list" in which MIS identified the information and sources it considered most important in the months immediately after Pearl Harbor. As a military intelligence service serving the needs of the U.S. Army, it first wanted intelligence on the armies and air forces American soldiers and airmen were likely to meet on the battlefield. Diplomatic traffic was a secondary concern, and even then the traffic of enemies or potential enemies (Vichy France) was of more interest than that of allies or neutrals. If MIS had consulted with SIS, it would have learned that these apparently reasonable wishes were, at least for the moment, beyond reach.

In the spring of 1942 SIS was not reading the army, air force, or military attaché traffic of *any* country, let alone Germany, Japan, and Italy, and success was not waiting just around the corner.[2] In the case of attaché messages, which usually ran along diplomatic circuits, the problem was largely cryptographic. No military attaché systems had been solved, although those of Japan were under attack and at least one German system had been identified. In the case of straight military traffic the more immediate problem was intercept. Since armies usually communicated across rather short distances, they relied on low-powered radios or landlines. In the early months of the war these communications were usually beyond the reach of American intercept stations; in fact, almost no German or Italian army or air force traffic was collected. To improve the situation, SIS would have to reorganize its network of monitoring stations, survey and construct new facilities (inevitably overseas) better situated to collect German and Italian army communications, and divert intercept positions currently assigned to diplomatic traffic. Given SIS's limited human, financial, and technical resources, a serious effort against Axis military communications would require it to abandon much of its work against diplomatic targets. This was an unattractive prospect.

SIS had always found diplomatic operations more rewarding than military. Diplomatic traffic was easier to intercept, and army codebreakers had significant experience and no little success in processing it. By April 1942 the codebreakers were able to read one or more of the diplomatic ciphers of Brazil, Chile, Columbia, France, Germany, Italy, Japan, Mexico, Portugal, and Spain. Success, however, was uneven. For some countries (Germany and Spain), only low-grade systems of relatively slight intelligence value were readable. For other countries (Italy and Portugal), several important ciphers remained unsolved. Still, on the basis of its growing experience and expertise, SIS could realistically anticipate further successes in the diplomatic area, especially against the codes and ciphers of the medium and small powers. It saw no reason, however, to plan its cryptanalytic operations around a handful of circuits as desired by army intelligence. For G-2 the traffic of a particular government (Portugal) over a particular circuit (Lisbon-Tokyo) might well have more intelligence value than the traffic of the same government over a different circuit (Lisbon-Montevideo). SIS, however, just wanted traffic; it did not particularly care from where it came. For the cryptanalysts, traffic of slight intelligence value was just as useful as traffic of high intelligence value in effecting solutions, recovering key, and reconstructing codebooks. Code values recovered on the Lisbon-Montevideo circuit could be immediately applied to reading messages from the Lisbon-Tokyo or Lisbon-Washington circuits. Once again the needs of intelligence officers failed to mesh with those of codebreakers, who were inclined by training and appetite to see their job as solving cryptanalytic problems rather than extracting nuggets of information for G-2. For the codebreakers, personal and organizational success was in large part a function of solution rates, and it did not matter much which codes and ciphers were solved.

To implement General Kroner's directive, SIS would have had to abandon or significantly reduce successful diplomatic operations in order to emphasize military operations that held little promise of success, at least in the foreseeable future. Continuity would have been sacrificed as SIS lost touch with, for example, Spanish or Portuguese cryptographic practices, a loss that would be difficult to make up should army intelligence later decide that it needed access to the diplomatic communications of Lisbon or Madrid. Moreover, the codebreakers would have had to adopt procedures, such as a focus on a few circuits, that made little cryptanalytic sense. In short, SIS would have had to stop doing what it did well in order to do what it wasn't sure it could do at all. In classic bureaucratic fashion, SIS accepted Kroner's priorities and then quietly replaced them with its own. The codebreakers preferred to play to their strengths by adopting a priority list that allowed them to continue what they were already doing.

SIS effectively reversed the priorities of military intelligence by giving diplomatic communications precedence over military. It also attacked targets irrelevant to G-2's immediate needs. Contrary to specific directives from MIS, the Signal Intelligence Service did little work on Axis army and air force systems in 1942, and the work it did perform focused almost exclusively on the Japanese army. As a gesture to General Kroner's instructions, Arlington Hall made Japanese military attaché traffic its first priority (it was Kroner's second). Since these messages moved along diplomatic circuits, they were relatively easy to intercept, and SIS already had a team under Sam Snyder working the traffic, although there had been no breakthrough.

SIS focused the bulk of its effort on purely diplomatic operations. PURPLE remained the single most valuable source of signals intelligence, so Japanese diplomatic communications (on all circuits) became the second priority. German diplomatic traffic was the third priority, but only the messages passing in FLORADORA, since the codebreakers had abandoned, for the time, the Reich foreign ministry's other high-grade system (OTPs) as too difficult to crack. Italian diplomatic ciphers were fourth on SIS's priority list, followed (in order) by the diplomatic ciphers (many of which were already being read) of Vichy France, Spain, Portugal, Finland, Argentina, Chile, and, finally, a catchall category of more than a dozen governments, including Bolivia, Brazil, Bulgaria, China, Colombia, Cuba, Dominican Republic, Guatemala, Peru, Sweden, Turkey, and the Vatican.[3] Some of these targets (e.g., Bulgaria, Cuba, Dominican Republic, Bolivia) were marginal to the concerns of American diplomatic and military policy in 1942. Their presence on the codebreakers' priority list and the simultaneous absence of Axis military targets are testimony to the assertion of cryptanalytic considerations over intelligence requirements.

The issue of priorities resurfaced early in 1943. In January Alfred McCormack circulated a paper endorsing General Kroner's directive of the previous year specifying that Axis military and military attaché traffic should be, respectively, the first and second priorities of army signals intelligence, but suggesting changes in subsequent priorities that would increase the focus on the Far East. Believing that the Japanese would continue to be the best source of information about themselves, McCormack argued that Japanese diplomatic and administrative traffic within the Far East, especially that between Japan and China, was most likely to produce the information required to fight the Pacific war and should become the third priority. Non-Japanese diplomatic traffic (Vichy French, German, Italian, and neutral) on Far Eastern circuits might also generate useful information about Japanese activities and intentions and should be next on the list. Diplomatic communications in and out of Europe would follow, with traffic between Europe and the United States receiving preference.[4]

On 1 February representatives of SIS and Special Branch discussed McCormack's proposal. Adopting the perspective of the codebreakers, the representatives agreed that any priority schedule should take into consideration not only the potential intelligence value of any given traffic but also problems relating to cryptanalysis and interception. In a critique of McCormack's proposal (and, implicitly, General Kroner's earlier directive), Major Harold Brown, a senior intercept officer, noted:

> A list of priorities should come to us in very general terms, because it is obvious that we do not intercept and read any traffic that we may desire simply by picking it out and going to work on it. G-2 can give us a list of priorities in the order of importance as they see it from an intelligence standpoint. . . . However, we cannot follow such a list of priorities rigidly as it would not be profitable from a cryptanalytical and radio standpoint.

Major Brown emphasized that any schedule should acknowledge that not all traffic can be intercepted and not all intercepted traffic can be read. Referring to McCormack's interest in traffic between Japan and China, Brown said his stations could probably intercept such traffic if they abandoned other targets whose communications were currently being read, but there was no guarantee that the new traffic could be decrypted. "We could more or less fulfill G-2's interest in that type of material from an intercept standpoint," he concluded, "but they would certainly lose everything else that they were now getting."

Major Telford Taylor, the representative from Special Branch, seconded Major Brown's concerns, noting that it would be imprudent to divert resources from targets that were currently producing valuable intelligence to attack targets whose intelligence value and powers of resistance were undetermined.[5] Eventually such pragmatism won out. In March, Arlington Hall received from army intelligence a new directive that identified the following "Group A" priorities: (1) Japanese army communications; (2) European and African weather traffic; (3) diplomatic communications (including military attaché) between (in rank order) Japan-Russia (Japanese traffic), Japan-Germany (Japanese and German traffic), Japan-Italy (Japanese and Italian traffic), and Japan–Vatican City (Japanese traffic). German military traffic was placed among the secondary targets in "Group B."[6]

In its effort to reconcile intelligence needs with the day-to-day realities of intercept and cryptanalysis, the new directive was an improvement over General Kroner's earlier instructions. Group A traffic was already being collected and processed, so the directive would require the diversion of few, if any, intercept and cryptanalytic resources. The list was heavily weighted toward Japanese targets, a longtime specialty of army sigint.

Japanese army systems continued to resist solution, but by the spring of 1943 Tokyo's military attaché cipher had been solved and, of course, coverage of Japanese diplomatic systems was comprehensive. Most Italian diplomatic traffic was also read. High-grade German diplomatic ciphers remained impenetrable, but Berlin's diplomatic communications figured only modestly in the Group A schedule. As for the troublesome German army and air force Enigma traffic, it was safely relegated to Group B along with other unproductive targets, such as German and Italian military attaché systems. All in all, the priority schedule played to Arlington Hall's strengths and required little dislocation in current operations.

The situation changed dramatically in the summer of 1943. In April army codebreakers registered their first success against high-grade Japanese military traffic when they solved the Japanese army's water transport code, a solution achieved independently by the Central Bureau (Brisbane) and Britain's Wireless Experimental Center (New Delhi).[7] Successes against other Imperial Japanese Army systems followed, and by the end of the year Arlington Hall was scrambling to find the resources to exploit its newfound access to Tokyo's military communications.

The cryptanalytic units (B Branch) were again reorganized to reflect the new priorities. The division of labor into cipher and code solution was jettisoned in favor of a return to country desks. B-I lost its information and bulletin activities to the headquarters unit and now focused exclusively on the translation of Japanese diplomatic and military messages. B-II (under the supervision of Solomon Kullback) assumed responsibility for all Japanese army cryptanalysis. B-III (under Frank Rowlett) took over all other cryptanalytic problems (including Japanese diplomatic), a staggering assignment in view of the fact that in 1943 Arlington Hall was working the diplomatic and commercial traffic of more than thirty governments, some of which were using more than a dozen systems to protect their communications. B-IV became a traffic analysis section as all machine operations were eventually assigned to B-III.[8]

The redistribution of tasks, however, did not solve the resource problem. Even before the break into Japanese army systems, as much as 75 percent of all intercepted traffic remained unprocessed for lack of cryptanalysts and translators. In August, four months after the solution of the water transport code, SIS estimated that Imperial Japanese Army work alone would require the processing of up to three hundred thousand messages a month, a herculean task that would require as many as two thousand additional staff, an increase that would more than double the personnel in the cryptanalytic branch.[9] The War Department authorized Arlington Hall to hire more personnel, but the increase would go into effect only at the beginning of 1944 and would be implemented in increments over the first three months of that year. Additional time would be consumed in training the new recruits as they trickled into Arlington Hall. In the short run, therefore, the only solution was to shift trained staff from diplomatic operations.

William Friedman recommended a drastic solution. Noting that Arlington Hall and Berkeley Street substantially duplicated each other's effort in the interception and processing of diplomatic traffic, Friedman proposed that SIS simply abandon most diplomatic cryptanalysis and leave the work to the British. He acknowledged that in certain areas, specifically the attack against Finnish and Swedish Hagelin machine traffic, Arlington Hall was ahead of its ally and should maintain operations, but this area involved only fifteen workers. If all diplomatic operations except Scandinavian were terminated, 563 people (cryptanalysts, clerks, machine operators, traffic analysts, and translators) would be free for assignment to B-II and the Japanese army problem. Friedman admitted that his proposal might have a detrimental effect on American signals intelligence as diplomatic intercept capabilities were allowed to atrophy and crucial continuity with diplomatic cryptanalytic problems was lost, but he believed that such issues could be resolved by closer collaboration with Britain. Specifically, there would have to be an agreement that Arlington Hall would receive not just the results (translations) of British diplomatic coverage but also all technical information concerning Berkeley Street's solution of foreign systems so that American capabilities, while dormant, would remain current in case the United States decided to resume independent coverage of diplomatic targets.[10]

Friedman's draconian proposal generated little enthusiasm in the corridors of Arlington Hall. Organizations, especially successful ones, resist drastic changes in their mission. Diplomatic cryptanalysis had been the principal (if not exclusive) focus of army signals intelligence since the creation of the Signal Intelligence Service in 1930, and its main successes (e.g., the solution of Tokyo's RED and PURPLE cipher machines) were in the diplomatic area. It was hard to convince senior officers, most of whom had grown up believing that nothing was more important than diplomatic operations, simply to walk away from that experience. There were also practical objections. For example, could Arlington Hall expect the British to share its interest in Latin American coverage? Could translators in Spanish and French simply retool with a crash course in Japanese?[11] Despite these concerns, no one could deny B-II's need for more people if the entry into Japanese army communications was to be exploited. In December Arlington Hall directed Friedman to chair a so-called Inquiry Committee of section chiefs to review the activities of B-III "with a view to determining what changes in coverage might be made in order better to cover Japanese activities."[12]

It is perhaps a sign of the internal resistance to downgrading diplomatic operations that the review came only several months after the problem of resources had been identified and Friedman had offered his unpopular solution. The Inquiry Committee worked its way through the various geographic (Italian, Chinese, Near Eastern, etc.) and functional (machine operations, weather ciphers, commercial codes) sections in Frank Rowlett's sprawling unit, interviewing desk chiefs and reviewing operations in an effort to evaluate the relative importance of the various activities. After several days of meetings, the committee issued a report that proposed to divert additional personnel to the Japanese army problem by pruning, in some cases lopping, diplomatic operations. Some units, such as the machine section with its vital rapid processing capabilities, and the Japanese diplomatic section, which remained the single most important source of diplomatic intelligence, were spared reductions in staff. The committee proposed to reduce other sections, such as the German desk, to the minimum staff necessary to maintain production in currently readable systems. A few sections, such as the unit working commercial codes and all desks in the Latin American section except those responsible for Argentina and Brazil, were marked for closure. In three cases (Spain, Near East, and weather ciphers), the committee was inclined to recommend substantial reductions or, in the case of meteorological ciphers, closure, but it requested guidance from higher authority. If the committee's recommendations were accepted, a minimum of 121 experienced personnel (and as many as 231) would be available for reassignment to the Japanese army problem.[13]

In the end, the Inquiry Committee had little impact. A handful of people were reassigned here, an operation was scaled back there, but there was no significant realignment of cryptanalytic work. The few sections that were closed (e.g., Near East) soon reopened for business. Four months after Friedman's committee recommended significant reductions in diplomatic operations, B-III was working the diplomatic traffic of at least thirty-one countries, roughly the same number it had been working before the committee began its review.[14] By 1945 the number of diplomatic targets had almost doubled compared with 1943 levels. Once again it was apparent that in a cryptanalytic agency it was enormously difficult to overcome the professional resistance to terminating operations that were showing cryptanalytic results, even if those operations produced little in the way of intelligence. As far as the codebreakers were concerned, if a desk was solving systems, it was successful, and you don't walk away from success. And there were so many successes.

The Signal Intelligence Service scored its first cryptanalytic success against Japanese ciphers, and over the years Tokyo's traffic remained the single most important source of diplomatic signals intelligence. After the solution of the PURPLE cipher machine in September 1940, American codebreakers never lost access to Japan's diplomatic communications. For lack of traffic a handful of systems remained unsolved at the end of the war, but the flow of intelligence was hardly affected.[15] For its most secret communications the Japanese foreign ministry relied throughout the war on PURPLE, which Arlington Hall continued to read even after Tokyo introduced certain modifications in the middle of the war. The scale of the American success against the Japanese target is revealed in the numbers. In the first six months of 1944, Arlington Hall produced full translations of 11,452 Japanese diplomatic messages and summaries of another 8,077. In the same period of 1945, the figures were 15,501 translations and 9,331 summaries.[16]

The messages of Japanese representatives in Bern, Lisbon, Madrid, Moscow, Stockholm, and the Vatican appeared frequently in the signals intelligence summaries and provided useful information on Japanese diplomacy and the affairs of their host governments. Japanese intercepts were especially valuable for generating intelligence on governments, such as the Soviet Union, Sweden, and the Vatican, whose traffic remained largely unreadable at Arlington Hall. The traffic of the Japanese embassy in Berlin, however, was consistently Arlington Hall's best intelligence source. Tokyo's wartime ambassador in Hitler's capital, General Oshima Hiroshi, sympathized with the ambitions of National Socialism, believed that the destinies of Germany and Japan were linked, and worked diligently to foster close relations between the two countries. A trusted confidant of Foreign Minister Ribbentrop and a favorite of Hitler, he had access to military and political deliberations that were closed to most senior German officials, let alone foreign diplomats. His correspondence with Tokyo also provided insights into Japanese political and military planning, since the imperial foreign ministry kept its ambassador in Berlin informed of most (though not all) important initiatives. In late July 1942, for instance, Arlington Hall decrypted a PURPLE message from Tokyo directing Oshima to inform the Germans that Japan would not join their war against the Soviet Union. In a rare instance of the president acting upon signals intelligence, Roosevelt promptly passed this news to Stalin without revealing the source but insisting that it was "definitely authentic."[17]

A conscientious and hardworking ambassador, Oshima deluged Tokyo (and Arlington Hall) with detailed reports on a wide range of topics. Some, such as his report on Hitler's "Atlantic Wall," the fortifications intended to repulse an Allied invasion of France, or his descriptions of Allied bombing raids on Berlin in the winter of 1943–1944, when cloud cover complicated post-mission assessments by Allied reconnaissance aircraft, directly assisted Allied military planners. Others, such as his reports on Hitler's attitude toward a separate peace with Russia, provided insights into German political calculations and strategic plans. A few, like his messages describing the attempt on Hitler's life and abortive coup in Berlin in July 1944, exposed political developments otherwise closed to American intelligence. Of course Oshima was not an infallible source. He was not always privy to important plans, and he tended to accept at face value Berlin's perspective on events. Occasionally his assessments were so blatantly unrealistic that they drew criticism from his own foreign ministry.[18] For all these deficiencies, the Japanese ambassador in Berlin remained for American policy makers (in the estimation of General George C. Marshall, the U.S. Army chief of staff) the "main basis of information regarding Hitler's intentions in Europe."[19]

Japanese diplomatic traffic also provided a window on Tokyo's espionage program. In January 1943, for example, Ambassador Oshima hosted a conference of intelligence officers from Japanese embassies in Bulgaria, Italy, Portugal, Spain, Sweden, Switzerland, Turkey, Vatican City, and Vichy France. For two weeks these officers discussed the state of Japan's intelligence effort and the requirements for the future. By monitoring Oshima's radio traffic with Tokyo, American signals intelligence was privy to the deliberations of this conference, including decisions to intensify efforts to crack Allied ciphers, to increase the number of intelligence officers working against the Soviet Union from centers in Bulgaria, Sweden, and Turkey, and to utilize news agencies and journalists to collect information.[20]

Japan's diplomatic traffic also exposed specific efforts to establish espionage networks in the United States. Three days after Pearl Harbor, the foreign ministry in Tokyo sent a circular to all its diplomatic missions, emphasizing the importance of improving intelligence collection capabilities and instructing each mission to determine whether its host government would be willing to contribute to those capabilities. The foreign ministry hoped, for example, to use pro-Axis Chilean officers, particularly military and naval attachés, to collect intelligence from Chile's embassy in Washington.[21]

Nothing came of this or many similar initiatives. The embassy in Madrid, however, reported some promising developments. The government of General Francisco Franco was already collaborating with German intelligence and also had indicated a willingness to cooperate with Japan. On 9 January 1942 the Japanese ambassador in Madrid, Suma Yakichiro, informed Tokyo of a visit from Angel Alcazar de Velasco, a Spanish intelligence officer who, until his expulsion from Britain, had worked in his country's London embassy under the cover of press attaché. Claiming to act at the request of Spain's foreign minister, Ramon Serrano Suner, the visitor offered Spanish assistance in collecting intelligence in the United States. Thus, was born the so-called TO network. Originally, Spain intended to base this net on intelligence officers working in the United States and Canada under diplomatic and consular cover, but relatively soon the plan was expanded to include journalists writing for Spanish newspapers and press agencies. In this scenario expenses, including payments to subagents, would be financed by funds transmitted by Spanish diplomatic pouch. The agents would file their reports through Spanish diplomatic channels or through open codes inserted in otherwise innocuous press dispatches. In Madrid Alcazar de Velasco would pass to Suma any reports of interest to Tokyo.

Many of the details of the operation were exposed in the fall of 1942 when a Spanish journalist destined for espionage work in the United States informed the American embassy in Madrid of his assignment and revealed some of his contacts and communications procedures. Of course decrypts of Ambassador Suma's messages to Tokyo had kept the Signal Intelligence Service informed of the plot since its origin. SIS intercepted its first TO intelligence report in June 1942 and thereafter closely monitored the flow of intelligence from Madrid to Tokyo. From various sources, including "a major in the office of the Chief of the Air Branch," "the manager of a Scranton munitions factory," and "a certain officer in the War

Department," Spanish agents working inside the United States on Japan's behalf allegedly collected a wealth of information on such subjects as arms production, convoy sailings, troop movements, and military planning. The information was so rich that TO became Tokyo's principal source of intelligence concerning the United States. It proved, however, a poor source. A study by American counterintelligence of Suma's decrypted messages concluded that "usually they are either vague or quite inaccurate. Only occasionally has a report been partially correct and of some importance. . . . where facts are lacking the writers draw on their imaginations."[22]

The Japanese seem to have fallen for a confidence game. There can be no doubt that Spanish agents actively collected intelligence in Britain and North and South America, and Madrid may well have passed some of this information to Berlin and Tokyo.[23] The TO network, however, seems to have been largely a fiction contrived by Angel Alcazar de Velasco for financial gain. The Spanish intelligence officer assured Suma that his agents communicated with Madrid through the telegrams and mail of the Spanish embassy in Washington and the consulate in New York. Arlington Hall was reading Spanish cable traffic, and American intelligence was opening Madrid's diplomatic bag, but no messages corresponding to the TO reports passed by Suma to Tokyo were ever discovered. A close analysis of press dispatches and commercial cables filed by Spanish journalists and businessmen also failed to reveal any secret communications. When, in the summer of 1944, Suma began receiving from the Marquis de Rialp, the press officer of the Spanish foreign ministry, summaries of what the marquis insisted were messages from Madrid's ambassador in Washington, Arlington Hall could find no such messages in the traffic of the Spanish embassy. Once again, the gullible Suma seems to have fallen victim to a fabricator.[24]

To finance intelligence activities in Europe and North America, Tokyo tried to smuggle valuable pearls through the Allied blockade for clandestine sale in Lisbon, London, and Paris. A consignment of pearls worth approximately ten thousand dollars, sealed in a nondescript shipping envelope and addressed to the Lisbon representative of Mikimoto, a Japanese dealer in cultured pearls, was entrusted to a Spanish diplomatic courier traveling from Tokyo to Madrid, via Africa and North America, on the diplomatic exchange ship *Gripsholm*. The Spaniards were informed only that the packet contained "official business." When the envelope reached Japanese hands, the pearls were missing. Urgent inquiries at the Spanish foreign ministry led to an investigation and an exchange of messages with Ambassador Cardenas in Washington, through whose embassy the diplomatic pouch had passed.

The ambassador soon uncovered the story. The Spanish diplomatic bag had been surreptitiously opened by American intelligence when the *Gripsholm* put into American port. Agents had discovered the pearls and removed them from the bag. Sometime later, the State Department delivered to the Spanish embassy in Washington a package of pearls, along with a chilly note insinuating that the department was aware of the purposes for which the pearls were intended. Ambassador Cardenas, who at the time knew nothing about the smuggling scheme and was surprised to have a package of pearls delivered to his doorstep, was furious that the Japanese should compromise Spanish neutrality in so blatant a manner. The ambassador believed that by agreeing to be the neutral "protecting power" for Japanese interests in the United States, Spain already risked alienating American opinion. Association with Tokyo's intelligence escapades only multiplied the risks. The ambassador was also experienced enough to realize that, having discovered the pearls, American intelligence would thereafter search every Spanish diplomatic pouch it could get its hands on.

During a home leave to Madrid, Cardenas spoke bluntly to Ambassador Suma. He curtly informed the Japanese representative that the pearls were in a safe at the Spanish embassy in Washington and would remain there until after the war. With more than a touch of malice he also remarked on how curious it was that the Americans always managed to find out about such matters and wondered aloud if Japan had been paying attention to its ciphers. Undeterred, Tokyo made several further attempts to smuggle pearls into Europe. A consignment was entrusted to the captain of a blockade-runner that sailed from Yokohama in September 1942. The pearls disappeared when the vessel was intercepted by British vessels in the Atlantic and scuttled by its crew. Eventually at least one shipment of pearls reached the European markets, and the proceeds from their sale were delivered to Japanese representatives in Lisbon for intelligence purposes.[25]

Although PURPLE and other embassy traffic produced the richest intelligence, nondiplomatic traffic also contributed nuggets of information. Japanese military attachés, especially those in Axis capitals, regularly submitted reports on military events on various fronts, the condition of strategic industries in Germany and Italy, civilian and military morale, the development of new weapons, and the preparation of fortifications and defensive lines. Arlington Hall solved several military attaché ciphers, and one, known to the Americans as JAS, produced surprising intelligence. During the war, the signals intelligence services of the various Axis powers collaborated against Allied and neutral communications. Although this collaboration never matched the scope and success of Anglo-American cooperation, it did score some notable cryptanalytic successes. German, Finnish, and Japanese codebreakers worked closely on several projects, and the liaison channels to Tokyo were the Japanese military attachés in Berlin and Helsinki, who used JAS exclusively to transmit cryptanalytic material.

Sometime in late 1942 or early 1943, Arlington Hall began to read the messages in JAS, and what the codebreakers saw set off alarms across Washington. The JAS traffic passing along Berlin-Helsinki-Tokyo circuits revealed that, in addition to successes against British, Russian, and Turkish communications, the Axis had cracked several American diplomatic ciphers, including the so-called strip cipher that carried the State Department's secret messages. This news caused consternation at State, but it was seized upon with unseemly glee by Arlington Hall. With scarcely a thought for the leakage of American diplomatic secrets, the codebreakers realized that if the Axis were exchanging decrypted American radiograms, they could advance their recovery of JAS key and code by using copies of State Department cables as cribs. In early 1943 Tokyo introduced a second military attaché system (JAT) for signals intelligence liaison messages. Initial efforts against this system were retarded by lack of traffic and the pressure to exploit the success against JAS, but by late 1944 the codebreakers were reading their first messages in the new system. The solution of JAS and JAT provided American intelligence a unique opportunity to monitor Axis efforts to penetrate Allied communications. It also allowed the American codebreakers to advance their work against certain targets (e.g., Turkey and the Soviet Union) by learning from the experience of their Axis counterparts. In this case the enemy became the unwitting collaborator of American signals intelligence.[26]

The success against the military attaché ciphers was jeopardized in the summer of 1943 when intercepted Italian traffic indicated that Italian intelligence had warned Tokyo that cryptographic materials at the Japanese legation in Lisbon had been compromised. In fact, the Office of Strategic Services had an informant inside the office of the legation's military attaché and this individual, a Portuguese stenographer, pilfered documents from the trash basket of his Japanese superior. The haul included cryptographic materials, possibly the plaintexts of encrypted messages sent to Tokyo. How the Italians uncovered this clandestine operation is anyone's guess. Tokyo was sufficiently alarmed that it demanded a report from its minister in Lisbon. When the report, essentially a long description of security measures in place at the mission, proved unsatisfactory, the foreign ministry directed its ambassador in Madrid to dispatch an officer to Lisbon to investigate the situation. The investigator found no evidence that any cryptographic materials had been compromised, and Tokyo's concern faded. Attitudes in Washington, however, were not as sanguine.

In late spring 1943, OSS had passed to the chief signal officer a report on its clandestine acquisitions in Lisbon and had received in response a polite acknowledgment that suggested the material was not sufficiently important to justify further efforts. By early June, at least a month before the Japanese received the warning from Italian intelligence, the OSS report reached the desk of Colonel Carter Clarke, the commander of Special Branch, who immediately recognized a threat to Arlington Hall's cryptanalytic programs. If Tokyo discovered that its communications had been compromised, it might revamp its cryptographic procedures and replace existing ciphers, including PURPLE, with new systems. Clarke immediately alerted General George Strong, the imperious chief of army intelligence, who may well have been the last serving officer to have actually campaigned against the indigenous tribes of the old American West. Strong's abhorrence of OSS was equaled only by his dislike of its director, William Donovan, and he seized the opportunity to savage the upstart intelligence agency and its ambitious chief. After a cursory investigation, Strong sent a scathing (and somewhat misleading) report to General Marshall, the army chief of staff, charging that a "group of amateur spies" had recklessly jeopardized America's most precious intelligence source by purloining the cipher of the Japanese military attaché in Portugal and condemning OSS as a "menace to the security of the nation."[27]

The codebreakers at Arlington Hall knew nothing of the battle shaping up among the intelligence chiefs and nothing of the OSS operation against Japan's mission in Portugal. Apparently the OSS report on its Lisbon operation never filtered down to the cryptanalytic desks. The analysts first became aware of the "Lisbon affair" when it unfolded in Japanese decrypts, even though by then General Strong had launched his assault against OSS. They were puzzled and then alarmed by the messages passing between Tokyo and its representatives in Lisbon, Madrid, and Rome. The Japanese foreign ministry had recently withdrawn from service a cipher (known to the Americans as J-19) that ranked just below PURPLE in importance. Could the abandonment of J-19 be related to events in Lisbon? If Tokyo suspected a compromise, would it next question the integrity of PURPLE? Suddenly, the codebreakers faced the prospect of losing the goose and all its golden eggs. They were relieved to decrypt the report of the investigator from Madrid, who assured Tokyo that he did not think there had been a compromise of cryptographic materials. When after several weeks PURPLE remained on line and Japanese traffic revealed no hint of major cryptographic changes, Arlington Hall concluded the danger had passed. For its part, OSS escaped serious repercussions by demonstrating that General Strong had been kept informed of the Lisbon operation and that the army's intelligence chief knew that the cryptographic material consisted only of messages recovered from wastebaskets. The affair, however, did result in a strict prohibition against any OSS operations to purchase or purloin foreign cryptanalytic material.[28]

Before America's entry into the war, SIS had had only modest success against German diplomatic ciphers. In the months after Pearl Harbor, the German section solved two versions of a Kryha cipher machine used by German commercial attachés to communicate with the foreign ministry in Berlin. In 1943 SIS solved a minor diplomatic system known as FELIX, and by the following year (with significant assistance from GCCS) Arlington Hall was reading another secondary system, SANTA ISABEL, as well as the Enigma machine cipher used by German military intelligence. The primary effort, however, focused on FLORADORA (also known as the Keyword system), one of Berlin's two most important diplomatic systems. SIS had long understood that this was a double-additive system and in July 1940 had actually obtained from the FBI (which had rifled the baggage of a German courier transiting the Panama Canal) copies of additive keys scheduled to enter service in 1941. Hopes were high for the new year, but when it began the purloined keys unlocked no messages.

Eventually it became apparent that Berlin, suspecting that some of its cryptographic materials had been compromised, had made slight changes in the use of the keys. With the aide of cryptographic materials recovered from German consulates in Iceland and Liberia, and in close consultation with their counterparts at GCCS, American cryptanalysts slowly developed procedures for recovering the additive keys. By the late spring of 1943, Arlington Hall was decrypting 25 percent of current traffic in FLORADORA and had read 50 percent of back traffic. By the summer of 1944 most messages in the system were readable.[29] The solution of FLORADORA was the first success against Berlin's high-grade diplomatic traffic, and it provided a useful window on German activities, especially in Argentina. FLORADORA traffic, for instance, led to the seizure of platinum and other contraband goods bound from Argentina to Germany and the exposure of pro-Axis Argentine diplomats who arranged these clandestine shipments.[30] The achievement was limited, however, by the fact that by 1944 FLORADORA was in service mainly between Berlin and a handful of secondary capitals (e.g., Buenos Aires, Dublin, and Kabul).

For all this success, Berlin's most secret diplomatic communications remained closed to American and British intelligence. For its most sensitive messages the German foreign ministry relied on the OTP system, a theoretically unbreakable cipher. Once they suspected the nature of the system they were facing, both SIS and GCCS had abandoned a problem they felt offered no solution in order to concentrate on more promising targets such as FLORADORA. The problem, however, fascinated Ruth Jache, Juanita Moody, and Thomas Waggoner, three young cryptanalytic aides in Arlington Hall's German section, who challenged the popular wisdom that the German OTPs were unsolvable. In September 1943 the three quietly took up the problem, staying on at their desks after their colleagues had left for the day and often working into the early morning hours.

One night an officer, attracted by the lights burning late in the work spaces of the German section, asked the trio what they were doing. Impressed by their youthful enthusiasm and their scorn for colleagues who refused to even attempt the OTP problem, he wrote a short note to Colonel Preston Corderman, the commander of Arlington Hall, noting that three young aides were working on their own time on an important target that no one seemed to care about, and that they had come up with some interesting observations. The next day, Colonel Corderman paid a surprise visit to the German section and astonished the senior cryptanalysts by announcing that he wanted to talk to the aides who were working on the OTPs. Most of the staff were unaware that any such work was in progress. When the confusion was resolved and the trio were introduced to Corderman, Tom Waggoner lifted Juanita Moody onto a vacant table, and said, "Tell him." Moody said that the trio suspected the German cipher key, which in a true OTP is random, was in fact not random and that it could perhaps be predicted. If they were right, then Arlington Hall might duplicate the key used by Berlin to encipher its messages. Corderman was impressed and announced on the spot that the problem was henceforth the first priority of the German section.[31]

The suspicions proved true. In a major cryptanalytic effort that at one point employed 123 personnel, the German section determined the process by which the German foreign ministry's printing machine produced the sheets of key. This crucial discovery allowed the analysts to recover previous key and anticipate future key.[32] The first message in the system that was now known at Arlington Hall as "GEE" was read in February 1945, although the solution was only partial. Partial translations were increasingly available in March, but none were deemed sufficiently important or complete to go beyond the corridors of Arlington Hall.[33] In fact, a significant cryptanalytic feat proved only a modest intelligence victory. By the spring of 1945, German diplomatic representation had been reduced to a handful of posts (Tokyo, Bern, Stockholm, Lisbon, and Madrid), which were increasingly isolated and marginalized as the Thousand-Year Reich began its death throes.

Despite the solution of GEE, non-German traffic remained the principal (if not always certain) source on developments in Germany in the last weeks of the war.[34] For example, by reading the reports of the Spanish ambassador in Sweden in the spring of 1945, American intelligence first learned that Prince Hesse had arrived in Stockholm from Berlin on a secret mission to sound out prospects for a negotiated peace. On the other hand, the reports of the Chinese ambassador in Bern suggested that the prince's presence in Sweden had nothing to do with peace feelers. French traffic supported the Spanish appraisal of the situation by reporting that Nazi foreign minister Ribbentrop hoped to arrange a last-minute settlement and had sent a representative to Sweden for that purpose.[35]

Italy had been a target of American cryptanalysts since the late 1930s, and operations against fascist communications accelerated once SIS began cooperating with GCCS. By the summer of 1943, all high-grade systems of the Italian foreign ministry were readable. In their study of fascist codes the cryptanalysts were aided by deficiencies in Italian cryptographic practices. Code clerks were frequently careless in preparing messages and following prescribed security procedures. More damaging was the foreign ministry's practice of routinely distributing detailed instructions for new systems in older systems, some of which had been in service so long that there should have been a presumption of insecurity. A review of Italian operations at Arlington Hall noted that, as a result of this practice, the Italian section "was in possession of most of the essential facts about a new system before any messages were sent in it."[36] The intelligence value of Italian diplomatic traffic, however, was modest. There was little to interest American intelligence in Rome's routine diplomacy in Ankara, Lisbon, and Madrid. The traffic of the embassy in Berlin might have attracted attention, but this traffic usually moved along landlines and was not accessible. Important political events, such as the fall of Mussolini in July 1943, were conspiratorial affairs that did not surface in any traffic at all.

For a time after the armistice in September 1943, Italian traffic largely disappeared, and Arlington Hall effectively closed its Italian section and transferred the staff to other operations. The armistice regime under Marshal Pietro Badoglio, which had established itself in Allied-occupied southern Italy, maintained occasional contact with a handful of embassies, but it did so in the clear or with ciphers deposited with American and British authorities. When, in September 1943, Mussolini established a rump government in northern Italy, the so-called Republic of Saló, the codebreakers promptly solved one of his regime's cryptosystems but could not accumulate enough traffic to crack the others.

Although the American attack against enemy diplomatic communications focused on Japan, Germany, and Italy, minor powers associated with the Axis did not escape notice. Finland, which had joined Germany in attacking the Soviet Union in 1941, received early attention, mainly because it remained at peace with the United States, and until late in the war its embassy in Washington generated a large amount of accessible traffic.[37] Helsinki's ambassadors and military attachés used a Hagelin cipher machine for their most confidential communications. Arlington Hall began work on this machine in the fall of 1942 and was reading messages in the system by May 1943. This success proved especially useful in February and March 1944 when, at American urging, Helsinki opened secret conversations with Moscow on the possibility of Finland's withdrawal from the war on terms short of unconditional surrender. Although ultimately futile, these negotiations attracted so much interest in Washington that at Arlington Hall the Finnish desk established around-the-clock watches, a schedule normally in place only in the high-priority Japanese section.[38] Several other Finnish systems were solved in 1944–1945, including another version of the Hagelin introduced by the Finns in December 1942 for high-grade traffic between Helsinki and Bern, Lisbon, Madrid, and the Vatican.[39]

Other hostile governments managed to escape attack until 1944, mainly because Arlington Hall lacked specialists with the requisite language competencies. In September 1944, after six months of effort, the codebreakers solved a high-grade Hungarian diplomatic cipher used exclusively on the Budapest-Tokyo circuit. That fall they also made entries into two other Hungarian systems, although one disappeared from Hungarian circuits in December. By April 1945, when most of the country had been occupied by Russian forces, all Hungarian diplomatic traffic had disappeared from international radio circuits.[40] Arlington Hall did not take on Bulgarian communications until the spring of 1944. With significant assistance from GCCS, the Hall was reading some messages in Sofia's main diplomatic system by September 1944 when the Bulgarians surrendered in the face of Soviet invasion. The spring of 1944 also witnessed the first American effort against Romanian ciphers. Once again, the British provided important assistance, including photographic copies of several codebooks. After some success, the effort ended in August 1944 when, after the Soviet entry into the country, encrypted Romanian diplomatic traffic disappeared from the airwaves.[41] In general, the traffic of Hitler's east European allies produced little intelligence. By the time the ciphers of Bulgaria, Hungary, and Romania were solved, these governments were diplomatically isolated, and their few remaining diplomatic missions communicated with their foreign ministries mainly over landlines. Consequently, Arlington Hall relied on Japanese and neutral traffic to learn of major events and issues in the region, such as Hungary's secret efforts to withdraw from the war in the late summer of 1944.[42]

The Latin American problem vividly demonstrates how signals intelligence operations were driven by bureaucratic inertia as much as intelligence requirements. The codes and ciphers employed by the countries of Latin American were relatively simple; indeed, many continued to rely on cryptographic practices that had been the height of sophistication at the Congress of Vienna. When solution was retarded, it was invariably because capitals such as Ascension, Managua, and Port-au-Prince generated little diplomatic traffic. Nevertheless, by April 1942 American codebreakers had solved Brazilian, Chilean, Colombian, Mexican, and Venezuelan systems. By August, Argentine, Dominican Republic, and Ecuadoran ciphers had been added to the list of readable cryptosystems.[43] Before the end of the war, that list included codes and ciphers from every country south of the Rio Grande, although occasionally an individual system resisted attack because of insufficient traffic.[44]

The intelligence significance of the Latin American targets, especially after 1942, was modest. For a time early in the war, Washington had been preoccupied by the threat of Axis espionage and subversion in the Southern Hemisphere, but SIS had remained on the periphery of this issue, allowing the Coast Guard, the FBI, and the Radio Intelligence Division of the FCC to intercept and decrypt clandestine espionage traffic. To be sure, the activities of Argentina, a neutral with pro-Axis sympathies, required constant surveillance, and the various hemispheric conferences generated episodic interest in the communications of the southern republics. In the fall of 1944, for instance, Arlington Hall monitored the reaction of Latin American governments to Argentina's call for a Pan-American conference to discuss Washington's criticisms of pro-Axis sympathies in Buenos Aires. Washington hoped to avoid any conference, but decrypts of Argentine, Chilean, Colombian, Uruguayan, and Venezuelan traffic provided early evidence of significant support for the Argentine proposal. Sigint was probably one of the factors that encouraged the State Department to abandon outright opposition to a conference in favor of Mexico's suggestion of a conference that would discuss a wide range of hemispheric issues.[45] Generally, however, Latin American traffic produced little to capture the attention of intelligence officers. In late 1943 two appraisals of the intelligence value of all systems then being worked by Arlington Hall concluded that, with the exception of Argentine and Brazilian traffic, Latin American communications had little value.[46] William Friedman's Inquiry Committee considered this traffic so marginal that it recommended that Arlington Hall discontinue work on all Latin American communications except for those of Buenos Aires and Rio de Janeiro. Apparently, such appraisals had little impact, since B-III's Latin American desks continued to attack their targets without pause. In the year after the Inquiry Committee recommended the discontinuance of all Latin American work except Argentine and Brazilian, B-III desks exchanged with their British counterparts recovered values and cryptanalytic observations for new Bolivian, Colombian, Guatemalan, Mexican, Peruvian, and Uruguayan systems, in addition to Argentine and Brazilian.[47]

The communications of the European neutrals (Ireland, Portugal, Spain, Sweden, Switzerland, Turkey, and the Vatican) received special attention. Throughout the war these neutrals maintained their diplomatic representation in Berlin, Rome, and Tokyo, and the confidential telegrams of their embassies offered Washington an insight into the political, military, and economic affairs of the enemy. The reports cabled to their respective foreign ministries by neutral ambassadors in London and Moscow also usefully supplemented the information reported by American diplomats in those capitals, thereby providing an additional perspective on the attitudes of alliance partners. The surveillance of neutral communications also alerted intelligence officers to the activities of the legion of spies, revolutionaries, secret emissaries, and confidence tricksters who found Bern, Istanbul, and Lisbon secure, lucrative locales for their intrigues. Finally, the neutrals were, each for its own reason, potentially significant factors in the diplomatic, economic, and military calculations of the Allies. The Vatican wielded a moral influence that, if thrown onto the scales of war, could outweigh any number of army divisions. Spain and Turkey occupied strategic positions at either end of the Mediterranean and disposed of armed forces that no military staff could ignore. Ireland and Portugal (with its Atlantic islands) faced the critical Atlantic sea routes. Portugal, Spain, Sweden, and Turkey possessed important reserves of such strategic materials as chromium, iron ore, tungsten, and wolfram. Throughout the war Switzerland maintained its reputation as the financial capital and intelligence crossroads of the world.

Spanish communications received early attention not only because of Spain's strategic importance but also because Washington suspected the pro-Axis regime of General Francisco Franco of abetting Axis intelligence operations in Europe, Africa, and Latin America. In particular, American intelligence believed that Axis agents in Latin America used Spanish diplomatic channels to communicate with Berlin.[48] During the war the Spanish foreign ministry employed two cryptosystems. For low-grade communications the ministry used "Code 04," an unenciphered code that had been in service since the First World War. For high-grade traffic Madrid employed a different code enciphered with additive tables. This system had been introduced in 1939 and was known to American codebreakers as "SPA." By early 1942 SIS was able to read most messages in Code 04 and had launched an attack against SPA. Initially, the effort against Madrid's high-grade system was retarded by the fact that each Spanish embassy used a unique set of up to one hundred additive tables to encipher the underlying code.

The attack against SPA accelerated significantly in the spring when, during his visit to SIS, Brigadier John Tiltman gave the Americans a copy of the codebook as well as additive tables in service at the Spanish embassies in Ankara, Bucharest, Buenos Aires, Helsinki, and Stockholm, materials that had either been reconstructed by GCCS or surreptitiously obtained by British intelligence.[49] On its own, SIS's Spanish desk recovered the tables used at other Spanish diplomatic posts, and by June 1942 American cryptanalysts were regularly reading the high- and low-grade traffic of Spanish embassies in several capitals, including Washington. That summer, however, the operation faltered when Madrid changed its encipherment by replacing the additive tables with long (ten-thousand-place), nonrepeating additive tapes. This was a significant improvement, since the nonrepetitive nature of the cipher key made solution through traditional cryptanalysis problematic. Fortunately, there were less traditional solutions.

As early as January 1942, William Donovan, then serving as coordinator of information for President Roosevelt, considered a proposal to acquire cryptographic material from the neutrals by clandestine means. By early spring American intelligence had prepared a plan to burglarize the Portuguese, Spanish and Turkish embassies in Washington. The plan was implemented one night in March when a team that included a safecracker and a photographer entered the Spanish embassy and photographed several hundred pages of secret documents, including codebooks and cipher tables. Despite this initial success, operations against the Portuguese and Turkish diplomatic missions were canceled because of opposition from the FBI, which resisted any encroachment on its prerogatives in the area of domestic intelligence operations.[50]

The FBI believed that if embassies were to be burglarized, the burglars should be bureau operatives. Although details of the program remain shrouded in secrecy more than fifty years later, it is clear that the FBI conducted its own operations against an unknown number of diplomatic missions in Washington, New York, and other North and South American cities. Operatives would enter the consulate or embassy at night, secure entry to the code room, crack the safe, and photograph cryptographic materials. Spain remained a favorite target. In August 1942, one month after the Spanish foreign ministry switched over to the additive tapes, the FBI passed to army intelligence photographic copies of cryptographic materials, including additive tapes, from Madrid's Washington embassy. The haul proved a godsend for Arlington Hall's Spanish desk, since solution of messages enciphered with the nonrepeating additive would have been unlikely without access to the tapes. Indeed, for the remainder of the war the codebreakers came to take such access for granted. In June 1944, for example, the Spanish desk informed its supervisor that the tapes then in service at the Washington embassy would soon run out and that it was time to acquire a copy of the next set of tapes. Soon thereafter, the FBI delivered copies of new Spanish additive tapes.[51]

Spanish cryptographic material also reached Arlington Hall as a result of other clandestine operations, such as the surveillance of Madrid's diplomatic pouch. Protected under international law from search and seizure, diplomatic bags were tempting targets for any intelligence service, not the least because they often contained cryptographic materials as foreign ministries distributed new codebooks and ciphers to their embassies and consulates. Neither Washington nor London was deterred by legal niceties. In October 1942, for example, the State, Navy, War, and Treasury Departments established a top secret committee to examine the diplomatic pouches of the Belgian, Dutch, French, Polish, Portuguese, Spanish, Swedish, and Swiss embassies in Washington.[52]

Under Allied blockade regulations, ships and aircraft serving Spain and other neutral countries had to touch at Allied ports or stations where their cargo, including mail, was subject to search. Although theoretically immune from search, diplomatic mail did not escape scrutiny. Spanish pouches received special attention, in part because Madrid tried to help Italian diplomatic missions evade Allied surveillance by including Rome's mail in Spanish bags. Crossing the Atlantic, Spanish steamships had to put into Bermuda or Trinidad, where all mail, including diplomatic mail to and from Spanish embassies in the Western Hemisphere, was taken ashore by British authorities and held until the vessels' scheduled departures. Although the seals and straps on the returned pouches were always intact, the Spaniards correctly surmised that the bags had been expertly opened and resealed. At times, surveillance of Spanish diplomatic mail abandoned all discretion. On 2 October 1942 several unidentified men boarded the Spanish steamer *Magallanes* in New Orleans harbor, detained a Spanish diplomat who was a passenger, and confiscated (despite his resistance) two sealed parcels containing cipher material. After an energetic protest by the Spanish embassy over this violation of international law and diplomatic custom, the parcels were returned (without explanation) to the embassy's custody. Nevertheless, the Spaniards were outraged by clear signs that the packages had been opened.[53]

Such incidents, of course, only inspired the Spaniards to greater caution, and occasionally American intelligence fell victim to its own clandestine operations. In August 1942, for instance, the Spanish ambassador in Guatemala somehow learned that his encrypted communications with Madrid were read by American intelligence. The representative in Guatemala City wrote to the Spanish ambassador in Washington, asking his colleague to alert their foreign ministry. The latter dutifully forwarded the warning to Madrid by the next bag. He also informed the foreign ministry that, while he believed his own ciphers were secure, he would send important messages in the cipher tables reserved for the embassy in Mexico City (copies of which had been deposited in the Washington embassy) until an investigation was completed. This news discomfited American intelligence (which read this report after covertly intercepting and opening the Spanish diplomatic bag) because at the time Arlington Hall could not read messages in the Mexico City cipher tables. Consequently, there was an annoying blackout in Washington-Madrid traffic until those tables were solved or acquired.[54]

In spite of all these efforts, coverage of Spanish diplomatic communications was not comprehensive. Access to the additive tapes in service at the important embassies in Berlin and Rome was difficult, if not impossible. Until late in the war, communications between Madrid and its European embassies usually moved along landlines, which were impossible to monitor. Still, sufficient traffic was readable to allow American signals intelligence to observe Spain's diplomatic activity. This was especially useful at the time of the Allied landings in North Africa (Operation Torch) in the fall of 1942, when both London and Washington were deeply concerned about Madrid's reaction. Spanish traffic also helped policy makers monitor Spain's noncompliance with the so-called Allied-Spanish Agreement of 2 May 1944 in which Madrid undertook to expel from Spanish territory designated Axis intelligence agents, close certain Axis consular and commercial facilities used for espionage purposes, and reduce wolfram shipments to Germany. Finally, surveillance of Spanish diplomatic traffic, especially on the Washington-Madrid circuit, revealed that Japan's TO intelligence network, which allegedly utilized Spanish diplomatic missions and communications facilities in the United States, was largely a figment of the imaginations of certain Spaniards who profited financially from Tokyo's gullibility.

For all the attention given to Spain, American signals intelligence did not neglect the other Iberian power, Portugal. SIS briefly investigated Portuguese diplomatic systems in the spring of 1941, but all work on this project was suspended between January and August 1942, perhaps because analysts were needed for more pressing projects. When work resumed, progress was rapid, in part because Arlington Hall had obtained photographic copies of three of Lisbon's codebooks. By the end of 1944, Arlington's Portuguese section, working in close cooperation with its counterparts at GCCS, had cracked almost all Portuguese codes and ciphers, including nine of the ten systems in use at the Washington embassy.[55] American codebreakers considered Portuguese traffic an important source of diplomatic intelligence. Lisbon was well represented in Berlin, Rome, Tokyo, Vichy, and the Vatican, and its conscientious diplomats generated a stream of informed reports on political, economic, and social conditions inside the Axis alliance. In June 1943, for example, Arlington Hall decrypted and circulated the following items from Portuguese circuits:

- A report from the legation in Tokyo on the increasingly grave mood in Japan
- Information from the ambassador at the Vatican on the collapse of morale in Italy and the secret efforts by the increasingly discredited king to reach out to nonfascist circles in search of a solution to the political and military crisis
- A message from the ambassador in Berlin describing heavy casualties and "practically total" destruction from Allied air raids on Rhineland cities
- A report from the legation in Bucharest on Romania's weakening commitment to the war on the eastern front

In March 1944 intercepted traffic of the Portuguese legation in Budapest provided early intelligence on the German occupation of Hungary. Later that year the legation's reports offered a glimpse of the roundup and deportation of Jews from the Hungarian capital. On 19 October the Portuguese legation reported that all Jews were being deported "to an unknown destination." Ten days later the legation informed Lisbon that Germany had demanded the deportation of sixty thousand Hungarian Jews, and that fourteen thousand had already left on foot, presumably for Austria. Noting that the deportees had little food, the report concluded, "The great majority will not even live to reach the frontier."[56] The reports of Lisbon's ambassador in Berlin also provided some of the first reliable information on the attempt on Hitler's life in July 1944. Surveillance of the traffic of the Portuguese embassy in Washington satisfied American counterintelligence officers that Japan's so-called FUJI spy network, which purported to provide Tokyo verbatim messages from Lisbon's representatives in Washington, did not have access to real messages and was largely the work of confidence tricksters who fabricated and sold information to the Japanese.[57]

Turkish communications also proved a rich source of intelligence. Like Lisbon, Ankara was well represented in belligerent and neutral capitals, and the reports of its able ambassadors and military attachés provided significant insight into wartime events and personalities. Among all the neutral targets, Arlington Hall considered Turkish circuits "the most important as regards intelligence and the amount of traffic received."[58] GCCS led the effort against Turkish systems, and when Arlington Hall established a Near Eastern section in December 1942, it benefited greatly from British experience. In June 1943 GCCS passed to Arlington a complete copy of the low-grade ZAFER Code. That year the Americans solved another low-grade system as well as the high-grade system CANKAYA, although the latter success was qualified by the fact that CANKAYA was soon replaced as Ankara's high-grade system by another cipher, INONU. GCCS assisted the American attack against CANKAYA by responding to inquiries about Turkish cryptographic practices, confirming identifications of code groups, and providing three thousand groups recovered by its own analysts. The two allies collaborated closely in the solution of INONU, which carried 25 percent of the traffic on the Washington-Ankara circuit and 30 percent of the traffic on the Moscow-Ankara circuit. The allies also cooperated in solving the cipher used by Turkish military attachés. Messages in INONU and the attaché cipher were especially useful in providing information concerning political affairs in Moscow and the military situation on the eastern front.[59]

In comparison to Portuguese, Spanish, and Turkish communications, Switzerland's traffic proved disappointing as a source of intelligence. Arlington Hall set up a Swiss desk in January 1943, and within the year several Swiss diplomatic systems, most of modest sophistication, were readable. For its most secret communications the Swiss foreign ministry employed the Enigma cipher machine on certain circuits. By the fall of 1943 Arlington Hall was reading Enigma messages on the Washington-Bern circuit. While successful from a purely cryptanalytic viewpoint, operations against Swiss communications provided only modest results from an intelligence perspective. Messages were concerned primarily with Bern's efforts to protect Swiss trade, and secondarily with humanitarian programs and Switzerland's activities as "protector" of various countries' interests in belligerent states.

A selection of messages from the fall of 1943 suggests the nature of Swiss traffic: the Swiss foreign ministry forwards to its legation in Tokyo an inquiry from the Canadian government concerning repatriation of civilians interned by the Japanese; the Swiss legation in Rio de Janeiro informs Bern that it has succeeded in securing the liberation of Italian sailors interned in Brazil; the legation in Tokyo informs Bern that foreigners in Japan are now required to declare their real estate holdings, bonds, and other income.[60] An occasional message caught the attention of American officers. In the final months of 1944, for instance, the reports of the Swiss representative in Tokyo detailed the worsening economic and industrial situation in Japan. At one point the representative informed his foreign ministry that his legation was without heat because the Japanese authorities could no longer provide the necessary pipes. The diplomat added that the Spanish embassy had resorted to sending its staff to forage for wood in the parks and forests.[61] As a whole, however, the traffic was mundane. A review of November 1943 concluded that "the intelligence value of most messages in the Swiss systems is low," and the next month Arlington Hall's special Inquiry Committee recommended the termination of all work against Swiss communications except for messages originating in Japanese occupied territory.[62] A handful of analysts maintained a watch on Swiss communications through the end of the war, but the traffic was never a high priority.

Swedish diplomatic communications proved difficult to penetrate. By 1941 most of Stockholm's embassies were using Hagelin cipher machines for their secret messages. Although in November 1942 Arlington Hall received from the FBI information on Sweden's use of the Hagelin, the codebreakers made little progress against the system. By the last year of the war, the Hagelin section at Arlington Hall had largely abandoned the Swedish problem in order to focus on more promising studies of Dutch and French Hagelin traffic. The section occasionally returned to Swedish high-grade traffic, but as late as June 1945 no solution had been effected and none was anticipated. Arlington Hall had some success against secondary systems in part because in 1942 it secured a copy of a codebook used by the Swedish legation in Caracas, as well as copies of the correspondence of the Swedish military attaché in Washington.[63] The resulting translations contained no intelligence of significance.

American signals intelligence came late to Irish communications, in part because Ireland did not figure prominently in Washington's wartime concerns and in part because GCCS provided any coverage required. There was some work on this target in 1943 and 1944, and by the end of the war at least two of Dublin's systems were readable. The traffic was generally of low intelligence value, although the radiograms of the Irish legation in Berlin occasionally provided insight into conditions in Germany. A report from the chargé d'affaires on 19 November 1944, for example, informed Dublin that German civilian morale had improved in the wake of the V-2 rocket attacks against British cities. He also noted that Allied bombing raids had idled workers at many German defense factories. Generally, however, Irish systems never received more than intermittent attention at Arlington Hall, which was pleased to leave this target to the British.[64]

The communications of the Vatican, the world's smallest state, had always tempted American signals intelligence. Like most other capitals, Washington was convinced that the Vatican had unparalleled access to information from all parts of the globe and that the messages of papal representatives were rich in political and military intelligence. Like most other capitals, Washington was wrong in this belief, but that did not divert American intelligence from its plans. As early as the spring of 1942, the Vatican figured prominently among the sigint priorities of army intelligence, but operations were postponed as qualified personnel were required on more pressing problems. For some time after the United States' entry into the war, the FBI ran the only active American program against papal communications. In a clandestine operation whose details remain classified to this day, the bureau, suspecting (incorrectly) that Axis intelligence agents in North America used the papal diplomatic pouch to communicate with their controllers in Europe, placed the mail of the papal delegation in Washington under surveillance.[65] The situation at Arlington Hall changed in September 1943 when, after the Italian armistice and the occupation of Rome by German forces, encrypted Italian diplomatic traffic virtually disappeared from the airwaves. Several analysts were shifted from the now idle Italian section to a newly formed Vatican section.

The effort against papal ciphers was cloaked in particular secrecy for fear of the domestic political consequences should Catholics or congressional representatives from heavily Catholic constituencies learn that the U.S. government was eavesdropping on the confidential communications of the Holy Father. Senior officers probably also feared offending the many Catholics who worked at Arlington Hall. The word *Vatican* did not appear on any organizational charts or in any internal correspondence. Like a handful of other supersensitive projects, the Vatican problem was known only by a code word based on colors. According to this scheme, the unit working papal ciphers was designated "Gold Section." In other problems the cryptosystems were identified by trigraphs in which the first two letters were an abbreviation of the country and last letter indicated the particular system in the sequence in which it had been taken up by the cryptanalysts. Thus, the Spanish desk would be working SPA and SPE, while the Turkish group might be studying TUA and TUB. To obscure the source of the traffic from unindoctrinated staff, Vatican ciphers were assigned the innocuous digraph KI, a label that gave no hint of the target's identity.[66]

During the war the Vatican used several cryptosystems, each designated by a color. Gold Section first attacked the CIFRARIO ROSSO (RED Cipher), a low-grade cipher that had been in service since the early 1930s and was considered insecure by the Vatican. With the help of GCCS (which had been studying papal traffic since October 1941 and had recovered almost three thousand groups of RED), Arlington Hall was soon able to read most traffic in this system.[67] It was Arlington's (and Berkeley Street's) only success against the Vatican. Neither the British nor the Americans made much progress against the pope's high-grade ciphers. The analysts in Gold Section were surprised at the sophistication of the cryptosystems.[68] Explaining their lack of success, they noted that "the difficulties encountered showed that considerable intelligence was matched against the analysts'," concluding that they were dealing with "a cryptographer of no mean ability." The effort against papal ciphers was also undermined by the complete absence of compromised cryptographic materials. The papal Secretariat of State distrusted the security of the diplomatic pouch and preferred to distribute new cryptosystems to its posts by the hand of priest-couriers (usually papal diplomats traveling to their posts), who never allowed the cipher to leave their person. Papal diplomats also exercised strict communications discipline and kept their telegraphic traffic to a minimum. Consequently, relatively few messages were intercepted. The attack against the system known to Arlington Hall as KIH, a special cipher used by the Vatican to communicate with its representative in Washington, was constrained by the fact that after a year of surveillance only forty-six messages thought to be in this system had been intercepted, far too few to help the cryptanalysts. In the summer of 1944 Arlington Hall simply gave up on Vatican ciphers and transferred the Gold Section staff to other operations.[69]

Ironically, the codebreakers abandoned the effort precisely when policy makers were increasingly desperate for reliable intelligence on the Vatican. In the last year of the war Washington worried about the Vatican's posture on a range of important issues, including the political shape of the postwar world, the projection of Soviet influence into Eastern Europe, and the reorganization of Italy's government. After the liberation of Rome in June 1944, American intelligence intensified its operations against the Vatican. However, agents working on the fringes of the papal administration were largely ineffectual. As we shall see, the most important source became a serious embarrassment when his reports proved to be fabrications. Signals intelligence would normally have supplemented human intelligence and provided a check on suspect agent reports. Because Vatican ciphers resisted every attack, American intelligence not only lacked direct insight into papal diplomacy but also was forced to rely on unreliable sources.[70]

The special security surrounding Arlington Hall's attack against papal communications had a negative (though unintended) impact on another American intelligence operation targeted against the Vatican. The CIFRARIO ROSSO, the one papal cipher the codebreakers were able to read, was a low-grade system that usually carried traffic concerned with minor administrative, ecclesiastical, and charitable affairs. It was, however, the only cipher available to Monsignor Paolo Marella, the pope's representative in Tokyo. Apparently, during the war, the papal Secretariat of State was never able to arrange a secure channel for sending new, improved ciphers to its man in Japan. Most, if not all, of Marella's messages to Rome were read by Arlington Hall. These messages contained little of intelligence value, since Marella knew that his cipher was antiquated and entrusted nothing important to its security.[71] At the time that Arlington Hall was studying papal messages, another American intelligence agency, the Office of Strategic Services, was also operating against the Papacy. In the fall of 1944 the OSS station in Rome began to receive information from a source (code-named Vessel) inside the Vatican who apparently had access to the files of the pope's Secretariat of State. Among the documents provided by Vessel were copies of telegrams from Monsignor Marella detailing political and economic conditions inside Japan, speculating on Japanese policy toward Russia, and discussing the possibility of papal mediation of the Pacific War. These reports from an informed observer at the very heart of the Japanese Empire were considered so valuable that OSS sent them directly to the White House. Unfortunately, it was all a hoax.

There was no source inside the Vatican, and the documents were forgeries. In its eagerness to penetrate the secrets of the Vatican, OSS had fallen victim to the fertile imagination and skillful pen of Virgilio Scattolini, journalist, film critic, pornographer, and the most brazen intelligence fabricator of the Second World War. From his flat near the Piazza di Spagna, Scattolini had been concocting spurious "intelligence" and selling it to gullible "clients" since 1939; OSS was only the latest in a series of victims that included various intelligence services, embassies, banks, and newspapers. OSS might have been spared embarrassment if it had had closer relations with the codebreaking service, now renamed the Signal Security Agency (SSA). Arlington Hall was reading Monsignor Marella's messages from Tokyo at the same time that OSS was purchasing Vessel reports that purported to be verbatim copies of the same messages. A comparison of the decrypted messages with the purchased versions would have immediately exposed the latter as forgeries. Unfortunately, OSS knew nothing of Arlington Hall's work against papal communications. Relations between the codebreakers and the covert operators were distinctly cool, especially after the "Lisbon affair," in which an ill-considered OSS operation against the code room of the Japanese embassy caused Tokyo to consider changing its ciphers. The work against Vatican communications also was too sensitive to be shared with other agencies, especially one as notorious for leaks and misadventures as OSS. As a result, one American intelligence service swooned over elaborately detailed reports from the pope's delegate in Tokyo, while another held proof that those reports were forgeries.[72]

During the war American codebreakers worked the diplomatic traffic of a handful of Middle Eastern and African states that were neutral or nominally allied against the Axis. Arlington Hall had established a Near East section in December 1942, but the unit focused primarily on Turkish systems, although Iraqi and Iranian systems were also under study by the summer of 1943. Arlington Hall closed the section in January 1944 as part of the effort to free personnel for transfer to the Japanese army problem, but the section reopened in April. In their work against Middle Eastern targets, the Americans benefited significantly from the experience of their British colleagues. Before the war Britain had been the dominant power in the region, and in order to remain so both during and after the conflict, London took a special interest in the affairs of the local governments. The communications of Afghanistan, Iraq, and Iran were as important to London as those of Mexico and Brazil were to the United States; consequently, GCCS had long experience in solving the ciphers employed by Baghdad, Kabul, and Teheran. This experience saved the Americans a lot of labor. Berkeley Street, for example, passed to Arlington Hall copies of all the codebooks employed by the Afghan and Iranian foreign ministries. In response to a request from SSA in the spring of 1944, the British provided general information on Iraq's diplomatic systems that materially assisted the Americans in solving Baghdad's newest cipher in less than six days. British generosity was qualified only in the case of Egypt, home to the vital Suez Canal, Britain's lifeline to India. At the specific order of the Foreign Office, Berkeley Street was prohibited from sharing with Arlington Hall information on Egyptian ciphers. For their part, the Americans were generally cooperative and occasionally made original contributions as when, in April 1944, Arlington Hall passed to Berkeley Street information on the main Ethiopian cipher. The Americans, however, could also be reserved. In early 1945, for instance, Arlington Hall decided not to inform the British that they had identified the nature (double transposition) of Ethiopia's newest diplomatic cipher.[73]

Among these targets only Saudi Arabia attracted serious American attention. In early February 1945 army intelligence directed Arlington Hall to make Saudi traffic an immediate priority. President Franklin Roosevelt had agreed to meet the Saudi king, Abdul Aziz al Sa'ud, on his way back to Washington from the Yalta Conference that ended on February 11. The War Department decided at the last minute that Saudi communications in the days before the meeting might provide the presidential party with warning of what the monarch desired of the president. Previously Arlington Hall's Near East section had solved two Saudi substitution ciphers, but by 1945 both were obsolete. Two current systems, known at Arlington as ABA and ABD, had been solved by Berkeley Street and shared with the United States. ABA was a letter code, while ABD was a substitution cipher that replaced each letter with two digits. The president's visit with King Abdul would provide an unexpected insight into how the Saudis used these systems.

On 13 February 1945 an American destroyer, the USS *Murphy,* pulled alongside a pier at the small Saudi Arabian port of Jidda. The crew scrambled to catch a glimpse of the party waiting to board the vessel; it wasn't every day that an American warship took on a royal passenger. The *Murphy* had been dispatched to carry King Abdul Aziz al Sa'ud to the Great Bitter Lake north of Suez to meet President Franklin Roosevelt. Before the voyage the American ambassador to Saudi Arabia had discreetly hinted to the king and his advisers that a small retinue, no more than a dozen or so individuals, would suit both the occasion and the accommodations of the *Murphy.* The king, however, refused to economize when it came to image. When his royal highness boarded the ship, he was followed by an entourage of forty-eight people, including his foreign minister, his finance minister, two royal princes, the court astrologer, and an assortment of chamberlains, secretaries, bodyguards, coffee servers, and cooks. With their robes, scimitars, and bandoliers, the royal entourage attracted more than a little attention. One individual, however, was the focus of particular scrutiny. Mohammed Abdul Djither, the king's chief radio officer, had come aboard with a large leather satchel. This official and his two assistants were responsible for maintaining radio communications between the destroyer and Mecca. The leather satchel, which never left Djither's sight, contained cryptographic materials. Since the royal delegation used the *Murphy*'s radio facilities, the ship's communications officer set out to discover as much as possible about the communications procedures and cryptographic systems employed by the House of Sa'ud.

The destroyer's radio personnel kept the Saudi officials under close observation during the voyage and tried to overhear royal transmissions between the ship and shore stations. The Americans were unanimous in their praise for the efficiency of Saudi radio operations. Operators sent rapidly and well, used correct international procedure, maintained circuit discipline, and conformed to the highest standards of communications practice. When messages required encryption, Djither would remove a large, leather-bound codebook from his satchel. On one occasion the royal radio officer, in an uncharacteristic security slip, encrypted a message while the destroyer's communications officer lingered nearby. The American officer was able to catch a glimpse of the cryptographic materials. In a report to the Office of Naval Intelligence, subsequently forwarded to Arlington Hall, he noted, "Words and phrases in the book are assigned letter-group equivalents. These letter groups are then reenciphered by reference to the numerical reenciphering table to form two-digit groups." Arlington Hall and Berkeley Street believed that the Saudis used two systems: a code and a cipher. The destroyer's alert communications officer had observed the two systems being used in tandem, thereby saving the codebreakers time and trouble. The state visit proved to have cryptanalytic as well as political rewards.[74]

Arlington Hall came late to the study of Allied communications. This delay reflected less a squeamishness about treating friends like enemies than a need to employ scarce staff against more pressing problems. In the difficult months of 1942 and 1943, for example, no one was interested in diverting cryptanalysts from the Japanese army problem just so that Washington could read the communications of the Norwegian government-in-exile. Neither Carter Clarke, Alfred McCormack, nor any other director of army signals intelligence policy had reservations about eavesdropping on friends. When discussing the principles that should guide SIS after Pearl Harbor, both Clarke and McCormack insisted that the communications of those allied with the United States against the Axis should not be privileged. Wartime partners had mutual interests, but at times these interests diverged. Such divergence could be expected especially toward the end of the war, when the pressing military peril receded and the victorious powers considered the peace conference and the shape of the postwar world. In the meantime, signals intelligence provided a useful insight into alliance politics, a prudent check on an ally's good faith, and an early warning of political and economic decisions that affected American interests.

Aside from a handful of Latin American republics (Mexico, Brazil, Dominican Republic) that declared war on the Axis soon after Pearl Harbor and whose diplomatic traffic received early attention, Allied governments escaped Arlington Hall's attention until midwar. Monitoring nets often scooped up the traffic of these governments, but the messages were merely dropped into the intercept files without analysis. In January 1943, as disagreements over American financial and military commitments strained relations between Washington and Chungking, SIS established a Chinese section.[75]

For two months a handful of linguists and cryptanalytic clerks sorted through the voluminous archive of Chinese traffic, classifying the messages according to external features, such as addressee. Although Herbert Yardley's Cipher Bureau had studied China's codes in the 1920s and had read at least three systems, the Signal Intelligence Service had not continued the work in the 1930s. The loss of continuity meant that the analysts had to start from scratch. They began by studying a nonsecret telegraphic code (designated MING) to familiarize themselves with Chinese code compilation practices. Work accelerated in March when a long report on Chinese diplomatic systems arrived from GCCS. Efforts focused on two systems, INVINCIBLE and WIN, each a one-part code with polyalphabetic encipherment. By the end of June, the section was decrypting messages in both systems.[76]

Like the French and the Portuguese, the Chinese believed that communications security was best served by using many systems simultaneously. Like the French and the Portuguese, they were wrong. By March

1944 Arlington Hall had solved eight of these systems. By June 1945 it had solved another four, including the principal foreign ministry system and the system used by Chinese military attachés, and had made entries into four more, including the cipher used by the chief of Chinese intelligence, General Tai Li, to communicate with his station chief in Washington. Solution of the military attaché cipher was facilitated by the discovery that the attaché in Washington routinely encrypted and forwarded to Chungking verbatim copies of the weekly situation reports distributed by General Dwight D. Eisenhower's command in Europe. By obtaining copies of these reports from the Joint Chiefs of Staff, American codebreakers had the perfect crib for reading the Chinese messages.[77] During the war Arlington Hall made no effort to read the communications of the Chinese communist forces operating under Mao Tse-tung against the Japanese in northern China, although glimpses of their activity (mainly military operations) occasionally appeared in intercepted Japanese traffic.[78]

In March 1943 Arlington Hall began studying the communications of the Free French government-in-exile of General Charles de Gaulle. Previously SIS had attacked the communications of the Vichy regime. With the aide of compromised codebooks generously furnished by GCCS and the second-story artists of the FBI, the codebreakers were eventually able to read more than a dozen Vichy colonial and diplomatic systems. Most were of marginal intelligence interest, but two in service on Vichy-Tokyo, Vichy-Hanoi, and Vichy-Shanghai circuits generated useful information concerning economic and political conditions inside the Japanese empire.[79] The Free French ciphers proved more resistant. Like their Vichy counterparts, the Gaullists believed that security was enhanced by the use of a large number of cryptographic systems, each carrying relatively few messages. As late as October 1943, none of the eighteen Free French systems then identified was readable at Arlington Hall, and the codebreakers provided little help to American diplomats then struggling to contrive a viable French policy.

Proud and irascible, General de Gaulle had been offended by the failure of London and Washington to consult with him before invading French North Africa in November 1942 and before securing a cease-fire there by cutting a deal with Admiral Jean Darlan, the commander in chief of Vichy armed forces and a notorious advocate of collaboration with Germany. Relations with the United States deteriorated further when Franklin Roosevelt, who challenged the general's vision of France as a great power and suspected him of harboring praetorian ambitions, refused to acknowledge de Gaulle's claim to sole leadership of the Free French movement and to recognize the French Committee of National Liberation as the "government" of Free France. "What to do with de Gaulle" was a question that bedeviled the White House and the State Department throughout 1943 and required extended discussion at the Anglo-American conferences at Casablanca (SYMBOL) in January, Washington (TRIDENT) in May, and Quebec (QUADRANT) in August. It was a question, however, that policy makers had to answer without the help of signals intelligence.[80]

The effort against Free French communications proved so unrewarding that at the end of 1943 William Friedman's Inquiry Committee recommended abandoning work on all French traffic except Vichy messages originating in Japanese-controlled territory.[81] Like most of the committee's recommendations, this one was never implemented, and work continued on Gaullist traffic. Progress, however, remained slow. In 1944 several low- and medium-grade systems were solved. The messages were, however, of modest intelligence value: the Gaullist representative in Stockholm requested additional funding for his mission; Free French headquarters in Algiers authorized its commercial agents in the United States to purchase three thousand barrels of rum; the Free French representative in the Dominican Republic sought guidance on a request from the local government to appoint the son-in-law of the Dominican dictator, Rafael Trujillo, as his country's ambassador to France, even though the young man had been in an altercation with the French police and had been shot and wounded by an officer.[82] Only at the end of the year did the more important high-grade systems begin to succumb to attack. The quality of political intelligence improved dramatically. For instance, by reading current and back traffic of de Gaulle's representative in Moscow, Arlington Hall became aware of Soviet efforts in 1943–1944 to woo France in order to secure a sympathetic power to the west of Germany in the postwar world. High-grade Gaullist traffic also allowed Washington to observe Paris's successful efforts to curry Chinese favor and secure Chungking's acquiescence in the reassertion of French imperial authority in postwar Indochina. Of more immediate interest to American authorities were decrypted messages that revealed French plans in the spring of 1945 to establish a clandestine intelligence network inside the United States. In addition to the intelligence officers working under diplomatic cover in French diplomatic and military missions, this network involved sixteen French citizens under academic, commercial, or journalistic cover, six of whom were present at the

San Francisco Conference. Paris directed the network to focus on American diplomatic plans, especially with regard to postwar colonies.[83]

To protect its access to Gaullist traffic, Arlington Hall preferred to keep its French ally at arm's length. In 1944 it turned aside an offer from Free French intelligence to collaborate on sigint operations against various targets including Japan and Spain, although in early 1945 it relented to the extent of allowing American sigint units in Europe to exchange information with their French counterparts, but only concerning German call signs, frequencies, and low-grade tactical systems. Cooperation was limited to German military targets. The Americans also failed to warn their ally that its communications practices were insecure. In September 1944, for instance, the cipher officer at Free French headquarters in Algiers allowed two American Signal Corps officers to inspect a modified version of the Hagelin cipher machine the French had just brought into service as their high-grade system. The Americans were impressed with the machine and its operators and said so in their report to the War Department. When the chief of cryptanalytic operations at Arlington Hall showed the report to Frank Rowlett (whose branch included the French desk), the chief of B-III assured his superior that the new French machine was not immune to attack. Rowlett's analysts cracked this machine, but Arlington Hall decided not to tell the French that their main system was insecure; it did, however, warn American military commanders in Europe who were operating with French units not to entrust any important messages to this system.[84]

While Arlington Hall attacked Chinese and Free French communications, minor allies did not escape attention. As early as March 1943, Arlington Hall solved a simple substitution cipher used by foreign representatives of the Polish government-in-exile in London for nonconfidential messages. The intelligence content of these messages was so low that only ten were published in the *Bulletin* between July 1943 and June 1944. In the spring of 1944 Arlington Hall opened an attack against the main diplomatic cipher of the London Poles. When initial efforts proved fruitless, the Americans requested and received from GCCS all available information on Polish codes and ciphers. Even with British assistance, the Polish problem lagged until the late summer of 1944, when the mission to Moscow of Prime Minister Stanislaw Mikolajczyk to discuss with Stalin Polish-Soviet relations coincided with the Warsaw Uprising (1 August–1 October 1944) to renew interest in Polish communications. In early September SSA solved a low-grade transposition cipher used mainly for consular and press affairs. At the end of that month the analysts solved an enciphered code used by the government-in-exile's treasury department, but the resulting intelligence was so trivial that they soon ceased decrypting the messages. The high-grade diplomatic systems and the military attaché system successfully resisted attack and remained unread through the end of the war.[85] In the months after the Yalta Conference of February 1945, when bickering over the postwar government of Poland would strain the Grand Alliance, the inability to read the leadership traffic of the Polish government-in-exile became especially troublesome to American policy makers.

The Signal Security Agency had more luck with the cryptosystems of the Czechoslovakian government-in-exile. In the spring of 1944 Arlington Hall established a Czech desk and requested and received from GCCS information on the exile government's ciphers. By June a low-grade diplomatic cipher had been solved, but the traffic (mainly consular and administrative) was trivial. By August SSA had solved a medium-grade diplomatic system and was sharing the product with GCCS. The Czechs' most secure system resisted attack through the fall, but by December this system also succumbed. By the end of the war, American access to Czech diplomatic traffic was largely complete.[86]

Cryptanalytic collaboration with a foreign partner did not preclude cryptanalytic operations against that partner. Before Pearl Harbor, American codebreakers had established contact with the Dutch cryptanalytic bureau in the Netherlands East Indies, which had been working with some success on Japanese diplomatic and naval communications. After Japan's conquest of the East Indies, elements of the Dutch unit escaped to Australia, and a senior officer, Colonel J. A. Verkuyl, worked for a time at Arlington Hall.[87] The Americans appreciated Dutch assistance but did not hesitate to place the Netherlands on the target list. In the summer of 1943 Arlington Hall asked Berkeley Street for information on Dutch diplomatic ciphers, especially the Hagelin cipher machine the Netherlands government-in-exile used for its secret communications. The British had had little success against this system, but they shared what they knew about its indicator system and keys. Unfortunately, the materials were misplaced at Arlington Hall and never reached the newly established Dutch desk until the American liaison officer at GCCS secured a duplicate set in the spring of 1944. By that time SSA had independently made substantial progress against the Dutch Hagelin. No Netherlands traffic had been decrypted before April 1944, but that month 963 Dutch diplomatic messages were decrypted and translated. The numbers for the following months were 1,062 (May) and 1,443 (June).[88] Arlington Hall was less successful with the communications of the Norwegian government-in-exile. Despite repeated efforts, neither the Hall nor Berkeley Street was able to read the Hagelin machine used by the Norwegians.

Arlington Hall gave new meaning to the adage that there are no secrets between friends. But what about really good friends? American codebreakers first took an interest in British codes and ciphers in the waning days of the First World War when the imminent collapse of the Central Powers raised questions about the inevitable peace conference and the political shape of the postwar world. On 1 November 1918 the State Department passed to the army's cryptanalytic bureau (MI-8) the text of a secret note handed by the department to the British and French embassies on 26 August, as well as copies of telegrams sent soon thereafter by the embassies to their governments. The State Department clearly expected the army codebreakers to use the note as a crib in their study of British and French ciphers. When MI-8's postwar successor, the Cipher Bureau, established itself in New York City, it continued the effort against British communications, focusing on both diplomatic and commercial systems. By the spring of 1921 the cryptanalysts were able to read a low-grade diplomatic code in service on the Washington-London circuit, but they had no success against the more secure systems.[89]

Soon thereafter, the Cipher Bureau abandoned the British problem in favor of more promising targets such as Japanese diplomatic codes. When, in 1930, the newly established Signal Intelligence Service inherited the records of the defunct Cipher Bureau, the folders of British material remained undisturbed in locked file cabinets. Japan remained the preoccupation of the army's handful of cryptanalysts. When, in the late 1930s, they expanded their operations to include other targets, they focused on those countries whose ideology (Nazi Germany, Fascist Italy) or geographic proximity (Mexico) most affected American security interests. Well after the German attack on Poland, SIS remained a small organization that lacked the resources to attack anything but a select list of targets. In 1940, for example, American codebreakers were still having difficulty with the handful of targets they had been working since the late 1930s, and they had neither the appetite nor the staff to add Britain to their list, especially when they could expect British ciphers to prove at least as intractable as the German and Italian ciphers they were futilely attacking. As late as 1 December 1941, a roster of SIS staff and their assignments contains no indication of work against British cryptosystems.[90]

Although the Signal Intelligence Service did not attack Britain's codes and ciphers before Japan's attack on Pearl Harbor, the subsequent record is less certain. On the one hand, the British do not appear in the wartime cryptanalytic records except as collaborators against other targets. Organization charts for Arlington Hall include no box labeled "British," and there are no Foreign Office messages in the decryption files. Neither the weekly reports of the various cryptanalytic sections nor the minutes of various cryptanalytic policy committees contain the slightest hint of anti-British operations, although other sensitive operations, such as the attack against Vatican ciphers, inevitably surface no matter how tight the security around them. Signals intelligence veterans who held senior positions at wartime Arlington Hall deny any knowledge of efforts against London's systems.[91] Claims by historians to have uncovered evidence that the United States was reading British traffic prove, upon closer examination, unfounded.[92]

Still, there are intriguing traces, rustlings that may suggest a shape behind the arras. A list of governments whose communications were "covered" in 1942–1943 includes "British Empire."[93] Then there is the question of intercept assignments. No later than September 1943, the Radio Intelligence Division (RID) of the FCC was intercepting British encrypted traffic. It was passing this traffic to the U.S. Navy, ostensibly to further the training of naval radio personnel who needed to identify various national "styles" in radio transmission. This rationale is supported by the fact that RID was sending the navy a variety of traffic, including some (Mexican diplomatic, Peruvian naval) that naval cryptanalysts were definitely not working. Nevertheless, the navy's concern for British communications is interesting, especially since it was not just interested in any Royal Navy traffic that RID might pick up (as might have been the case if it was only seeking samples of "national styles"); it requested RID to monitor specific Admiralty stations and provided frequencies and broadcast schedules.[94] It is also interesting that, by 1942, SIS had in its files a description (with sketches) of "Typex," the high-grade cipher machine used by London for its most secret communications. The pages of this report are stamped "U.S. Eyes Only," indicating that SIS did not want the British to know that the

Americans were interested in their cipher machine. By the spring of 1945 the naval cryptanalysts in OP-20-G had completed an analysis of Typex, although they were not sure how to break it.[95]

An even more provocative piece of evidence surfaces in the postwar testimony of Colonel Robert Schukraft, who directed army intercept in the period 1939–1942. In 1980 Schukraft was interviewed by historians from the National Security Agency as part of that organization's effort to record the experiences and impressions of wartime signals intelligence officers. The interview was classified and not intended for public viewing. Recently, however, portions of the interview were released, including intriguing references to British communications. When asked explicitly if army intercept stations monitored British traffic, Schukraft replied, "We never copied British at all. We never attempted to."[96] That seemed to settle the matter, and the interviewers moved on to other topics. However, later in the conversation, during a discussion of another matter, Schukraft spontaneously returned to the subject, generating the following exchange:

> Schukraft: "And some work was also done on British material."
> Interviewer: "In the early days?"
> Schukraft: [Several lines of reply, all blacked-out by censor.]
> Interviewer: "When was that, do you remember?"
> Schukraft: "About the beginning of the war . . . around . . . it probably would have been around March or April '42" (ellipses in original).[97]

Whatever the nature of the "work" done in early 1942, American signals intelligence maintained indirect surveillance of British diplomacy by monitoring the communications of third countries. From a message of the Free French representative in Washington on 8 September 1944, American intelligence learned that Sir Alexander Cadogan, permanent undersecretary at the Foreign Office and Britain's chief delegate to the Dumbarton Oaks Conference then in session in Washington, believed that "the duality and at times contrariety" of policy initiatives coming from the State Department and the White House seriously constrained the search for solutions to international problems. The French diplomat also quoted Cadogan as condemning Roosevelt's "obscure and illogical" policy toward de Gaulle and the French Committee for National Liberation and criticizing Washington's refusal to recognize the committee as the provisional government of France.[98]

Interest in London's activities seemed to have increased as the war wound down. On 20 April 1945, for example, Arlington Hall translated a message from the French foreign ministry to its ambassador in Washington indicating that although London had received evasive replies from Moscow concerning the mysterious disappearance of certain Polish politicians, it would not press the point for fear of jeopardizing chances for an Anglo-Soviet agreement before the San Francisco Conference. On 7 June 1945 the Brazilian ambassador in London informed Rio de Janeiro (in a message decrypted by Arlington Hall) that Prime Minister Winston Churchill wanted Washington to stand firm with London in insisting that the new Polish regime include noncommunist Poles and in resisting any effort to force Italy to relinquish to Yugoslavia the port city of Trieste. Indirect surveillance continued after the war. A summary of signals intelligence collected in late fall 1945 included a special section on British policy with subsections on Anglo-Turkish relations, Anglo-Greek relations, Foreign Office attitudes toward the Italian peace treaty, and recent policies of the Board of Trade. Information on these subjects came from reading Chinese, French, Greek, Italian, and Turkish traffic.[99] If Arlington Hall was not reading British communications, there can be little doubt that Britain was an intelligence target. In the case of Washington's other main ally, there can be even less doubt.

Chapter Six

The Russian Problem

In the spring of 1920 the State Department received a curious publication in the diplomatic pouch from its legation in Budapest. It was a pamphlet, "Documents Secrets de la Propagande Bolcheviste," by one Ladislas Szabo, a Hungarian newspaper editor and sometime professor of history, who had been active in the resistance against the short-lived (March–August 1919) Bolshevik government imposed on Hungary by Béla Kun in the aftermath of the First World War. The pamphlet eventually found its way to the War Department, where an officer in military intelligence noted to his surprise that the "secret documents" published by Szabo included a message that purported to be a decrypted telegram from Béla Kun to Vladimir Lenin, the leader of the Bolshevik movement that had seized power in Russia. Could a Hungarian intellectual have access to high-level communist communications? If he had secret messages in his possession, perhaps he knew something about the cryptosystems that protected them. Szabo's information might prove a windfall for American codebreakers who had been trying, with minimal success, to read the communications of the Bolsheviks. On 18 June 1920 Colonel Sherman Miles, the acting director of military intelligence, directed Major Elgin, the military attaché in Budapest, to conduct a discreet investigation of Szabo and to seek copies of any encrypted messages in the Hungarian's possession.[1]

From his contacts in Hungarian police and security agencies, the military attaché discovered that Szabo had a sound reputation; indeed, the prime minister himself vouched for his honesty. Elgin then approached the professor, who astonished the officer by revealing that he possessed not only dozens of telegrams exchanged by Béla Kun and Lenin but also the keys used to encipher those messages. The messages came from a former officer in the old Austro-Hungarian army who had been drafted into Kun's

Red Army to run the radio station outside Budapest. This individual was a devout Catholic (Szabo first encountered him praying in a Franciscan monastery) who wanted the world to know the truth about the godless Bolsheviks. The ciphers came from a clerk in Béla Kun's office whom Szabo saved from execution by pulling strings among his contacts in the Inter-Allied Military Mission that maintained an influential presence in Budapest in the years immediately after the First World War.[2]

Szabo readily agreed to give all these documents to Washington. In return he asked only for help with a personal problem. For some time he had been trying unsuccessfully to obtain a visa to relocate his family to the United States. Perhaps his new friends in the American army could intervene with the State Department on his behalf. On August 16 Szabo handed Elgin copies of messages Béla Kun had exchanged with Lenin and Georgiy Chicherin, the Soviet commissar of foreign affairs, on such matters as the movement of Bolshevik agents and funds into western Europe, the condition of communist parties in various countries, and the political situation in Czechoslovakia, Hungary, and Poland. The professor also provided eight Bolshevik ciphers, along with an explanation of their use. The attaché forwarded the collection to the War Department in the next pouch along with a recommendation that G-2 intervene with the State Department to secure a visa for his Hungarian source.[3] While it is unknown whether Ladislas Szabo achieved his dream of living in the United States, there can be little doubt that his material was a timely gift for American codebreakers.

Soviet communications had interested Washington since the establishment of the Bolshevik regime in November 1917. In the weeks following Lenin's seizure of power, Washington was largely cut off from its diplomatic and consular representatives in Russia and had to rely on press reports and dispatches from Sweden for news. As late as December, the State Department, struggling to reestablish secure communications and increase its official representation in Russia, remained uncertain about the state of affairs inside the country. Russia was suddenly an intelligence priority.[4] The Bolshevik revolution had followed the creation of the War Department's Cipher Bureau (MI-8) by only five months, and Bolshevik messages were among those collected and studied by Herbert Yardley and his staff in the early months of the bureau's existence. Given Washington's need for reliable intelligence on the new regime and its intentions, diplomatic systems received particular attention, and a handful of messages to Russian representatives in New York and Vancouver were read between

December 1917 and February 1918. The effort, however, was retarded by the lack of intercepts, the inexperience of the analysts, and the sophistication of the codes and ciphers.[5] There was no general entry into Bolshevik communications, and American codebreakers provided no insight into Lenin's intentions toward the Allies or the Central Powers and no intelligence support for American military units dispatched to Siberia in the summer of 1918. After the armistice in November 1918, the results would improve slightly, but progress was due as much to fortune as to cryptanalytic skill.

When the postwar Cipher Bureau established itself in New York, it continued to monitor Soviet communications. Indeed, these communications were now an even more important target, since Washington shared with London and Paris a concern that the Red revolution might spread beyond Russia's borders. Since the withdrawal of American diplomatic and consular officers from Russia in the summer of 1918, Washington had again been searching for an intelligence source more reliable than press stories and refugee reports. The Cipher Bureau tried to become that source. The navy contributed intercepts, and American diplomats and military attachés collected Bolshevik messages through clandestine means. In 1921, for example, the American embassy in Constantinople secretly employed a White Russian radio operator to intercept the traffic between Moscow and its representative in Berlin. In the same period the American military attaché in Czechoslovakia received from a Czech signals officer copies of all encrypted telegrams sent and received by Soviet representatives in Prague.[6]

From an examination of such traffic the Cipher Bureau concluded that the communist leadership in Moscow was using several systems to communicate with its diplomatic representatives and secret agents abroad. The materials provided by Ladislas Szabo allowed American cryptanalysts to read one system and to gain certain insights into the principles and practice of Soviet cryptography, but the Béla Kun messages did not prove to be the magic key to the communications of the new regime in Moscow. The ciphers were used only on the Budapest-Moscow circuit and were removed from service after Kun's political demise. Another opportunity in the summer of 1920 proved just as disappointing. Shortly before Major Elgin's first contact with Szabo in Budapest, Victor Weiskopf, an employee of the Justice Department on loan to Yardley's organization, solved a Russian transposition cipher with the assistance of papers recovered from passengers of a German plane forced down in Latvia while en route to Russia.

Once again, however, there was no breakthrough; Weiskopf's success could not be exploited into a general entry into Soviet cryptosystems.[7]

During the 1920s, Soviet codes and ciphers slipped in priority at the American Black Chamber, eventually falling behind British, French, German, and Japanese systems in importance. Given the modest staff resources of the office, this low priority ensured that Russia would receive scant attention. Only one member of the unit in New York was able to work in the Russian language, although Yardley occasionally gave the raw traffic personal attention. Solutions continued to evade the analysts, even though they received assistance from outside sources, which deluged the Cipher Bureau with unsolicited advice, leads, and copies of "authentic" Russian cryptologic material. Scandinavia was an especially fertile field for collateral information. In 1923, for example, the State Department forwarded to Yardley a letter from the American embassy in Sweden that contained a description of a cipher allegedly used by the Communist International (Comintern), the agency that supervised relations between Moscow and communist parties around the world. Since the Comintern was an arm of Soviet foreign policy and an instrument for fomenting international revolution, access to its ciphers would have been a windfall for any intelligence service. Unfortunately, the information from Sweden proved useless, since no traffic in this system was ever intercepted. In 1925 the Stockholm embassy submitted a report concerning yet another Russian cipher, and two years later a military attaché in the Baltic provided the War Department with information on Russian cryptographic practice as reported by Polish and Estonian intelligence.

From the opposite side of the globe, Yardley received a Bolshevik code used for clandestine communication with communists in the Netherlands East Indies. This system had been partially reconstructed by Dutch authorities, who had passed the information to Washington. In 1927 Chinese police allowed the American military attaché in Peking to study materials seized during a raid on the offices of Soviet commercial representatives in the Chinese capital, but the haul included nothing of cryptologic value. In the end, information from abroad (some of which may have been fabricated by con artists) made little difference. At the New York offices of the Cipher Bureau the Russian problem languished. Progress was so slow that as late as 1927 Yardley's team was still not sure whether the bulk of Soviet messages were transmitted in Russian, French, or German.[8]

In 1930, when he reviewed the files his fledgling SIS had inherited from the Cipher Bureau, William Friedman had no reason to believe that

Russian codes and ciphers would prove a promising exercise for his handful of aspiring cryptanalysts. Congress, however, forced Friedman to make
the Soviet Union his first priority. In the course of an investigation into
communist propaganda in the United States, the House of Representatives
had subpoenaed from American cable companies some three thousand
encrypted messages sent to Moscow by Amtorg, the Soviet trading organization in New York City. Suspecting that these messages contained evidence of subversive activities, the House had passed the material to the
navy's Code and Signal Section for study. After three months of effort, the
section had made little headway against the encryption despite the assistance of a former Amtorg employee who had once visited the agency's
code room and briefly observed its operations. Concluding that "solution
cannot be achieved by analytical methods," the naval cryptanalysts informed their superiors in the Office of Naval Communications that to
make any progress against the messages they needed access to the cryptographic materials in Amtorg's code room. Access could be obtained legally
by means of a subpoena or illegally by means of burglary. The first method
was dismissed as impractical, since Amtorg officials would certainly burn
their ciphers at the first hint of a subpoena. A clandestine raid, on the
other hand, was "feasible," especially since the former Amtorg employee
had volunteered information about the code room, its safe, and the work
schedules of the code clerks.[9]

The navy was no stranger to domestic clandestine operations. In
searching for cryptologic materials, ONI had run "black bag jobs" against
Japanese personnel and premises in the United States; only a year earlier,
naval agents had covertly entered and looted the New York office of the
American communist party.[10] The navy, however, decided against a noc-
turnal raid on the Soviet trade office in favor of an even more drastic expedient; in November 1930 it turned to the army for help in solving the
Amtorg messages. The navy was undoubtedly encouraged in its decision
by a recent gesture from its fellow service department. In October SIS had
passed to the Code and Signal Section a copy of what was purported to
be a cipher used by Amtorg to communicate with American communists.
Army intelligence had acquired this cipher from an unidentified source,
most likely an informant inside the party. According to information received, this system was to have gone into service in January 1928.[11] The
cipher proved useless to naval cryptanalysts, but the army's gesture was
appreciated.

There followed a brief but genuine display of interservice cooperation that would rarely be duplicated in subsequent years. Friedman set everything else aside and directed the entire energies of his small office against the new problem. He personally worked full-time on the messages for a month. His young staff, none of whom had been on the job for more than eight months, worked closely with their counterparts in the navy. They scoured Yardley's old files for leads and studied what was known about czarist ciphers. To beef up the translation capabilities of the program, I. Mishowt, a former captain in the Imperial Russian Navy, was hired as a temporary consultant. A suggestion that Amtorg might be using the "Russian Universal Commercial Code" set off a frantic search in libraries and publishing houses for a copy of this system. Without explaining the motive behind his inquiry, Friedman approached a former military intelligence officer, then in business in New York, about the code. This individual replied that he had never heard of it; wanting to help, though, he suggested that Friedman contact Amtorg! A copy was eventually uncovered without Amtorg's assistance, but it contributed nothing to the investigation.

At one point the cryptanalysts seem to have received from the British information concerning cryptographic materials seized during the 1927 police raid on Arcos, the Soviet trading company in London. Friedman even accepted unsolicited advice from amateur codebreakers who studied the Amtorg messages that were published in the *Saturday Evening Post*.[12] The Amtorg messages remained unbroken. Friedman expressed his frustration to Yardley, who had made a similar journey before him: "I will tell you quite frankly that without an inside track obtained by hocus-pocus, I feel that it may turn out that little or nothing can be done."[13] On 24 February 1931 Major D. M. Crawford, the chief of the Signals Intelligence Service and Friedman's immediate superior, advised the chief signal officer:

> The problem is apparently one of extreme difficulty because of the complexity of method and the absence of definite information relative to the basic system employed. . . . It is my belief that half-way measures and sporadic attempts will get nowhere in this case; nothing short of a deep, long-continued, and painstaking analysis has any chance of leading to a successful conclusion.[14]

Major Crawford had no intention of committing his unit to a "long-continued" effort against the Amtorg messages, since such an effort would distract the staff from their primary mission of compiling codes for the army. Noting that the matter had lost all urgency since the House of Representatives had completed its investigation of communist propaganda without the suspect messages, Crawford recommended that the Signal Intelligence Service abandon the project. Should Congress wish to pursue the effort, it might appropriate funds to hire Herbert Yardley as a special consultant. SIS would provide office space and clerical support. If after three months of concentrated study Yardley was unable to crack the Amtorg cipher, "the case may then be considered hopeless and be brought to a definite close."[15] The army accepted Crawford's recommendations. Congress agreed to offer Yardley one hundred dollars a week for a few weeks of his time. He declined. With the *Saturday Evening Post* about to publish the articles that would later appear as *The American Black Chamber,* Yardley had little interest in deviating from a path that promised literary fame and fortune to revisit the world of dusty intercepts and worksheets. Also, he probably realized that his position at SIS, though temporary, would be untenable once his revelations of American codebreaking secrets were published.

Major Crawford probably believed that Yardley's refusal closed the file on the Amtorg affair and that SIS would abandon Russian ciphers for more productive labors in code compilation. He was wrong. Friedman, at least for a time, continued to run the Russian problem. In June 1931 he opened a correspondence with I. Mishtowt, a shadowy individual who had worked briefly at SIS on the Amtorg messages. Through Mishtowt, Friedman communicated with an unidentified White Russian in Europe (one letter to Friedman was written from Berlin) who provided advice on Soviet ciphers at least until February 1932.[16]

Potentially more significant assistance arrived in November 1931 when Friedman received from the navy's Code and Signal Section photostats of an "Amtorg Code" and eight sets of cipher keys for use with that codebook. The navy had received this material the preceding summer from the naval attaché in Buenos Aires, who had obtained it from Argentine authorities after a police raid on Soviet offices.[17] The compromised material, however, produced no solutions and seemed to have had little impact on the effort against Russian codes and ciphers. Keys used on the Moscow–Buenos Aires circuit probably differed from those used on the Moscow–New York circuit, so that possession of one set would not provide access to messages encrypted by the other. Without a body of intercepted messages from the Moscow–Buenos Aires channel (which SIS did not have), the compromised material could not even be used to read Soviet communications with Argentina. Sustained study by a team of experienced analysts might have extracted from the compromised material insights into Soviet cryptology and communications practices, but in 1931 Friedman's unit of three junior cryptanalysts, one cryptanalytic aide, and a secretary had neither the experience nor the time for such study.

By 1932 SIS had abandoned the effort against Soviet codes and ciphers, a state of affairs that would continue for the remainder of the decade as the small unit focused its energies on exploiting its success against Japanese communications and, secondarily, organizing an effort against Germany and Italy, Tokyo's partners in the Axis alliance. There was sporadic coverage of Moscow's radio circuits, and Russian traffic occasionally found its way to Friedman's office. In 1932, for example, the military attaché in China obtained from White Russian sources several packets of encrypted Russian messages from Manchurian circuits. In its first months of operation (1933–1934), the Provisional Radio Intelligence Detachment counted 63 Russian messages among the 381 it intercepted. For a period in 1938, American operators were monitoring a Comintern radio station near Rocky Point, New York, that relayed clandestine traffic from Moscow to its agents in Latin America.[18] Such efforts, however, remained infrequent and unsystematic. Russian messages usually were intercepted as the unintended consequence of searching the ether for the radio transmissions of Japan or Germany. An army–navy study of intercept responsibilities in August 1940 recommended that "any Russian Government traffic *appearing* on circuits being covered by Army stations be intercepted and submitted . . . to the Navy" (emphasis added).[19] The wording suggests that the army did not specifically target Russian radio transmissions. It also suggests that the army had ceded to the navy cryptanalytic responsibility for Soviet communications. This suggestion is supported by the complete absence of Russian material in SIS files from the late 1930s.

At the turn of the decade there were small signs that the Signal Intelligence Service was renewing its interest in Russian communications. In April 1939 the chief signal officer, General Mauborgne, indirectly raised the matter with army intelligence. He had read in the *Saturday Evening Post* several articles written by General Walter Krivitsky, a senior officer in Soviet military intelligence who had defected to the West in 1937. Believing that Krivitsky might have information useful to the Signal Intelligence Service, Mauborgne, who was almost certainly acting at the suggestion of SIS, urged G-2 to contact the defector, who was then in the United States. There is no record that G-2 followed this suggestion.[20]

The Molotov-Ribbentrop Pact, the Russo-German partition of Poland, and the Soviet annexation of the Baltic republics had no immediate effect on SIS operations or priorities, but gradually the Soviet Union emerged as a feature, though small, on the sigint landscape. In October 1940 SIS directed its monitoring stations to copy Russian diplomatic traffic, the first time since the early 1920s that Soviet communications were an explicit intercept priority for the army. Additional diplomatic traffic was acquired by the clandestine photography of Russian embassy messages filed with American cable companies in Washington.[21] Curiously, SIS seems to have done nothing with the Russian messages that were soon filling its traffic files. There was no attempt at cryptanalysis. In 1940 the army's codebreaking effort focused on Japan, Germany, Italy, and Mexico (in that order). Even after the "expansion" that followed the outbreak of war, SIS had only forty-five employees in Washington, and not all of these were engaged in codebreaking. In a year that witnessed the main effort against the Japanese PURPLE machine, resources were stretched just to cover the established priorities. There was no slack to cover a new problem that lacked cryptanalytic continuity and promised a major challenge to the analytic and linguistic capacities of a service that was only beginning to free itself from peacetime limitations on budget and staff.

The following year the situation began to change. In January 1941 SIS hired forty-eight new personnel, more than doubling its staff in Washington. With the additional personnel it gradually expanded its cryptanalytic program to include new targets: Vichy France, Spain, Portugal, and Brazil. The Soviet Union now figured in SIS's plans. When Abraham Sinkov and his small team landed in Britain in February 1941 to initiate an exchange of cryptanalytic information with Bletchley Park, their "primary mission related to German, Japanese, Italian and Russian secret systems."[22] The British had been studying Soviet traffic since 1918, and throughout the twenties they scored important, albeit intermittent, successes against Moscow's diplomatic ciphers. This achievement was jeopardized in 1927 when official revelations in London of these successes caused the People's Commissariat for Foreign Affairs to review its cryptographic program. Although its access to Moscow's diplomatic traffic apparently ended in 1930, GCCS continued to read Comintern messages and had significant success against Soviet military and naval cryptosystems. At the time of Sinkov's mission, GCCS was studying Russian military, naval, and meteorological systems and was exchanging information with the efficient Finnish signals intelligence service, which specialized in Russian cryptanalysis.[23]

At Bletchley Park the Americans discussed Russian cryptosystems and communications practices with British codebreakers and received from their hosts copies of Russian codebooks and keys reconstructed by GCCS, including a meteorological cipher, three Red Army codes (including OKK-6, a system then in service for communication at the level of army, corps, and division), four naval codes (including the main systems then in service with the Baltic and Black Sea fleets), and an NKVD system.[24] The records are silent about what SIS did with the Russian material that Sinkov brought home in March 1941. The Red Army and NKVD codebooks would have been of little immediate use, since few, if any, Russian military and police messages were being intercepted by American monitoring posts. There can be no doubt, however, that the Soviet Union was receiving more attention at SIS. The Sinkov mission did not go to Bletchley Park on an open-ended shopping expedition. It returned with material specifically related to the current concerns of American cryptanalysts. It did not, for example, seek information concerning British progress against Chinese or Turkish or Greek systems, since these systems were not being studied at SIS. A comparison of the material acquired by Sinkov with the known cryptanalytic projects then in progress at SIS reveals that all items except the Russian can be related to specific projects. The inference is clear. In the spring of 1941 SIS was preparing to activate a Russian desk.

Yet for reasons that remain unclear, SIS shelved those preparations. Lack of traffic may have been a problem. While the telegrams of the Soviet embassy in Washington were available through covert arrangements with the cable companies, and occasional diplomatic messages were intercepted on radio circuits, there was little or no access to Soviet military and police traffic. In the Soviet Union such traffic moved along landlines or was broadcast on low frequencies that American intercept stations had difficulty hearing. The Red Army and NKVD codebooks acquired by Sinkov were of little use until intercept coverage of Russian communications could be expanded. Furthermore, no Soviet messages had been studied in SIS since the Amtorg affair ten years earlier, a serious loss of continuity that would have discouraged the most experienced cryptanalyst. The callow trainees who had been thrown against the Amtorg messages in 1931 were now the senior officers in SIS, and their memory of that fiasco (combined with the prevalent belief among cryptanalysts that Soviet diplomatic ciphers were unbreakable) could have caused them to draw back from a decision to revisit that experience.

Bureaucratic imperatives may have encouraged personnel to post-

pone tackling a tough problem when results (and credit) could more read-
ily be anticipated from a focus on systems less resistant than Russian.
Vichy and Spanish translations began to come on line in February and
March 1941. The effort against Italian systems suddenly accelerated when
Sinkov returned from GCCS with the results of British work on this tar-
get. In February the Italian section had penetrated two Italian systems; by
June it was recovering values in five.[25] It would have been natural to fo-
cus on exploiting these successes. Perhaps the War Department's interest
in Moscow's communications became less urgent after Hitler attacked the
Soviet Union on 22 June 1941 and Russia moved to the side of the angels.

After Pearl Harbor, American signals intelligence reconsidered its
priorities. Preoccupied with the mortal threat posed by the Japanese navy
in the Pacific and German U-boats in the Atlantic, the navy lost whatever
interest it had in Soviet codes and ciphers. In 1938 OP-20-G had opened
an attack against Russian diplomatic and naval communications, but the
effort, never a high priority for the navy's codebreakers, was without result. After Pearl Harbor the problem was shunted to the Italian desk,
where it languished. Naval stations continued to intercept Russian traffic,
especially on the Moscow-Tokyo circuit, but the accumulating messages
remained untouched for lack of staff.[26]

The situation was only slightly better in the army. In April 1942 SIS
reordered its cryptanalytic priorities to reflect the demands of active belligerency. The first three items on the target list were Japanese military attaché traffic, Japanese diplomatic communications, and German diplomatic traffic. Whatever resources were left over were assigned to such
targets as Italian diplomatic communications and the diplomatic messages
of secondary powers such as Vichy France and Spain.[27] Russian traffic did
not appear on the target list. Nevertheless, SIS did not totally abandon its
interest in Soviet communications. Interception continued, assisted by the
fact that wartime censorship regulations required all foreign governments
to file with censorship authorities copies of their communications. In
November 1942, for example, the Cable Censor passed to Arlington Hall
1,320 encrypted Soviet telegrams. This figure represented 18 percent of the
encrypted messages processed that month by the Cable Censor, even
though the Soviet Union was only one of fifty-six governments whose
communications were processed.[28]

There was also a residual interest in Russian cryptography. When
Solomon Kullback returned from his extended visit to GCCS in the summer of 1942, his baggage included a Russian meteorological code recon-

structed by the British. After the German invasion of the Soviet Union in June 1941, Prime Minister Churchill had directed GCCS to cease sigint operations against the new Russian ally. Although this directive was in the main implemented, Bletchley Park continued to work on Russian weather ciphers largely because Russian weather reports provided a crib for reading the main German weather cipher, which repeated Soviet weather messages intercepted and decrypted by German signals intelligence. The code provided to Kullback accelerated the work of SIS's weather section, which had independently broken a Russian weather cipher in June 1942 and had been reading encrypted Russian meteorological transmissions since that time.[29] The weather reports provided information useful for American air and maritime operations. For the historian, however, these brief reports, produced by a minor desk at Arlington Hall, have an additional significance. They were the army's first Russian decryptions since the creation of the Signal Intelligence Service, and perhaps the first Russian decrypts by American intelligence since Herbert Yardley read Béla Kun's telegrams to Lenin in 1919. They were also a harbinger.

On 1 February 1943, as newspapers trumpeted reports of Soviet advances along the entire eastern front and Russian troops mopped up the last German strongpoints in Stalingrad, two Americans appeared at the large office at Arlington Hall assigned to Major Geoffrey Stevens, the British liaison officer. Lieutenant Leonard Zubko, a Russian-speaking cryptanalyst from the Japanese diplomatic section, and his assistant, Miss Gene Grabeel, a new recruit only weeks from teaching school in Virginia, set about moving desks and cabinets and unpacking office supplies and files. Amid the constant shuffling and reshuffling of offices at Arlington Hall, the activity of two obscure employees would have attracted little comment. Even among the initiated there was probably little sense of the historic moment. Major Stevens was too discreet to ask what the two Americans were up to at the other end of his room. The truth would have sent him running for a secure line to Bletchley Park. Arlington Hall had activated a Russian section.

The creation of the Russian section has been ascribed, in part, to Colonel Carter Clarke's concern that Stalin might seek covertly to negotiate a separate peace with Germany. According to this explanation, Clarke anticipated that signs of such negotiations would appear in Soviet traffic, access to which would provide warning to London and Washington of Stalin's perfidy. Also, Arlington Hall had learned from intercepts that Japan and Finland were collaborating successfully in an attack on Soviet ciphers, and "this information was probably the immediate inspiration for SSA's [sic] examination of the Soviet telegrams."[30] The scenario is certainly plausible. Clarke was a tough, professional soldier who shared the conservative political values common to his profession and his social class. He and the senior officers at Arlington Hall were pragmatic enough to recognize the expediency of a wartime alliance with the Soviet Union, but they distrusted and disdained the Stalinist regime. In contrast to their cooperative attitude toward the British, they had no interest in cryptanalytic collaboration with the Russians. Recalling the Nazi-Soviet Non-aggression Pact of August 1939, Clarke and his team could readily imagine that Stalin might cut another deal with his fellow dictator, Hitler.[31] It is also true that Finland and Japan (together with Germany and Hungary) were working together on Soviet cryptosystems. It is unlikely, however, that either fear of a Russo-German peace or knowledge of Axis progress against Moscow's communications was the determining cause behind the new Russian section. For one thing, the timing was off.

Although the details remain vague and confusing, there is little doubt that in 1943 the Soviet Union and Germany (or elements in Germany), working through intermediaries, extended feelers on the subject of a negotiated peace.[32] Japan, which was at peace with the Soviet Union, had long encouraged such contacts in the belief that the Axis should turn all their resources against Britain and the United States. However, these peace feelers, which began in the spring and intensified in the summer and fall, occurred *after* the activation of the Russian desk in February 1943. Of course, ever since the German invasion of the Soviet Union in June 1941, American and British policy makers had worried that Stalin might cut his losses and deal with Hitler, and rumors of a possible settlement cropped up throughout 1942.[33] There was, however, no credible evidence before the creation of the Russian desk of Russo-German peace contacts; indeed, the best evidence pointed the other way. If the White House, the State Department, and the War Department worried about a separate peace on the eastern front in 1942, they did so despite overwhelming signals intelligence indicating that their concerns were baseless.

As early as April 1942, one of the first Magic diplomatic summaries reported a message to Tokyo from the Japanese ambassador in Berlin, Oshima Hiroshi, who dismissed any possibility of a separate peace.[34] In the months immediately preceding the establishment of the Russian section, American signals intelligence, the source Clarke would have found most convincing, consistently reported that a negotiated peace on the eastern front was extremely unlikely. In November 1942, for example, Ambassador Oshima sent Tokyo two messages (both decrypted by Arlington Hall) advising that it was futile for Japan to press for Russo-German peace talks. He reported that a separate peace was impossible, since Berlin would insist on such unacceptable terms as the cession to Germany of the Ukraine and the Caucasus. Oshima again dismissed the possibility of a separate peace in a message of 26 January 1943 in which he reported: "The German leaders have a deep determination to fight the war through. . . . They have determined never to compromise with either the Soviet [*sic*] or England and the United States—never!"[35] Japanese intercepts out of Russia indicated that a spirit of compromise was absent there also. On 21 December 1942 Ambassador Sato informed Tokyo that Soviet power and resolve were increasing and that Germany "cannot hope either to make Russia surrender or to reach a compromise peace." Japanese diplomats in Italy, the third partner in Axis alliance, were equally pessimistic.[36]

The first serious indication in the decrypts that there might be a basis for discussion was a message from the Japanese ambassador in Turkey on 29 January 1943. The ambassador reported to Tokyo that his German counterpart, Franz von Papen, believed a compromise peace with the Soviet Union was possible. In an editorial note appended to this item in the Magic Diplomatic Summary, intelligence analysts commented: "This is the *first* time that a statement of this nature has been attributed to a prominent German official in the available messages. Von Ribbentrop and lesser German representatives have repeatedly stated to the Japanese diplomats that Germany intends to continue the fight against Russia to the end" (emphasis added).[37] This message, however, was not translated at Arlington Hall until 7 March 1943, more than a month after the establishment of the Russian section.

The significance of Axis progress against Soviet ciphers is ambiguous. Why would the discovery of such progress, by itself, lead Arlington Hall to create a Russian section? After all, American cryptanalysts knew that the Axis powers were collaborating against British ciphers, but that knowledge did not result in the creation of a British section at Arlington Hall. Also, timing is again an issue. It is not clear that knowledge of Axis collaboration reached Arlington Hall in time to influence the decision to begin a Russian section. American intelligence learned of this collaboration by decrypting Japanese military attaché traffic on the Helsinki-Tokyo circuit. At first, Arlington Hall was interested in this traffic primarily to monitor Axis progress against *American* codes and ciphers. Many of the messages dealing with Soviet cryptosystems were not translated until 1944 or 1945, even though they had been intercepted in 1941–1942. Before the creation of the Russian section, the principal (if not only) insight into Axis progress is a brief summary of Japanese work against Russian diplomatic systems. This message was translated on 29 January 1943, only two days before the activation of the Russian section at Arlington Hall.[38] Perhaps there was sufficient time for the wheels of bureaucracy to turn and for senior officers to receive and consider the message, decide on a major policy initiative, and select Zubko and Grabeel to implement that decision. It is more likely that by 29 January a decision had already been made. It would appear, in fact, that a decision to create a Russian desk had been made by December 1942.

During his exchanges that month with Field Marshall Sir John Dill over the Turing affair and the general state of Anglo-American cryptanalytic cooperation, General George Marshall had specifically mentioned that Arlington Hall wanted "cryptographic material derived from Slavic Nations." Dill correctly interpreted "Slavic" to mean Russian, and he replied that Britain had shared with American representatives what it knew about Soviet codes and ciphers up to the German invasion of the Soviet Union, when sigint operations against Russia stopped.[39] Marshall would not have approached Dill on this subject unless American cryptanalysts had already decided they had a use for Russian cryptographic materials. Two other operations suggest an early decision to make the Soviet Union a target. In November 1942 the army asked the Radio Intelligence Division of the FCC to establish surveillance of a radio antenna the Russian embassy in Washington had received permission to raise at Bryans Point, Maryland. Also, by the fall of 1942 (at the latest), Arlington Hall had instituted traffic analysis of Russian communications to identify radio procedures and nets, almost certainly in preparation for launching a cryptanalytic attack.[40]

The decision to study Soviet codes and ciphers (which was made without informing the White House or the State Department) did not depend upon fear of a Russo-German peace or a desire to keep up with Axis cryptanalysis. The decision was the logical consequence of bureaucratic choices made in early 1942. As mentioned in chapter 4, Carter Clarke and his deputy, Alfred McCormack, shared with many senior officers at Arlington Hall a commitment to developing a comprehensive signal intelligence service that would serve American policy makers by providing information about the intentions and activities of all governments, not just those that were troublesome at the moment. Friends had to be watched as well as enemies because cordial relations did not suspend the need for diplomatic negotiations or preclude the possibility of clashing interests. Besides, today's friend could become tomorrow's enemy. Japan, after all, had been an ally in the First World War, while relations with France had changed dramatically after the authoritarian Vichy regime replaced the democratic Third Republic.

Clarke, for one, made no apology for this vision. In May 1942 he reminded McCormack, "Our primary task is to paint for our superiors as completely a realistic picture as possible of the activities 'behind the arras' of all those *associated with and against us*" (emphasis added).[41] McCormack needed little convincing. Clarke's deputy firmly believed that "the War Department must know as much as possible about the objectives, the psychology and the methods of our enemies and potential enemies (*and of our Allies as well*) in order to make the right decisions in military matters" (emphasis added).[42] No governments were immune in Clarke's mind, although intelligence priorities would reflect such factors as the availability of resources and the perception of relative threat. Clarke's approach to signals intelligence ensured that the Soviet Union would eventually have received Arlington Hall's attention even without a "peace-scare" on the eastern front or word that the Finns were reading a Red Army field cipher. In fact, as early as March 1942, Clarke had pushed to make Soviet traffic a sigint priority, but in those hectic months after Pearl Harbor, when the White House and the War Department were demanding information "yesterday" about Japanese and German intentions, circumstances were not favorable. The next year they were.

On 6 February 1943 the weekly activity report of Arlington Hall's second branch (B-II) carried a brief announcement: "Russian: This section activated during past week." The next report contained an equally cryptic notation: "Russian: Material edited and sent to machine room."[43] Then, as quietly as it had appeared, the Russian section disappeared from the record. Two weeks after its activation, the section was abruptly closed. The reasons behind this mysterious action remain veiled in secrecy. Lieutenant Zubko was transferred to an Army Air Corps mission in China, while Gene Grabeel was reassigned to the French section at Arlington Hall. Then, just as mysteriously, the section was reconstituted sometime in the spring of 1943 with Ferdinand Coudert, a scion of a politically and socially prominent New York family, as its new chief.

Coudert had recently joined Arlington Hall and had little experience in cryptanalysis, but he spoke Russian (as well as French, German, Serbo-Croatian, and Bulgarian) and had distant connections with Russia, the family law firm having represented the czarist government and the ill-fated Kerensky regime. Gene Grabeel returned from the French section, and gradually additional personnel arrived from other sections and projects. Arlington Hall now hid the very existence of the unit within layers of secrecy rare for even that security-obsessed organization. Initially the staff occupied a small room behind Arlington's maintenance unit.[44] Coudert was warned that no word of his section was to leak out, even within the service. Particular care was taken to keep the project from the British. To camouflage the section's true assignment, the traffic distribution office was instructed to forward to Coudert a variety of messages (e.g., Greek diplomatic) in addition to Russian.[45] The section's reports were not included, even under code names, in the weekly activity reports prepared by each branch but were passed to a handful of senior officers through a separate reporting channel. A box labeled "Russian" did not appear on any organizational chart; rather, the unit hid behind the unrevealing designation "B-II-b-9."

In the early weeks of the reconstituted section, the staff reviewed the files of stored and incoming messages, sorting the intercepts according to circuits and beginning the difficult process of distinguishing messages in one cryptosystem from those in another. Intercepted reports from Japanese military attachés were studied for what they might reveal about Finnish, German, and Japanese operations against Soviet ciphers. Progress was slow. At first the section focused on messages that carried the designation "Narkomindel," the cable address of the People's Commissariat of Foreign Affairs. Initially, Coudert's team believed that they were dealing with two diplomatic cryptosystems, which they labeled RUA and RUB. By the summer they had identified a third. The messages, however, remained impenetrable.[46]

The attack was constrained by the inexperience of the personnel and the absence of historical continuity in the effort. Mounting the first American attack on Soviet diplomatic ciphers since 1931, Coudert's group had no body of collective wisdom upon which to draw, no record of mistakes from which to learn. There were no veterans to tell them whether the Soviets traditionally used four- or five-digit groups, placed their indicators in the third or fifth group of a message, or preferred transposition to substitution as an encipherment. The team was on its own, and it was green. At Arlington Hall the experienced and accomplished cryptanalysts were all working the high-priority problems in the Japanese or German sections. While intelligent and hardworking, the staff of the Russian section (who numbered ten by August 1943) were mismatched against their opponent. In the late summer of 1943 Coudert confronted his superiors with the problem. Confessing that his unit had made little progress, he asked for more resources: "The aim is to break the systems and a staff of experts would be of value to the unit." If expert cryptanalysts were not forthcoming, Coudert hoped that his team might draw upon the knowledge of the British, who had studied Russian communications continuously between 1919 and 1941. He recommended that Arlington Hall ask GCCS for information and advice on Soviet diplomatic and commercial codes. The authorities rejected this recommendation out of hand, undoubtedly for fear of revealing to the British the existence of the Russian program.[47]

In September 1943 Arlington Hall acknowledged that the Russian problem required more attention. The Cryptologic Research Group, a committee of senior operations officers, decided that Russian diplomatic and military traffic should be exploited to the fullest, and to that end recognized the need to commit more resources to the problem. The committee also reaffirmed the policy of withholding from the British any information about the program.[48] To enhance the collection of Russian traffic, the War Department established an intercept station in the Aleutian Islands. Poor reception compelled the station to relocate to Fairbanks, Alaska, but by 1 January 1944 it was copying seven thousand code groups of Russian traffic a day.[49] At Arlington Hall the general reorganization of the cryptanalytic branch in September moved the Russian Section into B-III (General Cryptanalysis), the unit under Frank Rowlett now responsible for all cryptanalytic operations except Japanese diplomatic and military. Along with the desks for meteorological ciphers and German diplomatic systems, the section made up the "b" division of B-III. To camouflage its purpose it was known as "Special Problems," or simply "B-III-b-9," and it continued to report through special channels.[50] The cryptanalytic resources of the section received a boost with the assignment of experienced analysts from other programs. Lieutenant Richard Hallock, a Signal Corps reserve officer with a doctorate in ancient Near Eastern languages who had come to Arlington Hall from the Department of Archaeology at the University of Chicago, arrived from Rowlett's research staff to work on messages believed to carry the traffic of the Soviet trade and lend-lease missions in the United States. With the skill that made him an acknowledged authority on the decipherment of cuneiform tablets,

Hallock, within weeks of his arrival, made a discovery that would mark a watershed in the history of the Russian problem.

In early October Hallock arranged for the "trade" messages to be punched into IBM cards for machine sorting. His analysis of the results suggested a startling discovery—at least some of the messages had been enciphered with duplicate keys. Pure randomness is the bane of code-breakers, whose analytic success depends on pattern and repetition. Hallock's discovery, therefore, was a small but encouraging step forward for the Russian section. The news was sufficiently heartening that two senior cryptanalysts, Frank Lewis and Karl Elmquist, visited Hallock to review his work. Lewis's presence was an indication of the importance of the discovery. Then serving on the technical staff of B-II, the branch responsible for Japanese cryptanalysis, he had worked in signals intelligence since before the war and was considered one of the top codebreakers at Arlington Hall. Working together over several days, Hallock, Lewis, and Elmquist discovered that the use of duplicate keys in the trade messages was even more extensive than Hallock had surmised.

As gregarious as Hallock was reserved, Frank Lewis returned to B-II and reported the news to branch chief Solomon Kullback, a friend and colleague since prewar days. Kullback liked to know what was going on in other branches, and Lewis, a gifted cryptanalytic troubleshooter who was assigned to the most difficult and pressing problems at Arlington Hall, served as his eyes and ears in the organization.[51] Lewis could not have anticipated the results of his report. Later that day Kullback encountered Frank Rowlett in the men's room and announced with glee and more than a little exaggeration that one of his analysts had broken the Russian problem.[52] Rowlett and Kullback had been in the group of four young men recruited by William Friedman upon the creation of SIS in 1930, and their careers encompassed most of the history of American signals intelligence. Both had risen to senior positions in their arcane profession. It would have been remarkable if their long, productive professional association did not contain an element of competition. In any event, Rowlett's fiery response to Kullback's news certainly suggested more than a spark of competition. He was furious that another branch might claim credit for making an entry into a difficult and important problem that was really the responsibility of his branch. He returned to his office and promptly issued orders barring Lewis and Elmquist from any access to the Russian problem.[53]

Rowlett also took steps to place the Russian section more directly under his control. In the arcane numerology of Arlington Hall, the unit had been section 9 of "b" division in B-III (B-III-b-9) and had reported to Rowlett through Captain Wrigley, the chief of "b" division. Rowlett now detached the unit from Wrigley's command and made it an independent division (B-III-e) reporting directly to him. To reinvigorate the section's leadership, Rowlett replaced Ferdinand Coudert with William Smith, a supervisor in the French section. A former college professor and one of the country's few experts in the Breton language, Smith had joined the prewar SIS from an editorial post at Columbia University Press, where he had edited the *Columbia Gazetteer* and the press's famous one-volume encyclopedia. Coudert remained in the section as deputy chief and, happily free of administrative duties, organized an excellent Russian language and area studies program for the unit.

With Hallock's discovery and Smith's appointment, the Russian section moved into a more productive period. Over the next few months additional cryptanalysts arrived, including the veteran Genevieve Grotjan Feinstein, a member of the small team that had solved the Japanese PURPLE cipher machine in 1940, and Cecil Phillips, a chemistry student from the University of North Carolina who had joined Arlington Hall in June 1943 and cut his teeth on Japanese weather ciphers. The unit now shared the second floor of a wing in A Building with the meteorological section. The two sections were separated by only a corridor and high, movable plywood partitions, but security in the Russian section was so strict that the cryptanalysts solving German and Japanese meteorological ciphers knew nothing of the work going on only steps away. The only access to the section was through a narrow space where two of the partitions overlapped. Immediately inside, Smith sat at a long table, and no one entered the office without his knowledge and permission. If he had to leave the table for any reason, one of the section's supervisors took his place. Smith sat with his back to the partitions so that he could look out over his staff, who, like students in a classroom, worked at tables facing forward. To prevent conversations from being overheard in the corridor or in the weather section, Smith required voices to be kept low, and he would promptly admonish anyone for unnecessary conversation. Steps were taken to guarantee that nothing in the physical display of the office would reveal its mission to cleaning staff, messengers, or the simply lost who might appear at Smith's desk. There were no maps or charts on the walls. Each night the section's only Cyrillic typewriter and all Russian dictionaries were locked in containers. Before leaving at the end of the day, the staff sifted through the trash to ensure that it included no incriminating papers.[54]

With new leadership and additional resources, the section significantly expanded its operations against Moscow's communications. By the end of the year it was accelerating the effort against the systems used to protect the traffic of Soviet diplomatic and commercial missions in the United States. It had also opened an attack on the general administrative system used by the Soviet army, a system believed to be used by NKVD officers assigned to Red Army units in western Russia, and several low-grade military systems.[55]

In the first half of 1944 the Russian section began to register its initial successes.[56] By July it was able to read four Red Army operational systems, known to American codebreakers as ZMO, ZMP, ZMQ, and ZMR.[57] That same month Smith's team solved the transposition encipherment of another military system (ZMA) and began to recover the values of the underlying codebook. Some messages in this system were readable by November, and by April 1945 some two thousand code values had been identified. The section solved the encipherment of yet another Red Army cryptosystem (ZMT) in July 1944. Code recovery did not really begin until November, but the section was reading messages in this system by May 1945.

For all the interest in Soviet military systems, the section continued to concentrate most of its effort on the more difficult diplomatic and economic ciphers, especially the trade system known as ZET. Building slowly on Hallock's discovery of duplicate keys, the analysts had, by June 1945, recovered some fifteen thousand groups of key. They also now understood that they were dealing with not one but three trade codes, and they had begun the tedious process of reconstructing these books. Progress in one book, a one-part code known as RED, was especially encouraging, and by the end of the war enough key and code had been recovered that fragments of some trade messages were readable.[58]

Progress did not depend on access to compromised materials. The FBI, ONI, and the Office of Strategic Services (OSS) acquired foreign codes and ciphers by recruiting agents inside embassies or by dispatching operatives to burglarize embassy safes and photograph cryptographic materials. During the war, "bag jobs" (sometimes referred to as "second-story cryptanalysis") contributed significantly to the solution of several cryptanalytic problems. For example, the solution of the high-grade Spanish

diplomatic cipher would have been unlikely without photographic copies of the additive tapes provided routinely by the FBI's "confidential
sources." Soviet offices and personnel were certainly targets of clandestine
operations. In early 1944 the FCC's Radio Intelligence Division established contact with an individual whom it believed worked in the communications room of the Russian embassy in Washington. Unfortunately, this
clerk merely copied and translated Reuters press dispatches and had no
access to the embassy's cipher room or knowledge of its operations.[59]

In December 1942 FBI agents twice secretly entered a warehouse
rented by the Russian lend-lease mission in New York, and in 1944 bureau
operatives disguised as building inspectors unsuccessfully sought entry
into the Russian Consulate General in New York City.[60] The RID had located a clandestine radio station transmitting from inside the consulate,
and the operatives were on a reconnaissance mission for a planned burglary. These FBI operations produced no Soviet cipher material. At the
consulate general the agents were denied entry by suspicious Russian
officials. The operation against the warehouse, even if successful, would
have uncovered no cryptographic materials, since the Russians would
never have placed their code room in a distant annex separate from the
activity and security of their main office. There may have been other clandestine operations during the war, but Arlington Hall's Russian section
did not benefit from "wastebasket cryptanalysis." The early labors of the
section are not those of a unit with clandestine access to Soviet codes and
ciphers. If the section had had access to the cipher of the lend-lease mission, it would not have still been struggling in the summer of 1945 to read
its first trade message.

The Russian section also seems to have benefited little from Russian cryptographic materials available from European sources. One such
source was Axis intelligence traffic. In the early months of the war in the
east, Germany scored significant successes against Soviet army, air force,
and police communications. Sigint operations against the Soviet Union accelerated in the summer of 1941 when German signal intelligence services
began to collaborate with their counterparts in Finland, Hungary, and
Japan. The collaborators exchanged intercepts, recovered code values, and
cryptanalytic observations.[61] The Japanese military attaché in Helsinki
was Tokyo's principal channel for these exchanges. In late 1942 Arlington
Hall solved the special cipher, designated JAS by the Americans, used
by the attaché to transmit cryptanalytic intelligence. By monitoring the
Helsinki-Tokyo circuit, American codebreakers became silent beneficiar-

ies of the Axis effort against Russian codes and ciphers. The benefits, however, were modest. In February 1943, the month that Arlington Hall activated its Russian program, the Japanese dropped JAS and introduced a new cipher, JAT, for intelligence exchanges. Just when American codebreakers most needed the window into Russian cryptography provided by the Axis exchanges, that window closed. The Japanese section worked feverishly to crack JAT. By spring there had been significant progress, but more study was required to make the system completely readable. JAT traffic dropped off dramatically after October 1943, and Arlington Hall suspended cryptanalytic work until normal traffic resumed in July 1944. By then most messages were readable.[62]

Throughout its surveillance of the Helsinki-Tokyo circuit, Arlington Hall was primarily interested in what the traffic would reveal about Axis success against *American* codes. Information about Soviet codes was of secondary interest; indeed, most of the JAS/JAT messages dealing with Russian cryptosystems would not be translated until 1945. When the messages were consulted for what they could reveal about Moscow's cryptography, they proved uncertain guides. For example, the Germans, Finns, and Japanese collaborated extensively on the Red Army system known to Arlington Hall as ZMA. Searching for clues in the intercepts, American codebreakers in 1945 concluded, "Approximately sixty percent of the materials provided by reading the Japanese messages [were] wrong, misleading, incomplete, or so badly garbled as to be useless."[63] It is also important to note that Axis success was greatest against those Soviet systems (low- and medium-grade Red Army field codes) that were of less interest to American codebreakers than the high-grade diplomatic and trade systems that principally engaged the Russian section in 1943–1945.

The Finnish-Soviet armistice of September 1944 provided another source of Russian cryptographic material. Before the armistice, elements of Finland's small but accomplished signals intelligence service evacuated to Sweden in the steamship *Stella Polaris* and two smaller vessels. Their baggage included seven hundred crates of signals intelligence equipment and cryptologic documents, including dozens of Russian codes and ciphers solved or captured by their service.[64] Upon their arrival in Stockholm, the Finns offered to sell their documents to interested governments. Washington responded with alacrity. On short notice Lieutenant Paavo Carlson, a Finnish-speaking officer at Arlington Hall, was dispatched to the Swedish capital under State Department cover. There he joined the chief of the OSS station and the military attaché from the American embassy in debriefing the Finns.[65] The latter described their success against Soviet codes and for good measure threw in the news that they had also cracked several American diplomatic ciphers. They also sold some documents.

The Stockholm affair remains one of the most puzzling events in the intelligence history of the war. The standard account maintains that Wilho Tikander, the OSS station chief in Stockholm, informed his superiors that he had an opportunity to purchase Russian cipher materials from Finnish sources.[66] In Washington, William Donovan, director of OSS, passed this news to the State Department, which responded with the observation that any such transaction would be "inadvisable and improper." Despite this warning, Donovan could not walk away from an intelligence windfall. On his own authority he directed Tikander to close the deal, and in late November the station chief, who earlier had handed the Finns a suitcase full of American currency in return for a German Enigma machine with all its rotors, purchased fifteen hundred pages of Soviet cryptographic materials for an unknown sum.

On 11 December Donovan informed President Roosevelt that he had acquired and turned over to the State and War Departments one military and three diplomatic codes, although he refrained from mentioning that they were Russian codes. The State Department was both surprised and alarmed by the unannounced arrival of the codes, especially since it had assumed that its earlier position had quashed Donovan's initiative. On 23 December Secretary of State Edward Stettinius personally complained to Roosevelt about the dire impact upon U.S.-Soviet relations of Donovan's escapade. The president accepted Stettinius's complaint and directed the secretary of state to inform Moscow and to arrange the return of the materials to the Russians. Informed by State of the presidential directive, OSS notified General Deane, chief of the American military mission in Moscow, that it had acquired "from enemy sources" material "purporting to contain the key to certain Russian codes both military and NKVD." On 9 January 1945 Deane passed this information to General Fitin, the chief of the foreign intelligence department of the NKVD, who arranged for the Soviet ambassador in Washington to receive the material personally from Donovan.

The precise nature of the OSS purchase remains uncertain. Depending on the source, Donovan's organization acquired either fifteen hundred pages of cryptographic material or four codebooks or one codebook of fifteen hundred pages. The subsequent history of the material is also a subject for speculation. If, as historians assume, Donovan arranged to have the items copied before their return to Moscow, what happened to them? To what extent did the material advance the work of the Russian section? There can be little doubt that American signals intelligence eventually acquired Russian cryptographic material from the Finns. Arlington Hall's records include dozens of Finnish-sourced files, many of them explicitly marked "Stella Polaris."[67] These photostats include such items as "Russian Code Book VAK-38," "Russian Code 4-N," "Rules for the Use of Code Table KT," and "Report on the Encoding Methods of Russian Intelligence Groups."

Unfortunately, it is difficult to determine when these items reached Arlington Hall. Paavo Carlson brought no Russian cryptographic material from his mission to Sweden. Much of the material came after the war from the British, who had assumed some control over the Finnish assets.[68] Some of the files may represent Donovan's purchase, but given the antagonism that chilled relations between Arlington Hall and the OSS, it is unlikely that any files reached the codebreakers until after the war, when they would have been shared by the CIA, the postwar successor to OSS. Whatever its route to Arlington Hall, the *Stella Polaris* material had little perceptible impact on the wartime work of the Russian Section. The six Red Army systems and the Russian weather ciphers known to have been read before the end of the war were all solved *before* the Americans met the Finns in Stockholm. Hallock's crucial discovery of the use of duplicate keys in some Russian messages also preceded the Stockholm affair, as did the initial entry into the trade messages and the subsequent recoveries of key and code.[69] Moreover, in early 1945 the Finnish experience, with its emphasis on Russian army and air force tactical systems, was largely irrelevant to the Russian section's focus on diplomatic and trade systems.

The *Stella Polaris* affair may have had a negligible effect on wartime operations, but it led to a serious breach in the wall of secrecy that surrounded the Russian problem. In November 1945 Elizabeth Bentley, a veteran courier for Soviet intelligence, informed the FBI that Lauchlin Currie, a White House aide who passed information to the Soviets, had told his contact that the United States was about to crack a Russian diplomatic code. According to Bentley, this news set off a flurry of activity as Soviet agents rushed to inform Moscow and uncover additional information. Initially, Bentley could not remember the date of this incident, but in a subsequent interview with the FBI she guessed that it had occurred in the spring of 1944. Another bureau source, who worked closely with Currie during the war, recalled that the White House aide confessed to him that he had discovered that the United States had "broken the Soviet Diplomatic code," and, disturbed at this sign of mistrust toward an ally, he (Currie) had "tipped off" the Russians. This source thought the conversation took place in the spring of 1944, although he readily admitted that it could have occurred as late as the fall.[70] Such testimony, as well as the fact that on 1 May 1944, in apparent reaction to Currie's report, Moscow changed certain of its cipher procedures, has led intelligence historians to conclude that in the spring of 1944 Currie had somehow learned of Arlington Hall's work on Russian communications. In fact, it is more likely that Currie's betrayal occurred at the end of the year and that the *Stella Polaris* affair was the proximate cause.

Even if Currie had access to signals intelligence at the White House (an assertion that remains to be verified), it is difficult to see how, in the spring of 1944, he could have come across evidence of success against Russian ciphers. No Russian messages appeared in the army's Magic Diplomatic Summaries for the simple reason that no Russian messages (except weather reports) had yet been decrypted by American intelligence. For the same reason, no Russian items could have been included in the files of decrypts delivered to the White House each day by the navy. Currie could not have known about a success against Russian diplomatic systems in the spring because there had been no success. At that time the Russian section was nowhere near entering, let alone solving, Russian diplomatic ciphers. It is also unlikely that he somehow picked up word of the progress against the trade and military systems. As noted previously, the Russian program at Arlington Hall was highly compartmentalized and security was tight. In an exercise to test the security of various operations at the Hall, the Russian section was the only one to avoid compromise. Aside from the section staff, only a handful of senior officers were aware of the program. No reports went to the White House. It is difficult to understand how Currie could have heard about the work of Smith, Hallock, and Phillips when colleagues working only steps away from the Russian section remained in the dark.[71]

It is far more likely that Currie learned of OSS's purchase of Russian cryptographic materials from the Finns in December 1944, the only time we can be certain that documents relating to Russian ciphers circulated in the White House. He could have seen or heard about the correspondence on this subject that passed between the White House, the State Department, and OSS, communications that referred specifically to the acquisition of Russian diplomatic codes. To his mind the difference between acquiring a code and solving one may have seemed academic and unworthy of mention in the hurried report to his clandestine contact. In this scenario, Moscow's new cipher procedures (a modest change in the message starting point indicator, which seemed curious to American codebreakers, since it made no significant contribution to the security of the system) was not a reaction to a security crisis but some routine administrative adjustment in cryptographic procedures.

Material collected in Germany in the immediate aftermath of the Nazi surrender provided little short-term advantage to the Russian section. German signals intelligence services had run a major effort against Soviet communications and had achieved notable success against Red Army and Air Force cryptosystems, although their work against Moscow's diplomatic ciphers proved futile. Quantities of material relating to Russian communications and cryptography fell into the hands of investigators from the Target Intelligence Committee (TICOM), the joint Anglo-American operation that sent teams of specialists across the former Reich in search of German cryptographic personnel and archives. In one case a TICOM unit under Lieutenant Colonel Paul Neff discovered a photographic copy of a charred Russian codebook in the archive of the German foreign ministry's cryptanalytic bureau. The Germans had acquired this book from the Finns, who, upon the outbreak of the Russo-German war, had seized the Russian consulate in Petsamo before the staff could burn their codes and ciphers. Russian cryptographic material was also recovered in Schleswig by Lieutenant Oliver Kirby, another Arlington Hall representative on a TICOM mission. TICOM documents began to arrive at Arlington Hall at the end of May; they confirmed some of the early assumptions about Russian cryptography but provided no magic key to the systems then under attack in the Russian section. Once again there were no dramatic breakthroughs.[72]

While impressive, the achievements of the Russian section in 1944–1945 did not represent a general entry into Russian communications. Some systems resisted solution. For example, work on the Red Army's administrative system ceased in July 1944 for lack of results. For the same reason Arlington Hall, in March 1944, dropped work on the system used by NKVD officers in western Russia, although it would take up the problem again in July 1945.[73] Successes often proved limited. The Red Army codes readable by mid-1944 were of relatively low intelligence value. ZMO and ZMP were obsolete, having been removed from service by the Russians at the end of 1943. The traffic had carried only the minutiae of military administration: veterinary reports, repair of rolling stock, and the shipment of dehydrated vegetables. One message advised the intended recipient about good fishing spots.[74] ZMQ and ZMR were merely used for radio service messages ("Are you receiving me?" "Adjust your frequency," etc.); they carried no substantive information.[75] The progress against the high-grade trade (ZET) and diplomatic (ZDJ) systems promised the most in terms of intelligence, but the promise remained unfulfilled during the war. As late as August 1945, only portions of a few trade messages were readable, and these consisted almost entirely of lists of numbers representing units of lend-lease materials sent to Russia by the United States. Portions of a few diplomatic messages may also have been read, but almost certainly not enough to make the messages intelligible.[76]

By the end of the war, the Russian problem had grown far beyond its modest beginnings. The days when Leonard Zubko and Gene Grabeel shoved two desks and some file cabinets into a corner of an office and began leafing through intercept forms were distant indeed. At Arlington Hall more than a hundred people were now assigned to the problem. After the Japanese signed the surrender protocols on 2 September 1945, the Russian section received an influx of experienced cryptanalysts from the Japanese section, and the machine unit immediately shifted its emphasis to processing Russian traffic.[77]

Army codebreakers also established cooperative relations with other cryptanalytic services. In July 1943 the U.S. Navy had resuscitated its Russian program, which had languished for years from inattention and insufficient resources. Lieutenant Commander C. H. Taecker, a student of Slavic languages, directed the renewed effort. At first Russian naval traffic was monitored at the naval intercept facility at Bainbridge Island, Washington, by a carefully compartmentalized team of four operators, but expanding operations soon required additional personnel and stations. In April 1944 four more operators joined the Russian operation at Bainbridge Island, and in June four operators at the naval intercept station at Winter Harbor, Maine, began monitoring Russian broadcasts.[78] By late spring 1945, the navy had thirty-four operators working Russian traffic exclusively, and it planned to increase that number to two hundred to staff additional intercept positions at Bainbridge Island and newly established positions at Adak, Aleutian Islands. With these additional resources the navy in 1945 increased the number of Russian messages it intercepted from thirty-five hundred in May to fifty-five hundred in July.

The German surrender in May 1945 released cryptanalysts who had been assigned to German naval communications. Originally the navy expected to switch these codebreakers to Japanese codes and ciphers, but many were diverted to the growing effort against Russian systems. In July, for example, Atlantic commands made 146 yeomen and other specialists available to OP-20-G for work against Russian communications. An additional 153 personnel were undergoing training at Bainbridge Island for similar work. In a rare display of interservice harmony, the navy exchanged intercepts and cryptanalytic results with the army. Army and navy analysts, for example, collaborated in the solution of the encipherment protecting the Red Army system ZMA. On their own, naval codebreakers had some success against Russian coast guard and merchant marine systems, and in November 1944 they began publishing intelligence summaries based on Russian decrypts.[79] The information, however, was low-grade, consisting mainly of reports of movements of Russian coastal patrol vessels. As late as mid-July 1945, OP-20-G admitted that no significant intelligence had resulted from the expanded effort against Soviet communications.[80]

The Russian section's collaboration with other American agencies did not extend beyond the navy. The section, for example, played no role in joint FBI-RID operations against Russian consulates in New York City and San Francisco. At the end of January 1943, only days before Arlington Hall would secretly activate its Russian program, RID monitors picked up transmissions from an unregistered station broadcasting from the New York City area. Traffic consisted only of call and procedure signals and the repetition of the letter v.[81] Suspecting that it had stumbled across an Axis spy ring, RID made the location of this transmitter its highest priority and ordered around-the-clock surveillance. By the first week in February, monitors had determined that the unidentified radio was communicating with a station in the Soviet Union. Mobile units scoured New York seeking to pinpoint the location of the elusive transmitter. One evening an RID van, its rooftop aerial scanning the airwaves, stopped in a downtown alley behind a nondescript office building. The two agents in the vehicle were convinced that the radio was broadcasting from the building, and one left the car and ran around the corner to determine the street address. Within minutes he was back with surprising news: a plaque on the front of the building identified it as the offices of the Russian consulate. The Russians had a radio transmitter they didn't want anyone to know about. In fact, they had two.

On 16 March RID stations picked up transmissions from an unregistered station operating in the San Francisco area. Within weeks the monitors determined that the transmitter was inside the Russian consulate in that city and that it communicated regularly with a station in Siberia. The FBI was brought into the case of the clandestine Russian radios, and RID stepped out. By this time the Russian radio in New York was transmitting encrypted traffic to the Soviet Union in a cipher that could not be read by FBI cryptanalysts. The bureau established special radio surveillance of the consulates (the monitoring post in San Francisco was just down the street from the Russian mission) and continued, without success, to attack the ciphers. It made no effort to involve Arlington Hall. The Russian section knew nothing about the FBI-RID operations and received no traffic from them.[82]

In the spring of 1945 the army's Russian section acquired another partner when the British gingerly approached Arlington Hall about a joint effort against Russian communications. GCCS had aggressively attacked Soviet codes and ciphers in the interwar period. After Germany's attack on the Soviet Union in June 1941, Prime Minister Churchill had ordered Bletchley Park to cease Russian operations. In the face of this directive, the Park essentially abandoned the Russian problem, although it continued to read Russian meteorological ciphers. In the spring of 1942, however, the Radio Security Service uncovered traces of an extensive network of Russian clandestine stations in Europe.

The following year, British intelligence authorities decided to reopen the Russian program, at least to the extent of monitoring the clandestine communications. GCCS established a special section in London to study this traffic, and by January 1944 the first decrypts were available. The material (code-named ISCOT) consisted mainly of communications between Moscow and communist agents and resistance groups in German-occupied Europe. In late 1944 GCCS established another special unit in London (Sloane Square) to work internal Russian civil and military traffic. The British hid both of these operations from the Americans.[83] In the village of Stanmore the British nominally supervised the Polish Wireless Research Unit, remnants of the prewar Polish Cipher Bureau that had made the first important discoveries about the German Enigma machine. The small Polish party studied low-grade Red Army and Air Force ciphers. Bletchley Park considered Stanmore a cryptanalytic backwater and dismissed the effort there as little more than an excuse to keep the Poles occupied. In September 1943 Alistair Denniston, director of GCCS's diplomatic branch, confessed to an American liaison officer his concern that the Poles would prove a great embarrassment if word of their work leaked to the Russians.[84]

By the spring of 1945, suspicion of Moscow's intentions far outweighed any concern over possible embarrassment at both Bletchley Park and Arlington Hall. American codebreakers had long before abandoned any scruples about reading the secret communications of allies. Since the creation of the Russian section in February 1943, Moscow's messages were no more privileged than the Free French, Belgian, Dutch, Polish, or Czech messages that were read. Of course the Soviet Union was a more important ally, and for diplomatic and domestic political reasons Russian operations required a special degree of secrecy. There was, however, no question of principle. Long gone were the more innocent days when a secretary of state could close Herbert Yardley's Cipher Bureau because reading someone else's mail was ungentlemanly. The United States would accept the British suggestion of collaboration; the only question was the form such cooperation would take.

While there was some concern, especially in the navy, about revealing American cryptanalytic secrets to the British, American codebreakers believed that collaboration would significantly advance their work against Soviet cryptosystems. With the end of the European war, GCCS could contribute to the Russian problem dozens of veteran cryptanalysts who would share not only their skills but also the fruits of Britain's experience with Soviet ciphers in the 1920s and 1930s. The British could also contribute intercepts. British intercept stations were more favorably located to copy Russian radio transmissions, and British-owned undersea cables carried Russian telegrams around the globe. Finally, the allegedly worldwide reach of His Majesty's vaunted secret intelligence service enhanced the chances of acquiring Soviet codebooks and cryptographic materials through skulduggery.[85]

On 5 June General George Marshall, the army chief of staff, and Admiral Ernest King, the chief of naval operations, met to discuss the British initiative. They acknowledged that during the war Anglo-American sigint collaboration had often been undercut by U.S. interservice rivalries and each service's practice of dealing separately with the British. The service chiefs agreed that the United States should accept Britain's offer and that the Army-Navy Communications Intelligence Board (ANCIB) should be the authority to establish cooperation and supervise its American end. Arrangements were to remain informal; above all there should be no written agreements. To ensure secrecy, Marshall detailed an aide to communicate orally to the ANCIB the service chiefs' decision and directed him to burn any notes of the discussion.[86] On 12 June Admiral Hewlett Thebaud, chair of the ANCIB, invited Colonel H. M. O'Connor, a British liaison officer, to his quarters for a private conversation. Admiral Thebaud allowed the colonel to read (but not retain) a brief memorandum in which the ANCIB accepted on behalf of the army and navy the British offer to collaborate against Russian communications. The United States proposed "a full and frank exchange" of all Russian intercept material, any collateral information about Soviet cryptographic practice, all code and cipher recoveries ("reconstructed or otherwise obtained"), and any intelligence resulting from analysis of Moscow's communications. Cooperation should commence at the earliest possible date, at which time "all recoveries and technical details in possession of either side . . . shall be exchanged." The memo concluded with the assurance that army and navy sigint authorities were eager to discuss the details of collaboration. O'Connor immediately informed GCCS that "ANCIB have agreed verbally to complete cooperation at earliest practicable date." This news was "most welcome" at GCCS, where authorities immediately began discussing how to implement the understanding.[87]

As the first step toward collaboration, the two allies began exploiting an early British success against a Russian Baudot teleprinter. This machine, designated CAVIAR by GCCS, carried high-grade military traffic between Moscow and its army staffs in Russian-occupied territories. The attack against this encrypted traffic was probably the work of the special section established in great secrecy at Sloane Square in late 1944. By the Japanese surrender the British were intercepting quantities of traffic (particularly on the Berlin-Moscow circuit), had recovered some of the code that was used in conjunction with the machine encipherment, and were reading messages. Results were shared with Arlington Hall. Some of the intercepts revealed Soviet signals intelligence trying to spot transmitters and identify communications circuits in the American, British, and French zones of occupied Germany.[88]

Early Anglo-American cooperation against the Soviet target also involved joint efforts to identify clandestine stations servicing Russian agents and underground movements. During the war the FCC's Radio Intelligence Division had received regularly through liaison channels a "Suspect Schedule" of unidentified radio stations monitored by Britain's Radio Security Service. In return RID provided any information it acquired from its surveillance of these stations. Despite the general prohibition at

GCCS against Soviet operations, the British had maintained a watch on Soviet clandestine stations. Independently, RID had also noted secret stations in the Western Hemisphere communicating with the Soviet Union. By August 1945 RID was passing this information to GCCS.[89]

The increasing activity around the Russian problem had no effect on American foreign policy simply because, through the end of the war, the Russian section at Arlington Hall produced no political intelligence. As mentioned earlier, Moscow's diplomatic traffic remained impenetrable. The information extracted from the few Red Army systems that could be read was so insignificant that during the war no translations or summaries were published in the various intelligence bulletins disseminated to American diplomatic and military authorities.[90] No item from Russian communications appears in the Magic Diplomatic Summary, the principal instrument for circulating diplomatic signals intelligence to policy makers. The Russian section did not provide American policy makers with a "magic" key to unlock the secrets of Soviet behavior and intentions. When American presidents and their advisers faced Stalin across conference tables at Teheran, Yalta, and Potsdam, they did so without privileged access to Russian communications.

Despite the impenetrability of Russian ciphers, signals intelligence did provide an oblique view into Soviet behavior. During the war Arlington Hall intercepted and decrypted the secret communications of dozens of governments. These communications sometimes provided insights into Russian affairs as conscientious diplomats in Moscow or other capitals tried to keep their foreign ministries apprised of Soviet policies. Throughout the conflict, for example, Japanese diplomatic traffic out of Moscow produced information about military developments on the eastern front, prospects for a separate Russo-German peace, and the status of Russo-Japanese relations. In the last months of the war, as fissures began to appear in the anti-Axis alliance, non-Russian diplomatic traffic provided a useful perspective on Moscow's intentions toward a variety of contentious issues, including the reconstitution of Poland; the creation of postwar regimes in Bulgaria, Germany, Hungary, and Romania; the withdrawal of Allied forces from Iran; control of the Dardanelles; and the nature of a postwar international organization.

The radiograms of the Free French diplomatic mission in Moscow revealed Russian efforts in late 1944 and early 1945 to cultivate France's goodwill and separate Paris from London and Washington.[91] French diplomatic traffic also provided early evidence of Soviet intentions toward postwar Poland. Shortly before the opening of the Yalta Conference at which Britain, the Soviet Union, and the United States would discuss the future of Poland, the French representative to the Provisional Government of the Polish Republic that had established itself in the city of Lublin informed Paris that the Lublin Poles were totally subservient to Moscow, had little political legitimacy, and could sustain themselves in power only through the political and military support of the Soviet Union. Within two weeks of the conclusion of the conference, France's ambassador in Moscow reported that neither the Russians nor the Lublin Poles would accept measures to ensure the free and unfettered elections endorsed by the Allies. Throughout the spring of 1945, French and Turkish diplomatic traffic consistently affirmed that Moscow intended to control events inside Poland and would accept nothing less than a subservient regime.[92]

Diplomatic traffic also shed light on a variety of other issues that threatened to complicate U.S.-Soviet relations. In early August 1945 American intelligence received an early (and rare) glimpse into Russia's atomic weapons program when Arlington Hall intercepted an intelligence report radioed to Ankara by the Turkish embassy in Moscow identifying Pyotr Kapitsa and Abram Ioffe as leaders in Moscow's accelerated program to develop an atomic bomb.[93] Sigint also illuminated Soviet policies in the Balkans and the Near East. By eavesdropping on Persian communications, for instance, American codebreakers learned of Russian efforts to secure oil concessions in northern Iran and undercut American and British influence in that country. Greek and Iraqi diplomatic traffic from the summer of 1945 suggested that Moscow was fomenting civil unrest in northern Iran to advance its own political ambitions in the area.[94] Moscow's efforts in the spring and summer of 1945 to secure territorial concessions in eastern Turkey and the right to control passage through the Dardanelles was apparent in Turkish traffic as Ankara's conscientious ambassador in the Russian capital reported details of his conversations with the Soviet foreign minister, Molotov.[95]

French, Greek, Iranian, Japanese, and Turkish reports on Russian affairs filled the translation folders and appeared frequently in intermediate intelligence bulletins such as the RED Summaries, but few seem to have reached the highest levels of decision making. Aside from Japanese decrypts reporting the current state of Russo-Japanese relations or Tokyo's persistent fantasies regarding a separate peace between Berlin and Moscow, the Magic Diplomatic Summaries carry few items on Soviet foreign policy until the spring of 1945. As late as May 1945, the summaries devoted more attention to Paris's efforts to reassert French influence in the Levant than to Russian policies in the Balkans and Eastern Europe.

Because of routine delays in decipherment and translation, sigint on Russian activities was not necessarily more timely than intelligence from other sources. On 28 March 1945, for example, the Magic Diplomatic Summary reported (from Turkish traffic) that on 19 March Molotov had informed the Turkish ambassador of Moscow's intention to terminate the Soviet-Turkish Friendship Treaty of 1925, an act that would prove the opening move in a Soviet campaign to secure political and territorial concessions from Turkey. The State Department, however, had already learned of this Soviet démarche on 21 March when it received a cable from the American embassy in Moscow reporting that local papers had been carrying the story for two days. The diplomats scooped the cryptanalysts again on 22 June 1945 when the embassy in Ankara reported (three days before the news appeared in the Magic Summary) that Molotov was warning the Turkish ambassador in Moscow that negotiations concerning a new treaty of friendship could not go forward without territorial adjustments in Russia's favor.[96] Of course, the diplomats were not always first across the line. On 12 June 1945 Arlington Hall circulated a report from the Turkish ambassador in Moscow detailing a meeting with Molotov in which the latter first raised the matter of adjustments in the common border. The embassy in Ankara did not pick up this story until almost a week later.[97] Sigint also occasionally revealed information absent from diplomatic or press reporting. On 18 June Turkey's acting foreign minister discussed with the American ambassador the currently tense state of Soviet-Turkish relations. Seeking to attract Washington's sympathy and support, the Turk emphasized Moscow's demand that Ankara return certain territories ceded to Turkey in 1921. What the acting foreign minister did not say to the ambassador, but what was apparent to Arlington Hall from monitoring Turkish diplomatic communications, was that Ankara had been advised by its embassy in Moscow that the Soviets would not insist on border adjustments, that Molotov was merely fishing, and that there was no cause for alarm on this matter.[98]

In the end signals intelligence probably had little impact on American diplomacy toward the Soviet Union in the last year of the war. With Moscow's high-grade diplomatic and military traffic resisting Arlington Hall's attacks, Washington was denied access to the leadership traffic that would have revealed Russian intentions and activities. While useful, third-party traffic (French, Greek, Japanese, Turkish) was modest compensation for the inability to read Soviet communications. Usually this traffic merely confirmed intelligence gleaned from more traditional channels, such as embassy reporting. It is unlikely that it significantly altered the perceptions of policy makers already inclined by experience and current observation to suspect Soviet intentions. Even before Soviet activity began to feature prominently in such reporting channels as the Magic Diplomatic Summaries, senior officials such as Admiral William Leahy (chief of staff to the president), Averell Harriman (ambassador to the Soviet Union), George Kennan (embassy counselor in Moscow), General John Deane (head of the American military mission in the Russian capital), and Loy Henderson (director of the State Department's Office of Near Eastern Affairs) had developed serious concerns about Moscow's ambitions as Russian armies conquered and occupied Eastern Europe. Similar concerns were reported from Bucharest and Sofia by American diplomats in contact with Soviet occupation policies.[99] With the exception of Admiral Leahy, these officials had no access to signals intelligence, but they did not need special sources to alert them to Moscow's intentions toward Poland or Bulgaria or any of the proliferating flashpoints in U.S.-Soviet relations. While signals intelligence would have done little to change their attitudes, it certainly did not form them.

It would be a mistake to conclude that American efforts during the war to crack Soviet ciphers and read Moscow's secret communications reveal an early anti-Soviet attitude that betrayed the spirit of alliance and poisoned any hope of cooperation in the postwar era. As mentioned earlier, the decision to penetrate Soviet communications was made by signals intelligence officers without reference to the White House or the State Department, neither of which was aware during the war that Russian ciphers were under attack. Although these intelligence officers were anticommunist and suspicious of the Soviet Union, their decision reflected organizational imperatives more than ideological bias. The creation of the Russian section followed logically from Arlington Hall's decision to define its mission in the broadest possible manner. Once McCormack, Clarke, and Corderman concluded that to best serve the national interest Arlington Hall had to seek comprehensive coverage of the diplomatic communications of all governments, the effort against Moscow's codes and ciphers was no more anti-Soviet than the effort against the Vatican's codes and ciphers was anti-Catholic. In this context, the Russian problem at Arlington Hall was less a harbinger of the cold war than a herald of a new attitude toward intelligence and its potential role in American foreign policy.

Chapter Seven

A Usually Reliable Source

By the summer of 1945 the United States had developed a massive organization to intercept and process the diplomatic communications of foreign governments. The Signal Security Agency (as it was now called) directed the activity of eleven intercept stations, which enveloped the globe in an electronic net. From stations as close to Washington as rural Virginia and as distant as Asmara, Eritrea, and New Delhi, India, operators regularly monitored more than three hundred foreign transmitters and scooped from the ether up to 380,000 messages a month.[1] At Arlington Hall the cryptanalysts routinely dealt with 350 different codes or ciphers representing the cryptographic efforts of sixty governments or political entities, while the translators handled messages in twenty-five languages. The organizational effort was awesome, the technical achievements impressive, and the output enormous. The impact on American diplomacy was, however, limited by several factors, including the nature of the signals intelligence process, the nature of wartime diplomacy, and the nature of American decision making.

For all its successes, Arlington Hall revealed to American policy makers only a portion of the world at war. It is a truism that signals intelligence reveals only what is signaled. American codebreakers were deaf to important events and developments, such as the fall of Mussolini in July 1943 or the attempt on Hitler's life and abortive putsch in Berlin in July 1944, which, because of their conspiratorial nature, did not appear on communication channels. The events surrounding the removal of Mussolini in the summer of 1943 provide a case in point. Arlington Hall was as surprised as the Duce himself by King Vittorio Emanuele's decision to dismiss the fascist chief and acquiesce in his subsequent arrest on 25 July. Although it had been clear to observers for months that Italy's economic and military position was precarious, signals intelligence, reflecting the speculation in Allied, Axis, and neutral diplomatic circles, proved an uncertain guide to the political resilience and intentions of the fascist regime.

As early as December 1942, the intercepted reports of Axis and neutral ambassadors to the pope suggested that Vatican authorities believed that Italian governing circles were disillusioned with Mussolini's leadership and that papal officials anticipated significant political changes. Signals intelligence also provided fleeting glimpses of anti-Mussolini political machinations in Rome in the spring and early summer. On 10 June, for example, the Portuguese ambassador to the Vatican reported that the Italian king had approached nonfascist personalities, including former prime minister Ivanoe Bonomi, to explore a political solution to the increasingly desperate situation. Some intercepts suggested that the fascist regime intended to use the Vatican to mediate Italy's early withdrawal from the war. Since Arlington Hall was unable to read high-grade Vatican diplomatic traffic, it was difficult to confirm these rumors.[2] Other intercepts, however, suggested that, though discouraged, the regime faced no immediate threat and intended to continue the war. On 21 May, for instance, the Argentine embassy in Rome informed Buenos Aires that Mussolini retained the loyalty of the Fascist party and the masses, and that his hold on the country remained firm. In early July the Japanese ambassador in Rome advised his foreign ministry that, while opinion in the capital was gloomy, the people in the provinces were still resolute in their attitude toward the war.

Not a single message predicted the events of 25 July because the decision to depose Mussolini was made in secrecy by a handful of individuals, none of whom announced their intentions on internal or international radio circuits. In retrospect, a few indications could be gleaned from the mass of intercepts. On 22 June the Portuguese legation in Rome warned Lisbon to expect a reorganization of the Italian government. Two weeks later the legation reported that twenty prominent figures, including a former prime minister, two generals, and several senators, had signed a petition to the king demanding political reform and a suspension of hostilities. On 24 July, the day before Mussolini's fall, the Japanese embassy in Rome informed Tokyo that confidence in the fascist leader was weakening significantly. These reports were as close to a warning as Arlington Hall would come. Unfortunately, the warning came too late. By the time the Japanese message had been decrypted, translated, and circulated to American decision makers, Mussolini had been under arrest for twenty-four hours. The Portuguese messages were not available until 29 July, four days after the dictator's fall.[3]

Of course, what is signaled is not always accessible. Throughout the 1930s SIS had struggled to secure reliable and productive sources of traffic, and at times the absence of an effective intercept network had undercut its ability to perform its mission. Even after Pearl Harbor, when the army committed resources to building new intercept facilities and training the personnel to staff them, coverage was less than complete. For much of the war, most messages between Berlin and Rome passed along landlines beyond the reach of American and British intercept operators so that Allied signals intelligence was unable to eavesdrop on diplomatic exchanges between the Axis partners. Until late in the war the Allies faced similar obstacles in their effort to monitor communications on other important European circuits, such as Berlin-Bern, Berlin-Budapest, Berlin-Helsinki, and Berlin-Stockholm.

Even when accessible, communications often proved unreadable. The notable achievements against PURPLE and Enigma obscure the fact that many important targets successfully resisted cryptanalytic attack. There were always blank spots on the signals intelligence map, and all too often these spots coincided with important diplomatic concerns. During the bitter contest of wills between President Roosevelt and General de Gaulle in 1943, Arlington Hall had to admit that it could not read a single Free French message. There were no Chinese decrypts to help the White House in the winter of 1942–1943 when Generalissimo Chiang Kai-shek's strident demands for more financial and military assistance threatened a crisis in U.S.-Chinese relations. At the very time in 1944 that American policy makers became more concerned about the Vatican's attitude toward the political shape of postwar Europe, the codebreakers concluded that their effort against papal ciphers was hopeless.

Even when messages were readable, their meaning was not always unambiguous. Signals intelligence provides a window not so much on what foreign governments are thinking as on what they are saying, and what they are thinking may not be clear from what they are saying. Additionally, intercepted messages may simply mirror indecision, disagreement, and confusion among authorities in the targeted government. The flurry of Japanese "peace messages" in the summer of 1945 provides a case in point.

As early as the summer and fall of 1944, non-Japanese diplomatic traffic out of Tokyo revealed signs of an interest within elite circles in a negotiated end to the war.[4] In July 1945 similar signs began to appear in Japanese traffic. Communications on the Moscow-Tokyo circuit indicated that Japan hoped to enlist the Soviet Union on behalf of a negotiated settlement. Exchanges on the Bern-Tokyo circuit revealed Japanese officials in the Swiss capital seeking to open a channel to Washington through Allen Dulles, chief of the OSS station in Switzerland. The messages, however, were tentative and vague, revealing little except that the Japanese were dithering over peace and arguing over everything except the rejection of unconditional surrender. One intercepted message said that Japan would accept a peace based on no annexations of territory, another indicated that only a peace compatible with the national honor would be acceptable, a third suggested that the Atlantic Charter would be an appropriate basis for negotiations, a fourth advised that Japan would not present any terms at all but would wait for preliminary discussions with the Russians, while a fifth opined that the Potsdam Declaration (26 July 1945) might serve as a basis for negotiations and that the foreign ministry would "collect the views of all quarters on the matter of concrete terms." A hodgepodge of suggestions, fantasies, and platitudes, the decrypts could not reveal Japanese policy because the Japanese were unable to decide on a policy.[5]

Not all traffic was as problematic as the Japanese peace exchanges. The least ambiguous messages, however, were frequently the least relevant to the needs of policy makers. Each day Arlington Hall decrypted hundreds of messages that impinged hardly at all on the concerns of American wartime diplomacy: the Uruguayan legation in Lisbon informs Montevideo of its expenditures during the last quarter of 1944; the Swiss consul in Johannesburg reports on the care and feeding of Italian internees in South Africa; a Mexican trade delegation reports from Santiago on a luncheon hosted by the Chilean Association of Manufacturers. These were not messages likely to seize the imagination of policy makers or to receive space in the Magic Diplomatic Summary, but they represented the bulk of traffic processed each day by Arlington Hall. It is easy to forget that, even in wartime, the majority of communications passing along diplomatic circuits were concerned with administrative trivia or minor political and commercial affairs. Such messages, however, had to be processed if only to confirm their banality.

Furthermore, Arlington Hall's commitment to global sigint coverage, combined with bureaucratic resistance to abandoning "successful" operations, resulted in a rather expansive approach to target selection. While never totally indiscriminate (if pressed, even the Latin American section would have agreed that Japanese diplomatic traffic was more important than Venezuelan), this approach encouraged the codebreakers to aggressively attack a country's traffic even if experience suggested that the intelligence product did not justify the effort. Additionally, the culture at the old Munitions Building and, after Pearl Harbor, Arlington Hall contributed to a work environment in which success was a function of the number of cryptosystems broken and messages read. Codebreakers were usually indifferent to the content of the messages.[6] The tendency to consider all targets technical problems to be solved rather than intelligence sources to be exploited created a cryptanalytic process in which a new Peruvian cipher was potentially just as "interesting" and worthy of attention as a Japanese cipher. This posture, which was further abetted by the security-induced isolation in which the codebreakers worked, dispersed scarce resources, undercut efforts to focus on a handful of priority targets, and padded the monthly decryption figures with messages from governments peripheral to the war effort. Finally, Arlington Hall, for all its wartime growth, continually lacked the personnel to process anything but a small percentage of the messages its stations intercepted. One authority has estimated that no more than 15 percent of the traffic intercepted was ever translated.[7] All these factors combined to produce for American policy makers a signals intelligence "horizon" on which only certain diplomatic events and issues were visible. Many of these events and issues were peripheral to the central concerns of American wartime diplomacy.

Two features of America's wartime diplomacy diluted the influence of signals intelligence. After Pearl Harbor the principal diplomatic imperative was the need to protect and nurture the Grand Alliance with Great Britain and the Soviet Union. The state of relations with London and Moscow preoccupied President Roosevelt and his principal advisers to the exclusion of almost all other issues. Occasionally, other subjects, such as relations with the Free French movement of General Charles de Gaulle or disagreements with the Nationalist Chinese regime of Chiang Kai-shek, demanded attention, but such episodes never absorbed the energies of senior policy makers as did the politics of the Big Three. Unfortunately, signals intelligence provided, at best, only indirect support for American policy makers as they struggled with the diplomacy of the Grand Alliance. Unable or unwilling to read the diplomatic communications of London and Moscow, Arlington Hall could report only what outside parties, such as the neutrals, were speculating about the course of Big Three relations. At Washington, Quebec, Casablanca, Tehran, Yalta, Potsdam, and the other Anglo-American or Anglo-American-Russian conferences that were the diplomatic mileposts of the war, the codebreakers could provide the American delegations with no direct insight into the intentions and concerns of their British and Russian counterparts.

The commitment to unconditional surrender also diluted the influence of signals intelligence on American wartime diplomacy. There could be little influence when there was little diplomacy. The codebreakers had direct access to Axis (mainly Japanese) diplomatic communications, but since diplomatic contacts with the enemy were inhibited by the unconditional surrender formula, this access could have little impact on foreign policy toward Germany, Italy, Japan, and their minor partners. In a situation where Washington had not so much an evolving policy as a rigid posture toward Berlin and Tokyo, the only German or Japanese decrypt that could have much impact was one announcing, "We surrender."

Of course, coverage of Axis diplomatic circuits provided a window on, for example, Berlin's relations with neutral or friendly governments, but by the last year of the war, as more and more countries severed relations with Germany, and Hitler's minor allies fell by the wayside, these relations and activities diminished to the point of nonexistence. Even the insight into internal political conditions in Berlin and Tokyo was of limited utility beyond encouraging American policy makers in their anticipation of victory and providing grist for the psychological warfare mills. In purely diplomatic terms, it made little difference if signals intelligence revealed a peace faction in the Japanese government if Washington intended to do nothing about it. Axis diplomatic traffic proved much more useful in exposing Axis efforts at espionage and subversion, charting morale in Germany and Italy, and gaining an additional window on the activities of neutrals, especially Sweden and the Vatican, whose traffic remained largely unreadable.

Signals intelligence was most useful when American diplomacy had to focus on the medium and small powers whose traffic represented a rich hunting ground for American cryptanalysts. This occurred most frequently during large international conferences, such as the San Francisco Conference on the organization of the United Nations. Seasoned by its "intensive reading" of foreign communications during earlier international conferences, such as the Bretton Woods Conference on postwar economic cooperation (July 1944), the Dumbarton Oaks Conference on postwar international organization (August–October 1944), and the Chicago International Aviation Conference (November 1944), Arlington Hall began preparing for the San Francisco Conference well before the meeting's scheduled opening on 25 April 1945.[8]

Arrangements were made to obtain copies of every document and report published by the conference secretariat. Since the foreign delegations might include summaries or even quotations from these documents in their reports to their governments, these copies would serve as cribs for codebreakers seeking to crack the delegations' codes and ciphers, many of which had been introduced specifically for use during the conference. Details were collected on the procedures each delegation would use in communicating with its home government. The U.S. Army Communications Service graciously invited the various delegations to use its radio and wire facilities. Army communicators intended, of course, to provide Arlington Hall with copies of any messages entrusted to its channels.[9] The larger powers sensibly made their own arrangements. Arlington Hall noted that the French delegation installed a private teleprinter line between its headquarters in the Saint Francis Hotel and the French embassy in Washington. The Soviet delegation communicated with Moscow via a private teleprinter line linking the Russian consulate in San Francisco with the Russian embassy in Washington. As a backup, the consulate was also linked directly to a Russian vessel anchored in San Francisco harbor that could communicate by radio with the embassy. Even the British did not escape notice. American signals intelligence knew, for example, that Britain's Political Warfare Executive had a private line from 127 Montgomery Street in the financial district of the city to the British embassy in Washington and that the line was in service for ten minutes every day except Sunday.[10]

Although British and Russian (and some Chinese) messages remained impenetrable, Arlington Hall's coverage of conference traffic was sufficiently comprehensive to provide American policy makers with insight into the attitudes and intentions of most delegations on a range of contentious issues. Signals intelligence, for example, illuminated the efforts of Colombia and Ecuador to mobilize Latin American governments to secure for Argentina an invitation to the conference over the opposition of other states, most notably the Soviet Union, which objected to the pro-Axis posture of Buenos Aires during the war. Four Latin American states (Brazil, Chile, Mexico, and Venezuela) hinted that Soviet resistance to the inclusion of Argentina would convince them to oppose Moscow's bid to have two Soviet republics, White Russia and the Ukraine, invited to the conference. The Argentine question threatened to complicate not only the conference but also Great Power relations, since at the Yalta Conference (February 1945) Washington had endorsed the inclusion of the two Soviet republics. Access to the traffic between the Latin American delegations and their various capitals may have contributed to Washington's ability to formulate a compromise that resulted in the conference welcoming all three parties.[11]

Signals intelligence also forewarned Washington of simmering resentment among the medium and small powers over Great Power efforts to dominate the new organization through such devices as an exclusive veto in the Security Council. Intercepted traffic, including Chilean, French, Iranian, Mexican, Portuguese, and Turkish communications, revealed that Great Power pretensions irritated even some of Washington's most reliable allies, such as Australia, and that various governments were considering organizing the smaller powers to resist by enhancing the power of the General Assembly over the Security Council. For a time France, the only country with an appetite and the status to challenge the Great Powers, seemed inclined to speak for the disgruntled. Sigint revealed, however, a certain ambivalence among French officials and may have contributed to Washington's decision to defuse the opposition by convincing Paris to cast its lot with London, Moscow, and Washington. With their putative leader co-opted, the minor powers grudgingly acquiesced in the plans of the Great Powers.[12]

If signals intelligence ever had an impact on wartime American diplomacy, it was during multinational conferences such as the one in San Francisco. Nevertheless, assertions about the influence of codebreaking on American foreign policy must remain conditional or speculative, even in the case of international conferences. Historians hoping to connect a decrypt or set of decrypts with a particular foreign policy decision will almost always be disappointed. Except in a handful of cases (e.g., Roosevelt's assurances to Stalin in July 1942 that Japan would not attack the Soviet Union, and, less certainly, the decision in 1944 to "get tough" with Argentina for its pro-fascist posture), there is no evidence that signals intelligence directly influenced particular diplomatic decisions. On the other hand, in several instances Roosevelt and his diplomatic advisers, buffeted by political necessity, assured by personal conviction or intuition, or constrained by the paucity of viable alternatives, seemingly disregarded the sigint evidence when determining a policy. In 1941 the White House and the State Department clung to the hope that economic sanctions would restrain Japan even though Japanese intercepts clearly indicated that Tokyo would not be deterred by embargoes. After Germany's invasion of the Soviet Union, Roosevelt was not deterred from committing American supplies to Russia by signals intelligence (largely Japanese) indicating that the Soviets would quickly succumb to German attack. The specter of a separate peace between a beleaguered Soviet Union and a triumphant Germany haunted American deliberations over a second front despite consistent evidence from the decrypts that neither Berlin nor Moscow had any interest in a separate peace.[13]

To conclude simply that decision makers must have rationally and deliberately acted upon available signals intelligence is to confuse the mere existence of intelligence with its influence.[14] This approach begs several important questions: Did the relevant decision makers all receive the same signals intelligence at the same time? Was that intelligence unambiguous in its meaning? Did the decision makers all place the same credence in that intelligence? Did they all absorb that intelligence to the same degree? Was the available signals intelligence relevant to their decision priorities at any given time? Were there other influences that might have undercut the impact of signals intelligence? The problem is in part one of isolating and weighing any single element among the myriad factors that contribute to a decision. All too often the most that can be said is that sigint may have been one of several factors that influenced a decision or policy. Further complicating analysis is the fact that little is known about the process by which intelligence of any sort was integrated into decision making in the White House and the State Department. What little is known, however, suggests that the arrangements diluted the potential impact of signals intelligence.

The process by which signals intelligence was circulated to decision makers remains especially obscure. At a distance of more than half a century it is difficult to determine with any confidence who in the White House, the State Department, and other agencies had access to sigint. Each day Arlington Hall published the *Bulletin,* which contained all diplomatic and military messages completely solved and translated in the preceding twenty-four hours. Several copies of the *Bulletin* were distributed to the army's Special Branch and the navy's OP-20-G.[15] At Special Branch, editors condensed one or two dozen of the more important messages for inclusion in the Magic Diplomatic Summary, which circulated to the State, War, and Navy Departments. Since it is now impossible to reconstruct the list of individuals in these agencies cleared to read the Magic summaries, it is also impossible to identify which foreign policy decision makers, beyond the obvious candidates (e.g., the secretaries of state, war, and the navy), might have seen signals intelligence. Certainly the list included individuals below the level of department chiefs. The Magic distribution lists that survive (almost all from early in the war) are misleading. Before Pearl Harbor, for example, Secretary of State Cordell Hull was the only State Department official on the Magic list. We know, however, that at the time several other officers in the department had daily or at least occasional access to signals intelligence, including Undersecretary Sumner Welles, Assistant Secretary Adolf Berle, Chief of the Far Eastern Division Maxwell Hamilton, and Hull's two personal assistants.[16] That diplomatic signals intelligence circulated beyond a handful of top officials after Pearl Harbor is clear from a decision on 26 July 1945 to restrict access to any decrypts concerning Japanese peace initiatives to the "highest echelon" and to warn these privileged officials to withhold such decrypts from "other individuals in their offices . . . even though such individuals are authorized to receive Ultra information or have previously had access to the Diplomatic Summary."[17] On a range of issues, from the appropriate posture toward pro-Axis Argentina to planning for postwar Europe, senior advisers and midlevel officers in the White House and the State and War Departments exerted important influence on American diplomacy, but it is uncertain which of these officers had access to signals intelligence.[18]

The situation is slightly more clear in the navy. Under the terms of various interservice agreements, the army had assumed full responsibility for diplomatic signals intelligence with the understanding that the navy would receive copies of all diplomatic translations. The navy thus received diplomatic sigint from the army in both summary (Magic Diplomatic Summary) and raw (*Bulletin*) form. Since shortly before Pearl Harbor, the navy had been responsible for distributing this sigint not only within its own organization but also to the White House. It did so by circulating not summaries but actual decrypts selected from the total output of messages provided each day by Arlington Hall. The assumption, common among historians, that the Magic Diplomatic Summary (an army product) was the single instrument for disseminating diplomatic sigint throughout the government is therefore incorrect.

Each day the "I" (Intelligence Coordination) section of OP-20-G would review the hundreds of diplomatic translations sent over by Arlington Hall in the preceding twenty-four hours and select twenty to thirty of these for distribution to the White House and a short list of readers in the

Navy Department that included the secretary of the navy, the chief and vice chief of naval operations, the director and deputy director of naval intelligence, and the director of naval communications.[19] Not every "client" would receive every decrypt. On 20 July 1943, for example, OP-20-GI sent the White House only nine decrypts from that day's selection of thirty-two items, but it forwarded to the deputy director of naval intelligence nineteen items from the list. Roosevelt's allotment included three items from the Japanese embassy at the Vatican reporting on the pope's reaction to a recent letter from the president and the concern among papal officials over reports of Japanese atrocities in the Far East; a message from the Japanese ambassador in Italy indicating that financial markets were calm despite the Allied invasion of Sicily; a dispatch from the Japanese embassy in Bucharest speculating on German intentions on the eastern front; a radiogram from Tokyo's ambassador in Madrid summarizing Spanish news regarding the military situation in Sicily; a message from the German foreign ministry informing its representative in Nanking that henceforth Hitler would be referred to as "Führer of the Great German Reich" rather than "Chancellor of the German Reich"; a report from the Finnish military attaché in Tokyo concerning rumors of a Japanese-Soviet rapprochement; and a message to Lisbon from the Portuguese representative in Beirut reporting speculation that the Allies would cross into Italy from Sicily and then proceed across the Adriatic to invade Dalmatia.

From the list of twenty-one decrypts selected by OP-20-GI for distribution to its customers on 22 July 1943, the White House received seven, the chief of naval operations received nine, the deputy director of naval intelligence received eleven, and the secretary of the navy received none. That day the president's share of signals intelligence included three Japanese messages out of Rome indicating that the Italians were hard-pressed in Sicily and that Mussolini had appealed to Hitler for help; a message from Tokyo to its ambassador in Berlin forwarding advice from the imperial embassy in Moscow that while Russia's relations with its allies were warming, this trend would have no impact on the Soviet Union's relations with Japan; a "Fuji" intelligence report from the Japanese mission in Lisbon indicating that London was sending out peace feelers; a circular from the German foreign office directing its missions abroad to embark on a "whispering campaign" to promote the story that Russia was behind the air crash that killed Wladyslaw Sikorsky, the leader of the Polish government-in-exile; and a radiogram from the Portuguese embassy in Bucharest informing Lisbon that a Romanian delegation had departed for Italy and that Romania intended to withdraw some of its troops from the eastern front.[20]

Usually the White House received seven to ten translated diplomatic messages a day, although it was not uncommon for the number to slip as low as three or four. For all the expansion in American signals intelligence, the messages remained overwhelmingly Japanese in origin, just as they had been before the war when the Signal Intelligence Service labored with a modest staff against a handful of targets. For example, in June 1943, a month in which Arlington Hall decrypted and translated almost 7,500 messages, the navy sent the White House a grand total of 87 decrypts of which 73 (83.9 percent) were Japanese and the remainder were Portuguese (5), Finnish (4), Vichy French (2), Argentine (1), German (1), and Italian (1).[21] This sample suggests that Arlington Hall's cryptanalytic successes against dozens of foreign governments remained largely invisible to the White House, which saw only a relatively narrow range of results.

At the White House the president's naval aide delivered classified naval documents, including the diplomatic decrypts, twice a day. The president displayed a curious insouciance toward the signals intelligence. He frequently did not bother to read, let alone study, the decrypts. The morning briefing often took place in the presidential bathroom, where the aide would close the toilet lid, sit on it, and read aloud the foreign messages as the president shaved. In the afternoons the venue switched to an anteroom off the White House Map Room, where Roosevelt was content to listen to the oral report while he had his polio-wasted legs massaged or his troublesome sinuses packed by the White House physician.[22] The president did not retain any decrypts for study or future reference. At the end of the briefing, the naval aide would return the decrypts to OP-20-G for destruction.

When Roosevelt was resting at "Shangri-La," the presidential retreat in the Maryland mountains, the naval aide would read the decrypts to him over the phone. When the president traveled abroad to conferences, delivery of signals intelligence was even more problematic. The Map Room forwarded sigint to the naval aide with the presidential party in messages prefaced with the indicator "Colonel Boone." These messages consisted of cursory summaries of the more important decrypts. For example, during the Casablanca Conference (January 1943), one such message informed the naval aide, "From Colonel Boone. Jap[anese] Ambassador Berlin imploring his government consider attack on Russia and at least effect closer war plans with Germany."[23] The sigint reports to the traveling president were less substantial and also less frequent. During Roosevelt's discussions with Churchill at the Quebec Conference in August 1943, the president received only two Colonel Boone messages over the seven days of the meeting. During the Cairo and Tehran Conferences (November–December 1943), the Map Room sent sigint to the presidential party the slow way, by courier rather than radio. While he was aboard the USS *Iowa,* traveling to and from the conferences, Roosevelt received no signals intelligence at all during the eight-day transatlantic crossings between the United States and Africa.[24]

A comparison of naval routing logs with the Magic Diplomatic Summaries reveals that many of the decrypts circulated to the president were the same as those that served as the basis for the summaries distributed to the State and War Departments. Distribution, however, was not synchronized. It was not unusual for signals intelligence in the summary format to appear one or two days before (or after) the arrival of the relevant translation at the White House. On 22 July 1943, for example, the president received from the navy a translation of a message to Tokyo from the Japanese minister in Lisbon predicting Portuguese resistance to Allied efforts to increase their access to the Azores. This intelligence did not appear in the Magic Diplomatic Summary until 25 July.

Frequently the White House would receive decrypts that never appeared in the summaries at all. Just as frequently the summaries contained material that never reached the White House in the form of decrypts. A message from the Japanese ambassador in Berlin informing Tokyo of German appraisals of the military and political situation after the Allied invasion of Sicily is discussed in the Magic Diplomatic Summary for 19 July 1943, but the relevant intercept was never forwarded to the president. The summary for 24 July condenses two Japanese messages that contained information on Allied bombing of Indo-China. These messages appear among the items selected by OP-20-GI on that day for distribution to its customers; neither was earmarked for the White House, although both went to the chief of naval operations. The implication is clear. The White House (receiving decrypts from the navy) and the State Department (receiving the Magic summary from the army) were not necessarily reading the same signals intelligence, a situation not conducive to the effective integration of intelligence into the foreign policy process.

When, in February 1944, General George Marshall learned that the president was not receiving the Magic Diplomatic Summaries (known as the "Brown Books" from the color of their cardboard covers), he proposed binding the more important summaries into a slim pamphlet with black covers for delivery every day to the White House.[25] Apparently, no examples of these army "Black Books" have surfaced, so it is impossible to determine if or for how long this proposal was implemented. Since Roosevelt continued to receive signals intelligence through his naval aide until his death in April 1945, it is likely that the Black Books did not change the president's long-established practice of receiving actual decrypts from the navy. Of course, in the last few months of his life, the president's health was so precarious and his energy so easily depleted that he was able to devote less and less time to governmental affairs. It probably made little difference by then in what form signals intelligence arrived at the White House.[26]

The decision-making style of high authorities also undercut the impact of signals intelligence. For example, Franklin Roosevelt, who reserved for himself all important foreign policy decisions, was supremely confident of his ability to understand the international scene and his country's place in it. His approach to foreign affairs depended more on intuition than on information, and his posture toward certain countries (e.g., China and France) or issues (decolonization) was as likely to reflect personal biases as professional briefings.[27] In his dealings with foreign leaders he expected to prevail through the exercise of will and persuasive charm rather than the careful reading of intelligence reports and briefing books. When he wanted information, he tended to avoid formal intelligence channels, preferring instead to canvass indiscriminately the opinion of official and private visitors to the White House, some of whom had no more claim to his attention than an old school tie or a social relationship. His idiosyncratic decision-making style, with its reliance on personality and intuition and its abhorrence of system, made him a poor "customer" for the information services. One student of the president's attitude toward intelligence has noted: "He much preferred his own wide range of contacts—inside and outside government—from whom he gleaned bits and pieces of information. From these, and from his own instincts and preferences, FDR arrived at conclusions that were often at variance with intelligence analysis."[28]

Roosevelt was especially insensitive to the value of signals intelligence. He seems to have considered Arlington Hall's precious product as no more reliable than other forms of intelligence. There is little evidence that sigint engaged his attention, and there is no evidence that he ever specifically asked to see decrypts from a particular target. Content to have a handful of decrypts read to him while he completed his morning toilette or enjoyed an afternoon massage, Roosevelt received (and may have wanted) from the messages little beyond a general sense of that day's intelligence "headlines." This rather cavalier attitude denied him a full appreciation of the source and its importance. Indeed, even after years of receiving signals intelligence, Roosevelt seemed to have only the vaguest notion of what the codebreakers were doing for him. In November 1943, when sigint coverage of Tokyo's diplomatic communications was practically total and access to Japanese military traffic was increasing dramatically, the president complained to his secretaries of war and navy that the United States was getting "practically nothing from the inside of Japan" and urged Stimson and Knox to secure better information about Tokyo's capabilities and intentions. Characterizing the president's complaint as "a staggering statement given both the quality and quantity of Japanese SIGINT that reached him daily," one historian has concluded that "Roosevelt seems never to have grasped that SIGINT provided him with the best intelligence in the history of warfare."[29]

The president's failure to grasp the diplomatic advantage proffered by signals intelligence would have marginalized the codebreakers even if their efforts had not been constrained by operational difficulties. Together, the various factors ensured that, for all its expansion and achievement, signals intelligence would have little appreciable impact on American diplomacy in the period 1930–1945.

NOTES

Introduction

1. See, for example, Ralph Bennett, *Ultra in the West: The Normandy Campaign, 1944-1945* (London: Hutchinson and Company, 1980) and *Ultra and the Mediterranean Strategy* (New York: William Morrow, 1989). For examples from the Pacific theater, see Edward Drea, *MacArthur's Ultra: Codebreaking and the War Against Japan, 1942-1945* (Lawrence: University Press of Kansas, 1992); and Frederick Parker, *A Priceless Advantage: U.S. Navy Communications Intelligence and the Battles of Coral Sea, Midway, and the Aleutians* (Fort Meade, Md.: Center for Cryptologic History, National Security Agency, 1993).

2. An exception to this generalization is the pathbreaking study by Robin Denniston, *Churchill's Secret War: Diplomatic Decrypts, the Foreign Office and Turkey, 1942-44* (New York: St. Martin's Press, 1997).

1. Antecedents

1. For a history of cryptology, see David Kahn, *The Codebreakers: The Story of Secret Writing* (New York: Macmillan, 1967).

2. Ibid., pp. 176, 181-186.

3. Ibid., pp. 218-229.

4. Wayne G. Barker, ed., *The History of Codes and Ciphers in the United States Prior to World War I* (Laguna Hills, Calif.: Aegean Park Press, 1978), pp. 134-135. Parker Hitt wrote the *Manual for the Solution of Military Ciphers* (1916), a small classic in the literature of cryptology and the first book on the subject to be published in the United States.

5. In the summer of 1916 the army could identify only six officers who had any interest, let alone competence, in codes and ciphers. Barker, *History of Codes and Ciphers in the United States Prior to World War I*, p. 135.

6. Kahn, *The Codebreakers,* pp. 371–372; Wayne G. Barker, ed., *The History of Codes and Ciphers in the United States During World War I* (Laguna Hills, Calif.: Aegean Park Press, 1979), p. 6.

7. Barker, *History of Codes and Ciphers in the United States During World War I,* p. 23.

8. Ibid., p. 78.

9. Ibid., pp. 87–99; Kahn, *The Codebreakers,* p. 353. A cryptanalytic unit attached to American Expeditionary Force headquarters in France successfully attacked German army field ciphers.

10. Wayne G. Barker, ed., *The History of Codes and Ciphers in the United States During the Period Between the World Wars,* part 1, *1919–1929* (Laguna Hills, Calif.: Aegean Park Press, 1979), pp. 47–48.

11. Kahn, *The Codebreakers,* p. 355. The office later moved to East Thirty-seventh Street.

12. Barker, *History of Codes and Ciphers in the United States During the Period Between the World Wars,* p. 86.

13. Herbert O. Yardley, *The American Black Chamber* (1931; reprint, Laguna Hills, Calif.: Aegean Park Press, n.d.), p. 332.

14. Barker, *History of Codes and Ciphers in the United States During the Period Between the World Wars,* pp. 94–100; Kahn, *The Codebreakers,* p. 357.

15. Kahn, *The Codebreakers,* pp. 358–359; Barker, *History of Codes and Ciphers in the United States During the Period Between the World Wars,* p. 69.

16. John Chapman, "No Final Solution: A Survey of the Cryptanalytical Capabilities of German Military Agencies, 1926–35," *Intelligence and National Security* 1:1 (January 1986): 30–31; John Ferris, "Whitehall's Black Chamber: British Cryptology and the Government Code and Cypher School, 1919–29," *Intelligence and National Security* 2:1 (January 1987): 74ff.

17. Chapman, "No Final Solution," p. 27; Ferris, "Whitehall's Black Chamber," p. 71.

18. Robert G. Angevine, "Gentlemen Do Read Each Other's Mail: American Intelligence in the Interwar Era," *Intelligence and National Security* 7:2 (April 1992): 5–6.

19. Ferris, "Whitehall's Black Chamber," p. 89.

20. Barker, *History of Codes and Ciphers in the United States During the Period Between the World Wars,* pp. 70–73. During the 1920s, the Government Code and Cypher School ranged between eighty and ninety people, of whom approximately twenty-five were cryptanalysts. Ferris, "Whitehall's Black Chamber," pp. 61, 89.

21. Louis Kruh, "Stimson, the Black Chamber, and the 'Gentleman's Mail' Quote," *Cryptologia* 12:2 (April 1988): 68ff.

22. "Responsibility for the Solution of Intercepted Enemy Communications in War," 4 April 1929, Correspondence re Permanent Organization for Cipher Work, box 777, Historic Cryptologic Collection (HCC), National Security Agency, Re-

cord Group 457, National Archives and Records Administration (NARA), College Park, Maryland.

23. Quotes in Adjutant General to the Chief Signal Officer, 22 April 1930, Correspondence re Permanent Organization for Cipher Work, box 777, HCC.

24. "Memorandum recording conclusions of a conference in the office of the chief signal officer on 19 July 1929," Data on Personnel Assigned to MID, 1929–1937, box 777, HCC.

25. Ibid.

26. William Friedman to Swagar Sherley, 19 March 1924, box 1, Herbert Yardley Collection, National Security Agency, Record Group 457, NARA. Unless otherwise indicated, all details concerning Friedman's association with Riverbank Laboratories are drawn from this letter.

27. William Friedman to Herbert Yardley, 1 May 1919, and Herbert Yardley to William Friedman, 1 July 1919, box 1, Yardley Collection.

28. Herbert Yardley to William Friedman, 14 August 1919, Yardley Collection.

29. Kahn, *The Codebreakers,* p. 384.

30. Major J. O. Mauborgne to William Friedman, 16 October and 15 November 1920, box 1, Yardley Collection. In later years Friedman said that he was denied a commission because a physical exam revealed a heart condition.

31. Memorandum for the Executive Officer, 30 January 1939, SIS. General Files, 1939, box 779, HCC.

32. Kahn, *The Codebreakers,* pp. 384–385.

33. "Memorandum concerning conclusions of a conference in the office of the chief signal officer on 19 July 1929," Data on Personnel Assigned to MID, 1929–1937, box 777, HCC; Barker, *History of Codes and Ciphers in the United States During the Period Between the World Wars,* p. 127.

34. Thomas Parrish, *The Ultra Americans: The U.S. Role in Breaking the Nazi Codes* (New York: Stein and Day, 1986), p. 28.

35. Memorandum for the Executive Officer [from Major D. M. Crawford], 7 February 1930, Data on Personnel Assigned to MID, 1929–1937, box 777, HCC; Solomon Kullback oral history, NSA-OH-17-82, p. 2. All oral histories used in this study are from the Center for Cryptologic History, National Security Agency, Fort George Meade, Maryland.

36. Frank Rowlett, *The Story of Magic: Memoirs of an American Cryptologic Pioneer* (Laguna Hills, Calif.: Aegean Park Press, 1998), pp. 27–29. John Hurt was beloved for his eccentricities as much as he was respected for his language abilities. In the War Department cafeteria he would select several items, arrange the plates in a circle on his tray, and then take a bite from each plate in sequence. He never learned to drive, and he discomfited taxi drivers by forgetting his home address. As a pedestrian he paid scant attention to traffic, believing that a cold stare would stop any oncoming driver. On at least one occasion he was wrong. Knocked to the street after stepping in front of a moving vehicle, he was assisted to his feet by the

shocked driver. To the driver's anxious inquiry, "Are you hurt?" he calmly replied, "Yes, John B." and entered the folklore of the Signal Intelligence Service. Kullback oral history, NSA-OH-17-82, pp. 15–16.

2. *Launching a Service*

1. Frank Rowlett oral history, NSA-OH-01-74, vol. 1, p. 21c.

2. Ibid.; Solomon Kullback oral history, NSA-OH-17-82, p. 4. Unless otherwise indicated, the description of the training program depends on the Kullback and Rowlett oral histories.

3. "Current Activities of the Signal Intelligence Section," 8 March 1934, SIS General Files, 1934, box 778, HCC; Frank Rowlett, *The Story of Magic: Memoirs of an American Cryptologic Pioneer* (Laguna Hills, Calif.: Aegean Park Press, 1998), pp. 59ff.

4. The Amtorg affair is discussed in chapter 6.

5. A substitution cipher replaces a letter in a message with another letter or a number (*attack* = 1 20 20 1 3 11). A transposition cipher scrambles the letters of a message (*attack* = tktaca).

6. "Current Activities of the Signal Intelligence Section," 8 March 1934, SIS General Files, 1934, box 778, HCC; "Current Activities of the Signal Intelligence Section," 7 March 1935, General Files, 1935, box 794, HCC.

7. John Hurt, "A Version of the Japanese Problem in the Signal Intelligence Service," pp. 1–2, box 1413, HCC.

8. In a monoalphabetic cipher, each letter of a message is replaced by one cipher equivalent ($a = 1, b = 2, \ldots, z = 26$). In a polyalphabetic cipher, each letter of the message may be replaced by two or more cipher equivalents in a prearranged pattern ($a = 1$ or 27 or 53, $b = 2$ or 28 or 54, $\ldots, z = 26$ or 52 or 78).

9. Kullback oral history, NSA-OH-17-82, p. 13.

10. SRH-001, "Historical Background of the Signal Security Agency," vol. 3, p. 273, Record Group 457, NARA. All SRH items are archived in the National Security Agency's Record Group 457 at the National Archives.

11. Ibid., pp. 276, 282. The school moved to Fort Monmouth and began to train enlisted personnel in 1939.

12. Memorandum from J. W. McClaran, 10 April 1933, SRH-200, "Army-Navy Collaboration, 1931–1945," part 1, SRH-200.

13. Annual Report of War Plans and Training Division, FY 1931, General Files, SIS, 1931, box 752, HCC.

14. Adjutant General to the Chief Signal Officer, 22 April 1930, Correspondence re Permanent Organization for Cipher Work, box 777, HCC.

15. Major W. Simpson to Major R. Halpin, 1 October 1930, Correspondence Providing Direction to Army Intercept Stations, box 751, HCC.

16. Major D. M. Crawford to Chief Signal Officer, 30 November 1931, General Files, SIS, 1931, box 752, HCC.

17. For a sample of compilation activities, see "Current Activities of Signal Intelligence Section," SIS. General Files, 1934, box 778, HCC.

18. A one-part code arranges words and letters in strict alphabetical order and their code equivalents in strict numerical sequence (A = 0001, Aachen = 0002, etc.). A code in which the plain-language elements are arranged alphabetically but the numerical equivalents are mixed (A = 2471, Aachen = 6101) is known as a two-part code because it requires two books, the encoding book in which the plaintext is arranged in alphabetical order and the decoding book in which the code values are arranged in numerical order.

19. Kullback oral history, NSA-OH-17-82, p. 22.

20. SRH-001, "Historical Background of the Signal Security Agency," vol. 3, pp. 73ff.

21. Adjutant General to Chief Signal Officer, 22 April 1930, Correspondence re Permanent Organization for Cipher Work, box 777, HCC.

22. J. O. Mauborgne to G-2, Ninth Corps Area, 12 September 1932, Intercept/Crypto Correspondence, 1927–1941, box 781, HCC.

23. Captain John Ferriter to Department Signal Officer (Philippines), 1 August 1932, SIS. General Files, 1934, box 778, HCC.

24. Memorandum by Major Akin for the Executive Officer, 25 August 1932, and the Adjutant General to the Commander, Philippines Department, 26 October 1932, SIS. General Files, 1932–1939, box 778, HCC.

25. "Report on Provisional Radio Intelligence Detachment, 1 October 1933 to 17 October 1934," and "Report on Radio Intercept for the Period 1 October 1933 to 1 July 1934," Reports on Radio Intercept, 1934, box 781, HCC.

26. C[ommander] in C[hief] Asiatic Fleet to Chief of Naval Operations, 2 August 1933, and Memorandum by Major W. B. Sullivan, USMC, 16 March 1933, SIS. General Files, 1934, box 778, HCC.

27. Lt. Col. Dawson Olmstead to Assistant Chief of Staff, G-2, 19 September 1934, SIS. General Files, 1934, box 778, HCC; "Review of Signal Intelligence Activities in the Philippines, 1934–41," box 954, HCC.

28. W. Preston Corderman to Chief Signal Officer, 28 March 1936, and Prosser to Chief Signal Officer, 23 February 1937, Radio Intelligence Detachment File, 1930–1940, box 781, HCC.

29. Rowlett oral history, NSA-OH-01-74, pp. 171–173.

30. Ibid., p. 136; Kullback oral history, NSA-OH-17-82, p. 17.

31. SRH-361, "History of the Signal Security Agency, vol. 2: The General Cryptanalytic Problem," pp. 31–32.

32. "Report on Early Work Against Japanese Diplomatic Messages Enciphered by Machine," box 751, HCC. This report asserts that there was no effort to solve the RED machine until October 1936. Translation files indicate, however, that be-

fore that date as many as fifty RED messages were being read each month. See "RED Translations," National Cryptologic Museum Library, National Security Agency, Fort George Meade, Maryland.

33. Washington to Tokyo, 17 April 1936; Washington to Bogota, 7 April 1936; Tokyo to Washington, 25 April 1936, "RED Translations."

34. Tokyo to Bogota, 12 August 1935, "RED Translations."

35. Tokyo to Washington, 8 October 1936, "RED Translations."

36. For a survey of Roosevelt's early diplomacy, see Robert Dallek, *Franklin D. Roosevelt and American Foreign Policy, 1932–1945* (New York: Oxford University Press, 1979), parts 1, 2.

37. SRH-361, "History of the Signal Security Agency, vol. 2: The General Cryptanalytic Problem," pp. 34–35.

38. SRH-134, "Expansion of the Signal Intelligence Service from 1930 to 7 December 1941," p. 16; Kullback oral history, NSA-OH-17-82, p. 19.

39. "Panama Canal Department: Quarterly Report on Solution Activity, 1 October 1937–31 December 1937," box 706, HCC; SRH-001, "Historical Background of the Signal Security Agency," vol. 3, pp. 311–312.

40. Kullback oral history, NSA-OH-17-82, pp. 30–34; SRH-001, "Historical Background of the Signal Security Agency," vol. 3, p. 315.

41. Information from Samuel Snyder.

42. Ibid.; Kullback oral history, NSA-OH-17-82, p. 22.

43. "Intercept Activity of Signal Intelligence Detachment, Panama Canal Department," 26 January 1938, SIS. General Files, box 778, HCC.

44. General Mauborgne to Signal Officer, Eighth Corps Area, 11 January 1938; Colonel Compton to Chief Signal Officer, 23 February 1938; General Mauborgne to Signal Officer, Eighth Corps Area, 28 February 1938, SIS. General Files, box 778, HCC.

45. Major Eastman to Signal Officer, Hawaiian Department, 21 July 1938; General Mauborgne to Signals, Hawaii, 18 January 1938, SIS. General Files, 1938, box 778, HCC.

46. General Mauborgne to Signal Officer, Ninth Corps Area, 18 March 1939, SIS. General Files, 1939, box 779, HCC.

47. See, for example, "Special Report: Japanese Firm in Mexico," 18 April 1938, SIS. General Files, 1938, box 778, HCC.

48. Lt. Colonel Carr to the Adjutant General, 28 May 1938, SIS. General Files, 1938, box 778, HCC.

49. Major S. B. Akin to David Sarnoff, 14 July 1933, and Jewett to General Mauborgne, 15 July 1938, SIS. General Files, 1933, box 778, HCC.

50. SRH-001, "Historical Background of the Signal Security Agency," vol. 3, p. 300. In December 1938 the Signal Corps proposed a formal amendment to the Communications Act of 1934 that would exempt federal agencies from the prohibitions against intercepting and sharing private communications. When the Fed-

eral Communications Commission advised that exemptions would require explicit and detailed wording, the Signal Corps withdrew its proposal for fear of attracting public attention to its signals intelligence program. Memorandum for the Chief of Staff, 8 March 1939, SIS. General File, 1939, box 779, HCC.

51. Rowlett oral history, NSA-OH-01-74, pp. 71, 151; Earle Cook oral history, NSA-OH-14-82, pp. 21–23.

52. "Assignment of SIS Personnel, August–September 1938," box 751, HCC. Despite its title, this report actually describes assignments in 1939.

53. Tokyo to Rome, 30 September 1937, and Paris to Tokyo, 22 September 1937, "RED Translations."

54. Tokyo to Washington, 13 October 1937 and 16 October 1937, "RED Translations."

55. Information from Frank Lewis.

56. "Italian Codes and Ciphers, 1939–43," box 1388, HCC.

57. "Brief Summary of Solutions of Mexican Diplomatic Codes and Ciphers, 1922–1929," box 33, Yardley Collection.

58. David Kahn, "Roosevelt, MAGIC, and ULTRA," *Cryptologia* 16:4 (October 1992): 289. In the absence of documentary evidence, the date that the White House began receiving decrypts from SIS remains uncertain. Kahn depends on the memory of Frank Rowlett.

59. SRH-001, "Historical Background of the Signal Security Agency," vol. 3, p. 297; "History of Distribution of Intercept Traffic in SSA," box 1380, HCC.

60. Tokyo to Washington and Brussels, 13 October 1937, "RED Translations"; Grew to the Secretary of State, 13 October 1937 and 15 October 1937, *Foreign Relations of the United States, 1937,* vol. 4, *The Far East* (Washington, D.C.: Government Printing Office, 1954), pp. 74, 80.

61. The first decrypts concerning the agreement (the German-Soviet Treaty of Non-Aggression) were published on 28 August, four days after the world's press carried the story. See Moscow to Tokyo, 24 August 1939 [translated 28 August], Diplomatic Message Translations, box 287, HCC.

62. Grew to the Secretary of State, 1 October 1937, and Memorandum by the Chief, Division of Far Eastern Affairs, 28 October 1937, *Foreign Relations of the United States, 1937,* vol. 1, *General* (Washington, D.C.: Government Printing Office, 1954), pp. 606–608.

63. Tokyo to Berlin, 1 October 1937, Tokyo to Rome, 30 September 1937, Berlin to Tokyo, 19 October 1937, "RED Translations."

64. Paris to Tokyo, 25 August 1939, and Bern to Tokyo, 23 August 1939, "RED Translations."

65. For an appraisal of Roosevelt's biases in intelligence, see Christopher Andrew, *For the President's Eyes Only: Secret Intelligence and the American Presidency from Washington to Bush* (New York: HarperCollins, 1995), chap. 3.

66. On Austrian and Hungarian cryptanalysis, see David Alvarez, "Axis Sigint

Collaboration: A Limited Partnership," *Intelligence and National Security* 14:1 (Spring 1999): 2–4, 13. For British and German success against the RED machine, see Army Security Agency, *European Axis Signals Intelligence in World War II,* vol. 6 (Washington, D.C.: Army Security Agency, 1946), p. 29; and Cipher Deavours and Louis Kruh, *Machine Cryptography and Modern Cryptanalysis* (Dedham, Mass.: Artech, 1985), p. 215. I am indebted to Ralph Erskine for the Deavours-Kruh citation.

3. Toward Pearl Harbor

1. "Correspondence on the Expansion of the Signal Intelligence Service, 1939," box 1402, HCC.
2. General Mauborgne to the Assistant Chief of Staff (War Plans), 14 September 1939, box 1402, HCC.
3. General Tyner to the Adjutant General, 18 September 1939, SIS. General File, 1939, box 779, HCC. In 1938 the monitoring station at Fort Monmouth moved to Fort Hancock, twenty miles to the north.
4. William Lutwiniak oral history, NSA-OH-10-81, p. 2.
5. Colonel Eastman to G-2, 25 October 1939, SIS. General File, 1939, box 779, HCC; information from Frank Lewis.
6. General Mauborgne to Signal Officer, Panama Department, 23 October 1939, SIS. General File, 1939, box 779, HCC.
7. "The Status of the Cryptanalysis of Japanese, German, Italian, and Mexican Systems, August 1940," box 587, HCC.
8. Ibid.
9. Ibid.
10. Ibid.
11. William Friedman, "Preliminary Historical Report on the Solution of the B Machine," 14 October 1940, History of Japanese Cipher Machines, box 808, HCC; Berlin to Tokyo, 4 January 1939, Diplomatic Message Translations, box 286, HCC.
12. Los Angeles to Berlin, 16 April 1940 (translated 11 May); Guatemala City to Berlin, 6 May 1940; São Paulo to Berlin, 3 May 1940, Diplomatic Message Translations, box 288, HCC.
13. Washington to Rome, 3 May 1940, and Rome to Cairo, 8 May 1940, Diplomatic Message Translations, box 289, HCC.
14. Copenhagen to Mexican Government, 7 May 1940, and Mexican Government to Brussels, 11 May 1940, Diplomatic Message Translations, box 289, HCC.
15. Berlin to Hsinking (for Tokyo) and Vienna to Tokyo, 22 May 1940, and Rome to Tokyo, 29 May 1940, Diplomatic Message Translations, box 288, HCC. Compare the reports of William Bullitt, the American ambassador in Paris, in Orville Bullitt, *For the President, Personal and Secret: Correspondence Between Franklin D. Roosevelt and William C. Bullitt* (Boston: Houghton Mifflin, 1972), pp. 415, 419.

16. Prague to Tokyo, 17 May 1940, Diplomatic Message Translations, box 288, HCC.

17. Tokyo to Singapore, 10 April 1940, Diplomatic Message Translations, box 288, HCC.

18. SRH-134, "Expansion of the Signal Intelligence Service from 1930 to 7 December 1941," p. 22.

19. General Mauborgne to Signal Officer, Philippine Department, 6 December 1940, SIS General Correspondence File, 1940, box 779, HCC.

20. In 1930 a publisher had informed the War Department that Yardley was peddling a book about his intelligence work. An army officer met Yardley to express the War Department's concerns, but Yardley refused to allow the department to screen his writings. James Bamford, *The Puzzle Palace: A Report on America's Most Secret Agency* (Boston: Houghton Mifflin, 1982), pp. 18–19.

21. David Kahn, *Kahn on Codes: Secrets of the New Cryptology* (New York: Macmillan, 1983), pp. 67–68; Maochun Yu, "Chinese Codebreakers, 1927–1945," *Intelligence and National Security* 14:1 (March 1999): 201–213.

22. Information from Frank Rowlett; Rowlett oral history, NSA-OH-01-74, pp. 130–134; "Yardley Papers Submitted to General Akin," box 1, Yardley Collection. Another member of the Japanese section recalled that Yardley's report was of some use in gaining an understanding of Japanese military ciphers. Information from Samuel Snyder.

23. Once it had solved a Japanese diplomatic system, the navy usually did not decrypt and translate the intercepted messages because it lacked the necessary staff and had little interest in purely diplomatic intelligence.

24. Director of Naval Communications to the Secretary of the Navy, 21 January 1931, T5-710, Historical Collection, Center for Cryptologic History, National Security Agency. I am indebted to Bob Hanyok of the Center for Cryptologic History for calling my attention to this document.

25. The Amtorg affair is discussed in chapter 6.

26. Director of Naval Communications to the Chief of Naval Operations, 29 October 1931, General Files, SIS, 1931, box 752, HCC.

27. In 1931 Germany was not a world power, since Hitler had not yet taken office and embarked on the rearmament programs that would reestablish Germany's military strength.

28. Memorandum for the Director from J. W. McClaran, 10 April 1933, SRH-200, "Army-Navy Collaboration, 1931–1945," part 1. See also the correspondence in General Files, SIS, 1931, box 752, HCC.

29. Major W. Rumbough to Major Thomas Finley (G-2), 19 August 1935, SIS Historical Documents, 1930–1939, box 752, HCC.

30. Commander Kingman to Major Akin, 10 April 1934, SIS. General Files, 1934, box 778, HCC; Colonel Akin to Commander Safford, 1 December 1939, SIS. General File, 1939, box 779, HCC.

31. "Coordination of Intercept and Decrypting Activities of the Army and Navy, 25 July 1940," in SRH-200, "Army-Navy Collaboration, 1931–1945."

32. Robert Louis Benson, *A History of U.S. Communications Intelligence During World War II: Policy and Administration* (Fort Meade, Md.: Center for Cryptologic History, National Security Agency, 1997), p. 8 (hereinafter cited as *History*).

33. Ibid., pp. 9, 15; SRH-001, "Historical Background of the Signal Security Agency," vol. 3, p. 281.

34. Benson, *History,* pp. 8, 10.

35. Ibid., p. 13.

36. Bradley F. Smith, *The Ultra-Magic Deals and the Most Secret Special Relationship, 1940–1946* (Novato, Calif.: Presidio Press, 1993), p. 69.

37. J. Edgar Hoover to General Miles, 14 December 1940, and Colonel Akin to Assistant Chief of Staff (G-2), 16 January 1941, SIS. General Correspondence File, 1940, box 779, HCC; J. Edgar Hoover to General Miles, 19 June 1941, SIS. General Correspondence File, 1941, box 780, HCC.

38. Memorandum for Admiral Noyes, 27 July 1940. I am indebted to Stephen Budiansky, who kindly provided a copy of this memorandum.

39. Benson, *History,* p. 12.

40. Quoted in ibid., p. 17.

41. Alan Harris Bath, *Tracking the Axis Enemy: The Triumph of Anglo-American Naval Intelligence* (Lawrence: University Press of Kansas, 1998), p. 25.

42. Ibid., pp. 33–34.

43. Quoted in Benson, *History,* p. 16.

44. "Cooperation with GCCS," Clark Files: British Liaison, 1940–1945, box 1413, HCC. The Akin-Friedman memorandum is undated but is generally thought to have been written on or about 1 September 1940. See "A Chronology of the Cooperation Between the SSA and the London Offices of GCCS," p. 1, box 1, Yardley Collection (hereinafter cited as "Chronology").

45. Memorandum for the Chief of Staff, 9 September 1940, Clark Files, British Liaison, 1940–1945, box 1413, HCC; Benson, *History,* p. 18.

46. With the machine Tokyo also used a shorthand code of arbitrary letters to represent numbers, punctuation signs, and frequently used syllables and words (e.g., BKW = United States). This practice further complicated the work of the codebreakers, who could not be sure if they were correctly guessing the values of the 20's.

47. Frank Rowlett recalled the dramatic breakthrough in Theodore Hannah, "Frank Rowlett: A Personal Profile," *Cryptologic Spectrum* 11:2 (Spring 1981): 5. See also David Kahn, "Pearl Harbor and the Inadequacy of Cryptanalysis," *Cryptologia* 15:4 (October 1991): 284–285. For a technical description of the solution of PURPLE, see William Friedman, "Preliminary Historical Report on the Solution of the B Machine," 14 October 1940, History of Japanese Cipher Machines, box 808, HCC.

48. Smith, *The Ultra-Magic Deals,* pp. 50–51.

49. No copy of this alleged agreement survives in the documents currently available. Its existence is surmised from a reference in Henry Stimson's diary (16 May 1941) and in a postwar memoir by Laurance Safford, head of OP-20-G and a leading opponent of cooperation. See Dundas P. Tucker, "Rhapsody in Purple: A New History of Pearl Harbor, Part 1," *Cryptologia* 6:3 (July 1982): 193.

50. Kullback oral history, NSA-OH-17-82, p. 67. SIS originally intended to send Solomon Kullback in place of Friedman, but Kullback's wife objected, and he stayed home.

51. Smith, *The Ultra-Magic Deals,* pp. 54, 55.

52. Rowlett's appointment preceded Sinkov's and Kullback's by a few days, so technically he was senior.

53. The Voynich manuscript is an illustrated manuscript dating from the late Middle Ages. It is written in a secret language no one has been able to identify or decrypt.

54. Prescott Currier oral history, NSA-OH-38-80, p. 52.

55. Donald Gish, "A Cryptologic Analysis," *International Journal of Intelligence and Counterintelligence* 6:4 (Winter 1993): 387 n. 17. By January 1941, OP-20-G had recovered only about 3 percent of the values in JN-25B.

56. Prescott Currier oral history, NSA-OH-38-80, p. 56. Unless otherwise indicated, all details concerning the mission to Britain are taken from this oral history.

57. Address by Admiral (Ret.) Prescott Currier, Cryptologic History Symposium, 13 November 1991, National Security Agency. See also Ralph Erskine, "Churchill and the Start of the Ultra-Magic Deals," *International Journal of Intelligence and Counterintelligence* 10:1 (Spring 1998): 66.

58. [Abraham Sinkov], "Report of Cryptographic Mission," box 1296, HCC. This report summarizes the nonnaval results of the mission. Unless otherwise indicated, all details concerning the results of the Sinkov-Rosen mission are drawn from this report. See also "Chronology," p. 2.

59. An additive is a string of numbers added to a code group to provide a double layer of security. For example, if the word *attack* is represented in a codebook by 11625, another number, say 42224, could be added to the code group to create a new group, 53849. This last number is transmitted as the cipher text. A one-time-pad is a collection of pages, each covered with groups of numbers. The numbers are random, and, therefore, each page is different from all others, except for one copy, which is used by the recipient of the message for deciphering purposes. The sender uses each page once and only once as an additive to encipher a message, and then destroys the page. After the recipient deciphers the message, he destroys his copy of the additive page. The nonrepetitive nature of the additive makes it very difficult to solve the OTP system.

60. "Cryptographic Codes and Ciphers: Italian," box 1388, HCC; "Annual Report of the Chief Signal Officer and Miscellaneous Studies, FY 1942-1943," box 832, HCC.

61. General Mauborgne to the Assistant Chief of Staff (G-2), 30 April 1941, SIS. General Correspondence File, 1941, box 780, HCC; "Axis Material Sent to GCCS in 1941 and 1942," box 1371, HCC. In the Far East, naval cryptanalysts on Corregidor Island (Philippines) cooperated with their British counterparts at the Far East Combined Bureau (Singapore) on JN-25B, and in June 1941 OP-20-G began to exchange materials with Bletchley Park. Benson, *History,* p. 21.

62. Report by A. G. Denniston, 31 October 1941, HW 14/45, Public Record Office (PRO), Kew. All information concerning Denniston's visit is drawn from this report.

63. In October 1941, for example, a British officer delivered to SIS two large mailbags of Japanese army traffic as well as notes on British work against these messages. Undated memorandum, SIS Personnel, Organization and Duties, box 751, HCC.

64. General Mauborgne to the Assistant Chief of Staff (G-2), 28 October 1940, and Chinese Military Attaché to General Miles, 28 December 1940, "Sale to Chinese Government," box 790, HCC; General Mauborgne to General Shid-Ming Chu [*sic*], 10 July 1941, SIS, General Correspondence File, 1941, box 780, HCC.

65. Military Attaché, Union of South Africa Legation, to Colonel Arthur Harris, 29 November 1940, and Colonel Eastman to the Assistant Chief of Staff (G-2), 27 November 1940, SIS, General Correspondence File, 1940, box 779, HCC.

66. John Bryden, *Best-Kept Secret: Canadian Secret Intelligence in the Second World War* (Toronto: Lester Publishing, 1993), chap. 1.

67. General Mauborgne to the Assistant Chief of Staff (G-2), 20 November 1940, Canadian-US Intercept Matters, box 797, HCC.

68. Canadian Legation (Washington) to the Secretary of State for External Affairs, 3 May 1941, Canadian Correspondence, box 1358, HCC.

69. The army and navy representatives preferred to limit the new organization to clandestine traffic, but Yardley, perhaps hoping to establish an early track record, successfully argued for the inclusion of Japanese diplomatic, the area in which he had the greatest expertise.

70. Bryden, *Best-Kept Secret,* pp. 54, 70, 85.

71. Quoted in ibid., p. 64.

72. Department of External Affairs to the High Commissioner in Great Britain, 23 September 1941, Canadian Correspondence, box 1358, HCC.

73. "Memorandum on the visit to Washington," 26 November 1941, Canadian Correspondence, box 1358, HCC.

74. SRH-364, "History of the Signal Security Agency, volume 1: Organization (part 1)," pp. 90–91.

75. KW messages appear in "Diplomatic Message Translations, 1941," box 300, HCC. A later report, "Solution of the Kryha Machine Cipher," box 1394, HCC, asserts that KW and another version of the Kryha machine, KC, were solved in the

fall of 1942, but this is belied by the presence of KW messages in the translation files from the fall of 1941.

76. "Brazilian Codes and Ciphers, 1917–1945," box 1, Yardley Collection. For the monitoring station, see Colonel R. W. Minckler to the Assistant Chief of Staff (G-2), 24 September 1941, SIS, General Correspondence File, 1941, box 780, HCC.

77. For Colombia, see Bogota to Berlin, 12 March 1941, Diplomatic Message Translations, box 294, HCC. For Vichy, see Fort de France to Vichy, 29 September 1941, Diplomatic Message Translations, box 300, HCC.

78. There is no documentation to date this arrangement. David Kahn ("Roosevelt, MAGIC, and ULTRA," *Cryptologia* 16:4 [October 1992]: 292) believes that it dates from August 1940. Lou Benson (*History,* p. 13) suggests a date after 3 October, since the army–navy sigint agreement of that date includes no mention of the arrangement. I incline toward a date following the solution of PURPLE, since that solution created the conditions addressed by the arrangement.

79. "Handling and dissemination of certain special material," 25 January 1941, in SRH-200, "Army-Navy Collaboration, 1931–1945, part 1."

80. "Dissemination to White House," Pearl Harbor Investigation and Miscellaneous Material, box 1360, HCC.

81. Ibid.; Memorandum for GZ File, 15 May 1941, Pearl Harbor Investigation and Miscellaneous Material, box 1360, HCC.

82. For the Stimson episode, see Christopher Andrew, *For the President's Eyes Only: Secret Intelligence and the American Presidency from Washington to Bush* (New York: HarperCollins, 1995), pp. 107–108.

83. James Barros and Richard Gregor, *Double Deception: Stalin, Hitler, and the Invasion of Russia* (DeKalb: Northern Illinois University Press, 1995), p. 43.

84. The proposals are detailed in most histories of Pearl Harbor. See, for example, Herbert Feis, *The Road to Pearl Harbor* (Princeton, N.J.: Princeton University Press, 1971), pp. 295, 309.

4. Marching to War

1. The experience of MS-6 is described in "Second Signal Battalion: Historical Background Information," box 1432, HCC. See also Robert Louis Benson, *A History of U.S. Communications Intelligence During World War II: Policy and Administration* (Fort Meade, Md.: Center for Cryptologic History, National Security Agency, 1997), p. 31.

2. As late as May 1942 SIS had a backlog of over one hundred thousand messages that had not been processed to any extent. General Strong to the Chief of Staff, 27 May 1942, Special Branch, G-2, Military Intelligence Division, box 1305, HCC.

3. Information from Frank Rowlett.

4. Alfred McCormack to Generals Bratton and Lee, 12 February 1942, Special Branch, G-2, Military Intelligence Division, box 1305, HCC.

5. Quoted in Benson, *History,* p. 36.

6. Colonel Carter Clarke to Alfred McCormack, 6 May 1942, Special Branch, G-2, Military Intelligence Division, box 1305, HCC.

7. Magic Diplomatic Summaries, 20, 21, 22 March 1942, Record Group 457, NARA.

8. Magic Diplomatic Summaries, 5 and 6 November 1944.

9. "War Experience of Alfred McCormack," pp. 10–11, McCormack Papers, box 1097, HCC.

10. Ibid., p. 23.

11. The Military Intelligence Service (MIS) was created in March 1942 to "operate and administer the service of collection, compilation, and dissemination of military intelligence." The old MID remained as a small staff organization under the assistant chief of staff for intelligence (G-2), and MIS acted as its operational arm. MIS claimed control over army signals intelligence, but the Signal Corps successfully rebuffed such a claim. The Signal Corps retained administrative control over SIS, but in practice operational guidelines were set by MIS. Benson, *History,* pp. 34, 36.

12. "Expansion of the Signal Intelligence Service," box 1296, HCC.

13. In the spring of 1942 the FBI's cryptanalytic section was working Axis diplomatic, clandestine, and commercial traffic as well as domestic criminal traffic.

14. This description of the discussions over allocation depends on Benson, *History,* pp. 48–54.

15. "Directives of Army and Navy Monitoring Stations," 19 March 1942, Army-Navy Directive Study, box 1374, HCC.

16. "SSA, History of Communications Branch," box 1380, HCC; "Second Signal Battalion: Historical Background Information," box 1432, HCC; Colonel Bullock to Colonel Clarke, 28 May 1942, SIS Reports: Miscellaneous, 1940–1942, box 781, HCC.

17. SRH-349, "Achievements of the Signal Security Agency in World War II," p. 6.

18. Information from Ann Caracristi and Dale Marston.

19. Information from Ann Caracristi.

20. Information from Katharine Swift.

21. Information from Juanita Moody.

22. William Lutwiniak oral history, NSA-OH-10-81, pp. 3–5; Norman Willis oral history, NSA-OH-34-80, p. 8.

23. In June the Signal Intelligence Service was renamed the Signal Intelligence Division. In the next year it would be renamed the Signal Security Division, the Signal Security Service, and finally the Signal Security Agency.

24. SRH-361, "History of the Signal Security Agency: The General Cryptanalytic Problem," pp. 5–6.

25. As late as September 1942, the British liaison officer observed that "Kullback, who could be so helpful, is apt to believe that he has his finger on the pulse of everything; the organization being what it is he has not, and often there are cases of malnutrition that he has not noticed or deemed of no importance." Stevens to Denniston, 28 September 1942, HW 14/53, PRO.

26. William Friedman to Alistair Denniston, 13 November 1941, HW 14/22, PRO.

27. Earle Cook oral history, NSA-OH-14-82, pp. 51–52; information from Frank Lewis.

28. SRH-364, "History of the Signal Security Agency, vol. 1: Organization, Part 2," pp. 154ff.

29. Wilma Davis, who had joined SIS before Pearl Harbor, ran the Japanese army address problem, which had a staff of sixty. Delia Sinkov, the wife of Abraham Sinkov, supervised thirty people working Japanese army tactical systems. Mary Jo Dunning directed another unit in the large Japanese army section. Julia Ward, former dean of Bryn Mawr College, was probably the highest-ranking woman at Arlington Hall. She supervised the editing and publishing of all translations. Information from Ann Caracristi.

30. William Lutwiniak oral history, NSA-OH-10-81, p. 13.

31. Information from Juanita Moody.

32. Information from Katharine Swift and Kathleen Fenton.

33. Information from Kathleen Fenton.

34. Information from Katharine Swift.

35. Ann Caracristi, address delivered at the National Security Agency, 1998.

36. Intelligence Division Executive Council, Minutes of the Meeting of 24 May 1945, box 995, HCC.

37. One authority suggests that as early as January or February 1942 Canada's Examination Unit was passing to SIS decrypts of Vichy diplomatic messages. John Bryden, *Best-Kept Secret: Canadian Secret Intelligence in the Second World War* (Toronto: Lester Publishing, 1993), pp. 125–126. A document from the fall of 1942 suggests a date later in the year. T. A. Stone to Ronald Macdonnell, 12 October 1942, Canadian Correspondence, box 1358, HCC.

38. Frank Cain, "Signals Intelligence in Australia During the Pacific War," *Intelligence and National Security* 14:1 (Spring 1999): 40–61.

39. "To Chinese Government," 15 February 1942, Sale to Chinese Government—Correspondence with China, box 790, HCC. Most of the material provided by China dated from 1938 to 1939.

40. "Notes on diplomatic liaison with U.S.A.," enclosed with Denniston to Tiltman, 8 March 1942, HW 14/46, PRO.

41. "Report by Lieut. Colonel J. H. Tiltman on his visit to North America dur-

ing March and April 1942," HW 14/46, PRO. Unless otherwise indicated, the description of Tiltman's mission depends upon this report.

42. "Notes on diplomatic liaison with U.S.A."

43. The U-boat campaign also benefited from the solution by German naval cryptanalysts of the cipher used by the Allies to route convoys across the Atlantic.

44. Final Report, British-American-Canadian Radio Intelligence Discussions, box 1395, HCC. The description of the conference proceedings depends upon this report.

45. Some recommendations were definitely not implemented, such as the recommendation that the three governments establish a standing committee to coordinate sigint operations. On the plotting centers, see Alan Harris Bath, *Tracking the Axis Enemy: The Triumph of Anglo-American Naval Intelligence* (Lawrence: University Press of Kansas, 1998), pp. 75–76.

46. At the conference the Americans specifically acknowledged that they were currently receiving all the Italian and Spanish diplomatic traffic they desired, although those in OP-20-G said they wouldn't mind having more Italian naval.

47. In early 1942, as a result of perceived deficiencies in the administration of GCCS, Alistair Denniston was replaced as director of Bletchley Park by one of his deputies, Edward Travis. Denniston remained in GCCS as chief of civil (diplomatic) cryptanalysis, which was detached from Bletchley Park and relocated to Berkeley Street, London.

48. Solomon Kullback, "The British GC & CS," 1 August 1942, pp. 6–7, Sinkov Papers, box 1413, HCC. All information concerning the Kullback mission and its results is taken from this report.

49. "Diplomatic Work at the War Department, Washington, New Delhi and Melbourne," 21 October 1942, HW 14/58, PRO.

50. See the list of papers under cover letter from Captain Harold Hayes, 8 July 1941, HW 14/45, PRO.

51. The documentation concerning Tiltman's mission explicitly identifies various items he carried to Washington, but the papers (including Tiltman's final report) mention no reciprocal gifts from the Americans.

52. Minutes of 8 August 1942, HW 14/48, PRO.

53. Alistair Denniston to Geoffrey Stevens, 22 December 1942, HW 14/62, PRO.

54. Franklin D. Roosevelt to General George Marshall, 9 July 1942; General George Strong to the Chief of Staff, 9 July 1942; General George Marshall to Franklin D. Roosevelt, 11 July 1942; all in Clark Files, British Liaison, 1940–1945, box 1413, HCC.

55. Benson, *History,* pp. 98–99.

56. Dill's response can be found under "General Marshall's letter of 13/12/42," Sinkov Papers, box 1413, HCC.

57. During 1942 OP-20-G attacked the German naval Enigma. In September 1942 a GCCS delegation visited Washington and secured an understanding,

the so-called Holden Agreement, in which the British agreed to collaborate with OP-20-G against German naval (mainly U-boat) communications. Benson, *History,* pp. 60–61.

58. Ibid., p. 101.

59. Ibid., pp. 105–106.

60. In a memorandum to Clarke, Taylor argued, "What we really want at this time is to gain a foothold in ENIGMA and develop technical competence and gradually develop a supplementary operation so as to improve joint coverage. What we ultimately want is independence." Quoted in Ibid., p. 107.

61. "Excerpts from Cable 4782," 14 May 1943, Colonel McCormack Trip to London, box 1097, HCC.

62. Benson, *History,* p. 109.

63. Ibid., pp. 97, 113.

64. Between 31 May 1943 and 8 August 1943, Berkeley Street sent Arlington Hall 14,903 intercepted diplomatic messages representing thirty-eight countries. In that same period, Arlington Hall sent Berkeley Street 24,696 diplomatic messages representing thirty-two countries. Over half (53 percent) of Arlington Hall's contributions were Japanese messages. Memorandum for the record, 7 September 1943, UKUSA Liaison, box 800, HCC.

65. Radiogram of 26 May 1943, Friedman Correspondence While in England, 1943, box 1398, HCC; Benson, *History,* p. 113. The United States continued to withhold information concerning its interest in Russian communications, while Britain did not reveal its effort against the State Department's consular code. For the former, see chapter 6. For the latter, see John Croft, "Reminiscences of GCHQ and GCB, 1942–45," *Intelligence and National Security* 13:4 (Winter 1998): 137.

66. Monthly Information Letter, No. 8, 15 December 1944, Cryptanalytic Technical Exchanges Between SSA and GCCS, box 1328, HCC.

5. Targets

1. Alfred McCormack to Colonel Carter Clarke, 26 January 1943, Intercept Priorities Memoranda, 1943, box 1432, HCC. McCormack provided details of General Kroner's directive.

2. Some Mexican army traffic may have been readable. In October 1942 the Mexican military attaché in Washington was using a cipher formerly used by the Mexican foreign ministry for minor diplomatic affairs. This system had been solved in 1940, but it is not clear when it was adopted for use by the army. By the fall of 1942, Arlington Hall was reading a simple cipher used by the Mexican army for internal correspondence, but it is not clear when this system first became readable. "Mexican and Other Latin American Cipher Systems" and "Mexican Ciphers: MXC, MXE, MXH," box 1417, HCC.

3. Alfred McCormack to Colonel Carter Clarke, 26 January 1943, Intercept Priorities Memoranda, 1943, box 1432, HCC.

4. Alfred McCormack to Colonel Carter Clarke, Subject: SSB Priorities, 26 January 1943, SSS Intercept Priorities Memoranda, 1943, box 1432, HCC.

5. Major Brown to William Friedman, 28 January 1943, and Major Telford Taylor to Colonel Carter Clarke and Alfred McCormack, 3 February 1943, SSS Intercept Priorities Memoranda, 1943, box 1432, HCC.

6. Robert Louis Benson, *A History of U.S. Communications Intelligence During World War II: Policy and Administration* (Fort Meade, Md.: Center for Cryptologic History, National Security Agency, 1997), p. 83.

7. Ibid.

8. "SSA, Cryptanalytic Branch Annual Report, FY 1944," box 1115, HCC. In early 1944 another section, B-V, was created to handle all Japanese plaintext messages.

9. Lt. Colonel Earle Cook to C. O. Arlington Hall Station, 18 August 1943, Expansion of the Signal Intelligence Service, 1943, box 1296, HCC. In July 1943 Arlington Hall received 380,487 messages of all types, about half of which were Japanese army messages.

10. William Friedman to Chief, Signal Security Agency, 29 July 1943, Expansion of the Signal Intelligence Service, 1943, box 1296, HCC.

11. For a critical response to Friedman's proposal by a senior officer, see Lt. Colonel Earle Cook to Chief, Signal Security Agency, 31 July 1943, Expansion of the Signal Intelligence Service, 1943, box 1296, HCC. Cook was then chief of B Branch (all cryptanalysis).

12. B Branch Inquiry Committee, Meeting of 2 December 1943, Cryptanalytic Effort Underway in SSA, 1943, box 948, HCC.

13. B Branch Inquiry Committee, Meeting of 9 December 1943, Cryptanalytic Effort Underway in SSA, 1943, box 948, HCC.

14. "SSA, Cryptanalytic Branch Annual Report, FY 1944," box 1115, HCC. This report lists thirty-one countries whose messages were translated and published in March 1944. Since some countries may have had messages not worth publishing, the total number of targets might exceed thirty-one. The annual report for the preceding year recorded that Arlington Hall was solving the ciphers of "more than thirty nations." "Cryptanalytic Branch, Report for Fiscal Year July 1, 1942 to June 30, 1943," box 2, Yardley Collection.

15. In the summer of 1944 the Japanese foreign ministry had seventeen systems in service. Eleven of these were completely readable at Arlington Hall, including all systems used by Japan's European embassies. "SSA, Summary Annual Report for FY 1944," p. 70, box 1370, HCC. At least two of the unreadable systems were still unsolved in the summer of 1945.

16. "Cryptosystems (Foreign), 1942–1945," box 1023, HCC.

17. Carl Boyd, *Hitler's Japanese Confidant: General Oshima Hiroshi and Magic Intelligence, 1941–1945* (Lawrence: University Press of Kansas, 1993), p. 65. My evaluation of Oshima's position and activity depends on Boyd's excellent study.

18. Ibid., pp. 144–145. Oshima could be surprisingly uncritical in his reporting. In October 1943, for example, he assured Tokyo that Mussolini (then head of the so-called Republic of Saló, a rump fascist government in north Italy) would raise a trustworthy Italian army of three hundred thousand troops to fight alongside the Germans.

19. Quoted in ibid., p. 1.

20. Tony Matthews, *Shadows Dancing: Japanese Espionage Against the West, 1939–1945* (London: Robert Hale, 1993), pp. 113–114.

21. Magic Diplomatic Summary, 19 May 1942.

22. Magic Diplomatic Summary, 24 July 1943. The appendix of this summary has a long report on the TO affair.

23. At least one Spanish diplomat, the consul in Vancouver, was expelled for intelligence activities. A Spanish agent was also arrested by the FBI on charges of conspiring to smuggle strategic materials through the Allied blockade.

24. Magic Diplomatic Summary, 3 September 1944.

25. For the affair of the pearls, see Matthews, *Shadows Dancing*, pp. 76–80, 115, 166. When informed by Suma of Cardenas's insinuations concerning Japanese cipher security, Tokyo smugly assured its representative in Madrid that the affair could not have been the result of Washington reading Japanese communications.

26. "Report on JAT," box 1402, HCC. For Axis cryptanalytic cooperation, see David Alvarez, "Axis Sigint Collaboration: A Limited Partnership," *Intelligence and National Security* 14:1 (Spring 1999): 1–16.

27. Bradley F. Smith, *The Shadow Warriors: OSS and the Origins of the CIA* (New York: Basic Books, 1983), p. 220; Anthony Cave Brown, *The Last Hero: Wild Bill Donovan* (New York: Times Books, 1982), pp. 304–305.

28. "Messages Re Compromise of Japanese Codes in Lisbon," box 878, HCC; Brown, *The Last Hero*, p. 306; "Enemy Code and Cipher Systems," 25 May 1944, Rome X-2 Branch Reports, folder 827, box 108, Records of the Office of Strategic Services, Record Group 226, NARA.

29. For the American effort against FLORADORA, see "Annual Report of the Chief Signal Officer and Miscellaneous Studies, FY 1942–1943," box 832, HCC.

30. "SSA, Summary Annual Report for FY 1944," p. 74, box 1370, HCC.

31. Information from Juanita Moody.

32. For a technical description of the solution of the German one-time pad, see Cecil Phillips, "The American Solution of a German One-Time-Pad Cryptographic System," copy in the possession of the author.

33. Intelligence Division Executive Council, Meeting of 1 March 1945, Minutes Intelligence Division and Cryptanalytic Research Group, 1943–1945, box 995, HCC.

34. GEE back traffic on the Berlin-Tokyo circuit provided some information on Japanese production and technical developments. For example, GEE messages revealed that Japan was putting into service a new medium tank.

35. Stockholm to Madrid, 17 March 1945, and Bern to Chungking, 20 March 1945, Diplomatic Message Translations, box 482, HCC; Paris to Washington, 18 April 1945, Diplomatic Message Translations, box 483, HCC.

36. "Italian Codes and Ciphers, 1939–43 (with an epilogue: summer 1944)," p. 227, box 1388, HCC.

37. The United States finally broke relations with Finland in June 1944.

38. "SSA, Cryptanalytic Branch Annual Report, FY 1944," p. 28, box 1115, HCC.

39. "SSA, General Cryptanalysis Branch Annual Report, July 1944–July 1945," p. 17, box 1380, HCC.

40. Ibid., pp. 25–26.

41. Ibid., p. 13.

42. Magic Diplomatic Summaries, 28 August, 12 September, and 15 September 1944.

43. Determined from a survey of messages collected in Diplomatic Message Translations, 1942, box 307 (April) and box 318 (August), HCC.

44. For example, a cipher used by the Brazilian government since 1942 for especially secret communications with its embassy in Washington was not solved, in large part because as late as 1945 only seven messages in the system had been intercepted. "Brazilian Codes and Ciphers, 1917–1945," box 1, Yardley Collection.

45. See, for example, the Magic Diplomatic Summaries for 6 and 11 November 1944.

46. B Branch Inquiry Committee, Meeting of 3 December 1943, Cryptanalytic Effort Underway in SSA, 1943, box 948, HCC; memorandum for Lieutenant Cook, 11 December 1943, Coordination Section Correspondence and Reports, 1943–1944, box 1018, HCC. The only other traffic so ranked was Swiss.

47. Document headed "Governments on which there has been no substantial impediment to liaison," Clark Files, British Liaison, 1940–1945, box 1413, HCC.

48. "German Government Telegrams Sent in Spanish Government Codes," box 824, HCC.

49. "Annual Report of the Chief Signal Officer and Miscellaneous Studies, FY 1942–1943," box 832, HCC. One report indicates that the codebook and additive tables arrived from GCCS as early as January 1942. British intelligence obtained cryptographic material from an agent inside the Spanish embassy in London. Nigel West and Oleg Tsarev, *The Crown Jewels: The British Secrets at the Heart of the KGB Archives* (London: HarperCollins, 1998), p. 141.

50. Robin Winks, *Cloak and Gown: Scholars and the Secret War* (New York: Morrow, 1987), pp. 171–173.

51. Davis to OIC, B.III.a, 7 June 1944, and J. Edgar Hoover to General Bissell,

21 September 1944, Spanish Code, box 840, HCC. For a sample of photographed materials, see "Plain Text Messages and Additive Strips from Spanish Embassy, Washington," box 1358, HCC.

52. A[dolf] B[erle] to Secretaries of War, Navy, and Treasury, 5 October 1942, PSF. Safe: Miscellaneous, box 4, Franklin D. Roosevelt Library, Hyde Park, New York. I am indebted to Brian Villa for drawing my attention to this document.

53. Magic Diplomatic Summaries, 21 October 1942 and 10 January 1943.

54. Sanz-Agero to Cardenas, 14 August 1942, and Cardenas to Soraluce, 9 September 1942, Spanish Code, box 840, HCC.

55. "Cryptographic Codes and Ciphers: Portuguese Cipher Systems, 1941–1944," box 1376, HCC. During the war the Portuguese foreign ministry used several editions of a basic one-part code of fifty to sixty thousand groups. The earliest version (used during the war only for consular correspondence) had been in service since 1910, but new editions appeared frequently through the end of the war. Depending on the edition and the communications circuit, encipherment was by some mix of repagination, additive tables, substitution tables, and transposition.

56. Magic Diplomatic Summary, 2 November 1944.

57. "Foreign Cryptosystems, 1942–45," pp. 2–6, box 1023, HCC; "Diplomatic Translations of White House Interest," reports dated 9, 10, 24, and 30 June 1943, box 833, HCC; SSA, Semi-monthly Reports, December 1943–November 1944, reports dated 1 April 1944 and 14 August 1944, box 114, HCC; Magic Diplomatic Summary, 23 February 1943.

58. "SSA, General Cryptanalysis Branch, Annual Report, July 1944–July 1945," p. 29, box 1380, HCC.

59. "Progress of SSA and Cooperation with GCCS on Near Eastern Systems," box 843, HCC. Most Turkish diplomatic systems were one- or two-part codes enciphered by short (forty-place) repeating additives.

60. Bern to Tokyo, 19 October 1943, Rio de Janeiro to Bern, 15 October 1943, and Tokyo to Bern, 28 October 1943, Multinational Diplomatic Translation Summaries, box 883, HCC.

61. Magic Diplomatic Summaries, 19 November 1944 and 28 December 1944.

62. "Swiss Cryptographic Systems," in "Foreign Cryptosystems, 1942–45," box 1023, HCC; B Branch Inquiry Committee, Meeting of 9 December 1943, box 948, HCC.

63. "SSA, General Cryptanalysis Branch, Annual Report, July 1944–July 1945," p. 18, box 1380, HCC; "Swedish Codebook" and "Correspondence of Military Attaché, Washington, and Headquarters, Stockholm, 1940–1942," box 153, HCC.

64. Magic Diplomatic Summary, 22 November 1944; SSA, Semi-monthly Reports, December 1943–November 1944, report dated 16 October 1944, box 1114, HCC.

65. Memorandum for the Director from Edward Tamm, 28 September 1942,

and "Allegations of the Misuse of the Washington Papal Embassy Diplomatic Pouch" [date and author deleted by censor], documents released to the author by the FBI under the provisions of the Freedom of Information Act.

66. See, for example, the reports for 8 October and 5 November 1943 in SSA, B-III Weekly Reports, October–December 1943, box 1114, HCC.

67. Minutes of the Third Meeting of Directing Subcommittee of Research Section, 24 October 1941, HW 14/21, PRO.

68. The system known to Arlington Hall as KIF was a one-part, three-letter code of twelve to fifteen thousand groups. It was enciphered with twenty-five keys, each consisting of a combination of substitution tables and random mixed alphabets, and each using different nulls. Each papal nunciature (embassy) had a unique set of sixteen of these twenty-five keys and would use them on particular days of the month. A nuncio (ambassador) might begin a telegram in the assigned key for the day but then shift, as many as eight times, to other keys in the course of the message.

69. "Cryptographic Codes and Ciphers: Vatican Code Systems," box 1284, HCC.

70. For American intelligence operations against the Vatican, see David Alvarez, "A Few Bits of Information: American Intelligence and the Vatican, 1939-1945" (paper presented at the conference "FDR, the Vatican, and the Roman Catholic Church in America," 7-9 October 1998, Franklin D. Roosevelt Library, Hyde Park, New York).

71. The Vatican had become aware of the CIFRARIO ROSSO's insecurity no later than the spring of 1940. This cipher was certainly read by American, British, German, and Italian signals intelligence, and probably by Finnish and Hungarian.

72. For the Vessel affair, see Alvarez, "A Few Bits of Information."

73. Exchanges on various Near Eastern and African systems are described in the paper headed "Governments on which there has been no substantial impediment to liaison," Clark Files, British Liaison, 1940-1945, box 1413, HCC.

74. Staff Communication Officer to Director of Naval Intelligence, 25 February 1945, "Saudi Arabian Communications Aboard the U.S.S. Murphy," box 1340, HCC.

75. "Annual Report of the Chief Signal Officer and Miscellaneous Studies, FY 1942-1943," box 832, HCC. The section was also responsible for Thailand.

76. Ibid.; SSA, Intelligence Division, B-II, Semi-monthly Reports, September 1942–December 1943, box 1114, HCC. For the Cipher Bureau's work, see "Data on Miscellaneous Cryptographic Systems, 1917-1929," box 60, Yardley Collection.

77. "SSA, Cryptanalytic Branch Annual Report, FY 1944," p. 26, box 1115, HCC; "SSA, Annual Report: General Cryptanalysis Branch, July 1944–July 1945," pp. 26-27, box 1380, HCC.

78. See, for example, Magic Diplomatic Summaries for 26 and 28 November 1944.

79. "Survey of French Systems," 8 October 1943, pp. 3-4, in "Foreign Cryptosystems, 1942-45," box 1023, HCC. In September 1943 Arlington Hall's French sec-

tion held copies of six Vichy codebooks. Report of B-III-d, 24 September 1943, SSA, Weekly Reports, January to October 1943, box 1114, HCC. For a Vichy codebook obtained through British sources, see "B" to Denniston, 11 December 1942, HW 14/61, PRO.

80. On Gaullist-American relations, see Robert Dallek, *Franklin D. Roosevelt and American Foreign Policy, 1932–1945* (New York: Oxford University Press, 1979), pp. 376–379, 458–462; Warren Kimball, *Forged in War: Roosevelt, Churchill, and the Second World War* (New York: William Morrow, 1997), pp. 298–299.

81. B Branch Inquiry Committee, Meeting of 6 December 1943, Cryptanalytic Effort Underway in the SSA, box 948, HCC. In 1943 Arlington Hall solved two ciphers used by the Free French faction loyal to General Henri Giraud. These provided some insight into the struggle for power between Giraud and de Gaulle.

82. "French Diplomatic Translation Summaries," box 881, HCC.

83. "French-Russian Relations" and "Sino-French Relations," box 583, HCC; "French Intelligence Activities," supplement to the Magic Diplomatic Summary, 24 May 1945.

84. General Strong to G-2, 6th Army Group, 6 February 1945, and General Davis to Commanding General, 6th Army Group, 10 January 1945, "Memoranda Relating to French Interest in Sigint Intelligence [*sic*] Matters," box 1277, HCC; Frank Rowlett to Colonel H. G. Hayes, 9 November 1944, "French Use of Hagelin," box 1432, HCC.

85. "Polish Cipher Systems, 1942–1944," box 1284, HCC; SSA, B Branch Semi-monthly Reports, report of 30 September 1944, box 1370, HCC; "SSA, General Cryptanalysis Branch, July 1944–July 1945," p. 28, box 1380, HCC.

86. "SSA, Cryptanalytic Branch Annual Report, FY 1944," p. 29, box 1115, HCC; SSA, B Branch Semi-monthly Reports, reports of 30 September and 29 December 1944, box 1370, HCC.

87. John Prados, *Combined Fleet Decoded: The Secret History of American Intelligence and the Japanese Navy in World War II* (New York: Random House, 1995), pp. 247–248. SSA's annual report for 1945 notes that Colonel Verkuyl, "an Arlington Hall alumnus," had been placed in command of Dutch cryptologic operations in Australia.

88. "SSA, Cryptanalytic Branch Annual Report, FY 1944," p. 27, box 1115, HCC.

89. "British Cryptographic Systems, 1917–1932," box 1356, HCC. For decrypts of British messages from 1921, see "Translations of 'A' Code Messages, 1921," box 51, Yardley Collection.

90. The roster is filed in "Pearl Harbor Investigations and Miscellaneous Material," box 1360, HCC.

91. In an interview with me, Frank Rowlett insisted that British codes and ciphers were not attacked before or during the war. He claimed that cooperation with London was so close that the intelligence likely to result from an effort

against British communications would not have been worth the necessary resources. Frank Lewis and Al Snyder, both seniors at wartime Arlington Hall, separately told me that they were not aware of any operations against the British.

92. In his biography of Adolf Berle (*Liberal: Adolf A. Berle and the Vision of an American Era* [New York: Free Press, 1987]), Jordan Schwarz claims (p. 250) that during the 1944 Chicago conference on international civil aviation (at which Berle led the American delegation) the United States intercepted and read the secret cable traffic of the British delegation. The claim depends on a reference in Berle's diary to "the messages from London." The context of the entry, however, makes it clear that Berle was referring to American messages from the U.S. embassy in London, not to intercepted British messages. See Memorandum for the Secretary of State, 2 December 1944, Adolf Berle Diary, Franklin D. Roosevelt Presidential Library.

93. "Cryptanalytic Branch, Report for Fiscal Year July 1, 1942, to June 30, 1943," p. 2, box 2, Yardley Collection.

94. Captain W. Moore to George Sterling, 2 December 1943, FH-99X4, Navy Department, box 55, Intercepted Radio Transmissions, 1940–1945, Radio Intelligence Division, Records of the Federal Communications Commission, Record Group 173, NARA.

95. "Cryptographic Description, Type X Machine," box 1117, HCC; information from Ralph Erskine.

96. Robert Schukraft oral history, NSA-OH-36-80, p. 12.

97. Ibid., p. 94.

98. Magic Diplomatic Summary, 8 September 1944.

99. Paris to Washington, 16 April 1945, Translations of Intercepted Radio Traffic, box 2725, Records of the Chief of Naval Operations, Record Group 38, NARA; London to Rio de Janeiro, 7 June 1945, Diplomatic Message Translations, box 500, HCC; RED Intelligence Summaries, 3 December 1945, box 192, HCC.

6. The Russian Problem

1. Colonel Sherman Miles to the Military Observer in Budapest, 18 June 1920, Correspondence Regarding Béla Kun, box 48, Yardley Collection.

2. Ladislas Szabo, "My Hunting After the Secrets of the [*sic*] Bolshevik Diplomacy," Correspondence Regarding Béla Kun, box 48, Yardley Collection.

3. Major Elgin to the Director of Military Intelligence, 19 August 1920, Correspondence Regarding Béla Kun, box 48, Yardley Collection.

4. David Langbart, "Spare No Expense: The Department of State and the Search for Intelligence About Bolshevik Russia, November 1917–September 1918," *Intelligence and National Security* 4:2 (April 1989): 317–318.

5. Signal Security Agency, "Data on Soviet Cryptographic Systems, 1917–

1933," p. 3, box 2, Yardley Collection; "TRQ—Russian: Solution Dates of Certain Messages, 1917–1918," box 47, Yardley Collection.

6. Admiral Mark Bristol to the Secretary of State, 20 April 1921, and Lt. Colonel McCabe to the Director of Military Intelligence, 10 May 1921, "TRQ—Russian: Correspondence re codes and ciphers, 1920–1930," box 48, Yardley Collection.

7. "Data on Soviet Cryptographic Systems, 1917–1933," p. 5. The anonymous author of this study asserts that Weiskopf's success was the only solution of a Russian system by an American before the Second World War. This seems to ignore the fact that MI-8 solved several Russian messages between December 1917 and February 1918.

8. Ibid., pp. 9–11.

9. Director of Naval Communications to the Director of Naval Intelligence, 27 September 1930, box 2, Yardley Collection.

10. Jeffrey Dorwart, *Conflict of Duty: The U.S. Navy's Intelligence Dilemma, 1919–1945* (Annapolis, Md.: Naval Institute Press, 1983), p. 45.

11. "New Soviet System (Amtorg), 1928," box 750, HCC. The army's "Data on Soviet Cryptographic Systems, 1917–1933," errs in stating that this cipher was first obtained by the navy and turned over to the army in 1931.

12. Describing to Herbert Yardley the effort against the Amtorg messages, Friedman admitted, "We were misled by the simplicity of the stuff seized in the Arcos raids in London." William Friedman to Herbert Yardley, 5 March 1931, box 2, Yardley Collection. For an example of amateur advice, see the submission in box 3, folder 3, of the William Friedman Papers, George C. Marshall Library, Lexington, Virginia.

13. William Friedman to Herbert Yardley, 5 March 1931, box 2, Yardley Collection.

14. Major D. M. Crawford to Lt. Colonel O. S. Albright, 24 February 1931, box 2, Yardley Collection.

15. Ibid.

16. "Letters from a White Russian," box 750, HCC. In the records *Mishtowt* is sometimes spelled *Mistowt.*

17. Receipt signed by Major D. M. Crawford, 7 January 1932, for items received on 2 November 1931, Russian Code for Commercial Correspondence, box 138, HCC. This file contains a photostat of an Armtorg codebook, but it does not contain the eight sets of cipher keys that (as the above receipt specifically records) accompanied the book. The missing keys are almost certainly the eight packets of Russian additive received from the naval attaché in Buenos Aires and enclosed in folders labeled "Prefectura General de Policia." See "Captured Russian Additives," box 2, Russian Ciphers and Codes, 1907–1931, Record Group 457, NARA.

18. "Soviet Traffic: Manchurian Addresses," box 138, HCC; "Report on Radio Intercept for the Period October 1, 1933 to July 1, 1934," Report on Radio Inter-

cept, 1934, box 781, HCC; Lt. Cook to the Chief Signal Officer, 11 August 1938, SIS, General Files, 1938, box 778, HCC.

19. "A Study of the Radio Intercept Activities of the Army and the Navy, Part III: Recommendations," Army-Navy Directive Study, box 1374, HCC.

20. General Mauborgne to G-2, 27 April 1939, SIS, General Files, 1939, box 779, HCC. On 10 February 1941 Krivitsky was found dead in a New York hotel room. An apparent suicide, the case was sufficiently mysterious to encourage speculation that he had been murdered by Soviet intelligence.

21. Colonel Akin to the Commander, Second Signal Service Company, Ft. Monmouth, 8 October 1940, SIS, General Correspondence File, 1940, box 779, HCC; Robert Louis Benson and Cecil James Phillips, *History of Venona* (Fort Meade, Md.: National Security Agency, 1995), vol. 1, p. 10. I am indebted to Lou Benson for arranging the declassification of portions of this three-volume in-house history of the VENONA project.

22. "A Chronology of the Cooperation Between the SSA and the London Offices of GCCS," box 1, Yardley Collection.

23. John Ferris, "Whitehall's Black Chamber: British Cryptology and the Government Code and Cypher School, 1919–29," *Intelligence and National Security* 2:1 (January 1987): 74, 78; C. G. McKay, "British Sigint and the Bear, 1919–1941," *Kungl. Krigsvetenskapsakademiens Handlingar och Tidskrift* 2 (1997): 81–96.

24. "Report of Cryptographic Mission," box 1296, HCC. The naval codes were only partially reconstructed. One can be found, along with information on the Russian meteorological cipher, in "Russian Meteorological File," box 200, HCC. I am indebted to Ralph Erskine, who suggested that naval codebooks were passed to Ensign Robert Weeks, a naval representative on the American delegation.

25. "Italian Codes and Ciphers, 1940–43," Cryptographic Codes and Ciphers: Italian, box 1388, HCC.

26. Lt. Commander Henry Learned to Commander John Redman, 6 March 1942, "Activities of the Italian Cryptanalysis Section," box 147, HCC. For naval intercept of Russian traffic, see Stevens to Tiltman [n.d., but ca. July 1942], HW 14/47, PRO. In June 1942 the navy abandoned the Russian diplomatic problem when it transferred to the army all responsibility for diplomatic sigint.

27. See chapter 5.

28. Weekly Report: Diplomatic Traffic, Reports 1–6, box 851, HCC. In November 1942 the Soviet Union far outdistanced other governments in the number of encrypted cables passing through American censorship. It was trailed by Free France (704), China (598), Sweden (470), and the Netherlands (404).

29. "Report Pertaining to Meteorological Section," 7 May 1943, in "Annual Report of the Chief Signal Officer and Miscellaneous Studies, FY 1942–1943," box 832, HCC.

30. Robert Louis Benson and Michael Warner, eds., *Venona: Soviet Espionage*

and the American Response, 1939–1957 (Washington, D.C.: National Security Agency and Central Intelligence Agency, 1996), p. xiii. See also John Earl Haynes and Harvey Klehr, *Venona: Decoding Soviet Espionage in America* (New Haven, Conn.: Yale University Press, 1999), p. 8.

31. Information from Frank Rowlett. Discussing the attitude of army sigint authorities toward the Soviet Union, Rowlett recalled, "We looked on them as untouchables. We had no reason to trust them."

32. Gerhard Weinberg, *A World at Arms: A Global History of World War II* (New York: Cambridge University Press, 1994), pp. 609–610.

33. Warren Kimball, *Forged in War: Roosevelt, Churchill, and the Second World War* (New York: William Morrow, 1997), pp. 166, 177.

34. Magic Diplomatic Summary, 8 April 1942.

35. Magic Diplomatic Summary, 11 December 1942 and 28 January 1943.

36. Magic Diplomatic Summary, 31 December 1942.

37. Magic Diplomatic Summary, 7 March 1943.

38. This message is reproduced in Benson and Warner, *Venona,* pp. 43–45. The original translation seems to have been incomplete or in some other way unsatisfactory because a second version was completed on 6 February 1943.

39. "General Marshall's letter of 13/12/42," Sinkov Papers, box 1413, HCC.

40. Memorandum by G. Sterling, 11 November 1942, Intercepted Radio Transmissions, 1940–1945, Radio Intelligence Division, Records of the Federal Communications Commission, Record Group 173, NARA (hereinafter cited as RID); "Intercept Information: Russian Radio Operations," 26 January 1943, box 1128, HCC.

41. Colonel Carter Clarke to Alfred McCormack, 5 May 1942, Special Branch, G-2, MID, box 1305, HCC; information from Frank Rowlett.

42. Alfred McCormack to Generals Bratton and Lee, 12 February 1942, Special Branch, G-2, MID, box 1305, HCC.

43. SSA, Intelligence Division, B-II, Semi-monthly Reports, September 1942–December 1943, box 1114, HCC.

44. Robert Schukraft oral history, NSA-OH-36-80, p. 84.

45. Benson and Phillips, *History of Venona,* pp. 18, 25.

46. "Report Section, B-II," p. 2, in "Annual Report of the Chief Signal Officer and Miscellaneous Studies, FY 1942–1943," box 832, HCC.

47. "Survey of B Cryptographic Branch, August–September 1943," box 995, HCC; "US/British Agreements on Comint Effort, 1942–43," box 1328, HCC.

48. Meetings of 2 September and 9 September 1943, Minutes Intelligence Division and Crypt. Research Group, 1943–1945, box 995, HCC.

49. Unsigned and undated memorandum headed "MS-6" in SSA, General Correspondence File, 1944, box 1015, HCC. Plans for an intercept station in Alaska dated from the summer of 1942, when the Signal Corps proposed a station with thirteen directional rhombic antennae, two of which would be oriented toward Moscow.

50. The first weekly report of the newly constituted B-III-b stated, "A special report submitted by B-III-b is to be considered apart hereof." SSA, Weekly Reports, January–October, 1943, box 1114, HCC.

51. Information from Frank Lewis. The British liaison officer informed GCCS that Kullback was "apt to believe that he has his finger on the pulse of everything." Major Stevens to Alistair Denniston, 28 September 1942, HW 14/53, PRO.

52. Information from Cecil Phillips, who had the story from William Smith.

53. Senior officers at Arlington Hall were informed that Lewis and Elmquist had developed "definite leads" on the Russian problem, but that they were relieved of further responsibilities in that area because their skills were urgently required on the Japanese army problem. Meeting of 13 November 1943, Minutes Intelligence Division and Crypt. Research Group, 1943–1945, box 995, HCC.

54. Information from Cecil Phillips.

55. "Cryptographic Codes and Ciphers: Russian, B-01," box 1347, HCC.

56. The section's success is described in "SSA, General Cryptanalysis Branch, Annual Report, July 1944–July 1945," box 1380, HCC. In this report the section appears in a special addendum under the cover designation "Special Problems Section."

57. At Arlington Hall foreign systems were identified by trigrams. At the time Russian codes and ciphers were identified by Z. The letter M indicated a military system, D a diplomatic system, and E an economic or trade system. The third letter indicated the particular system in the functional category.

58. "SSA, General Cryptanalysis Branch, Annual Report, July 1944–July 1945," Special Problems Section, p. 5, box 1380, HCC. Information from Cecil Phillips.

59. Unsigned memorandum, Intercepted Radio Transmissions, 1940–1945, RID.

60. Robert Louis Benson, *The KGB and the GRU in Europe, South America, and Australia,* Venona: Historical Monograph No. 5 (Fort Meade, Md.: Center for Cryptologic History, National Security Agency, n.d.), p. 3; Benson and Warner, *Venona,* pp. 303–304. In a conversation with the author on 10 March 1998, Lou Benson confirmed that the incidents at the warehouse and the consulate general were FBI operations.

61. David Alvarez, "Axis Sigint Collaboration: A Limited Partnership," *Intelligence and National Security* 14:1 (Spring 1999): 1–17.

62. "JAT Write-up—Selections from JMA Traffic," box 1018, HCC.

63. "SSA, General Cryptanalysis Branch, Annual Report, July 1944–July 1945," Special Problems Section, p. 4 n. 2, box 1380, HCC.

64. "List of Russian Codes Read or Captured by the Finns," box 522, HCC.

65. Benson and Phillips, *History of Venona,* p. 50.

66. Bradley F. Smith, *The Shadow Warriors: OSS and the Origins of the CIA* (New York: Basic Books, 1983), pp. 353–354; Memorandum for the President [from Donovan], 11 December 1944, PSF, Subject File: OSS, box 151, Franklin D. Roosevelt Library.

67. See, for example, the files in box 1100, HCC. Some files carry the designation "267," which was a code term for *Stella Polaris* materials.

68. Benson and Phillips, *History of Venona,* pp. 50–53.

69. The report of the "Special Problems [Russian] Section" for the fiscal year 1944–1945 does not mention Finnish material, although it explicitly acknowledges the use of material extracted from Japanese messages. If the section had used Finnish material, it probably would have said so.

70. For the testimony of Bentley and other sources, see Benson and Phillips, *History of Venona,* pp. 36–37.

71. When questioned by the author, cryptanalysts who had worked in the wartime French, German, and Japanese sections admitted that until the end of the war they were completely unaware that Arlington Hall had a Russian section.

72. "SSA, General Cryptanalysis Branch, Annual Report, July 1944–July 1945," Special Problems Section, p. 7, box 1380, HCC. TICOM materials, especially the Petsamo codebook, would only prove useful long after the war.

73. "B-01" and "B-02," in "Cryptographic Codes and Ciphers: Russian, B-01," box 1347, HCC.

74. The subject matter of ZMO and ZMP traffic was so banal that, for a time, it aroused the suspicion of the analysts. One report noted, "There is some possibility that an open code underlies the plain text, but no proof of this exists. The only reason for this belief is that some of the material mentioned is rather unbelievable, and it is just possible that when an item such as 'red bilberry' is mentioned, it might have an entirely different meaning to the recipient of the message." "Minor Army Ciphers" in "Cryptographic Codes and Ciphers: Russian, B-01," box 1347, HCC.

75. "SSA, General Cryptanalysis Branch, Annual Report, July 1944–July 1945," Special Problems Section, p. 4, box 1380, HCC.

76. Cecil Phillips recalled that "no diplomatic or trade message was translated or published before September 1945, but it is possible that a few of the repetitive trade messages with lots of numbers were completely solved by then. All the number groups were solved by mid-1944, and there may have been enough nonnumber groups solved to permit such a solution. But there was no interest in publication of material that was already two years old and contained nothing but lists and quantities of material which we were supplying them." Cecil Phillips e-mail, 18 February 1998.

Lou Benson, the National Security Agency's leading authority on the early history of the Russian problem, confirmed that until the end of the war the intelligence extracted by army analysts from the Russian messages they could read in whole or in part was so insignificant that no translations were published or circulated at Arlington Hall. Information from Lou Benson.

77. Information from Cecil Phillips; Norman Willis oral history, NSA-OH-34-80.

78. Benson and Phillips, *History of Venona,* p. 22.

79. Ibid., pp. 46–47.

80. "Survey of OP-20-G by Naval Inspector General," box 1286, HCC; "RATTAN Liaison," box 1471, HCC.

81. Such transmissions are indicative of a station testing its equipment and its connections with another transmitter.

82. The story of the consulate radios can be traced in boxes 48–49, Intercepted Radio Transmissions, 1940–1945, RID. Cecil Phillips and Lou Benson confirmed that Arlington Hall knew nothing about this operation until after the war.

83. Benson and Phillips, *History of Venona*, pp. 30–31.

84. Taylor to Strong (for Clarke and Corderman), 14 September 1943. Ralph Erskine kindly shared the contents of this letter.

85. Memorandum for F-20, 21 May 1945, "RATTAN Liaison," box 1471, HCC.

86. Memorandum from the Chief of Staff to Admiral King [undated], "Memoranda Re U.S. Army Signal Intelligence Activities in India and Australia, 1943–1945," box 1383, HCC.

87. Memorandum by Admiral Hewlett Thebaud, 12 June 1945, and Memorandum for Admiral Thebaud and General Clarke, 16 June 1945, "RATTAN Liaison," box 1471, HCC.

88. "Russian Y Service Reports," box 202, HCC; "Baudot Charts," box 1473, HCC.

89. "British Security Coordination, June 1 1945–December 31 1945," box 62, RID.

90. Information from Lou Benson. The navy may have published some translations; if so, they do not survive in the available documentation.

91. RED Intelligence Summaries, 3 October 1944, 21 November 1944, and 30 January 1945, box 192, HCC. In this case "RED" does not refer to the Soviet Union. It is a code name for another publication that summarized sigint from around the world.

92. Moscow (Garreau) to Paris, 16 January 1945, Translations of Intercepted Radio Traffic, box 2725, Records of the Chief of Naval Operations, Record Group 38, NARA; RED Intelligence Summaries, 27 February 1945; Magic Diplomatic Summary, 3 April 1945.

93. RED Intelligence Summaries, 23 August 1945.

94. Ibid., 14 August 1945.

95. Ibid., 18 June 1945 (Special Supplement) and 26 June 1945.

96. Harriman to the Secretary of State, 21 March 1945, *Foreign Relations of the United States, 1945,* vol. 8, *Near East* (Washington, D.C.: Government Printing Office, 1969), pp. 1219–1220; Wilson to the Acting Secretary of State, 22 June 1945, *Foreign Relations of the United States, 1945,* vol. 1, *The Conference of Berlin* (Washington, D.C.: Government Printing Office, 1960), pp. 1024–1026; Magic Diplomatic Summaries, 28 March 1945 and 25 June 1945.

97. Magic Diplomatic Summary, 12 June 1945; Wilson to the Acting Secretary of State, 18 June 1945, *Foreign Relations: The Conference of Berlin,* pp. 1020–1022.

98. Wilson to the Acting Secretary of State, 18 June 1945, *Foreign Relations: The Conference of Berlin,* pp. 1020–1022; Magic Diplomatic Summary, 15 June 1945.

99. Hugh De Santis, *The Diplomacy of Silence: The American Foreign Service, the Soviet Union, and the Cold War, 1933–1947* (Chicago: University of Chicago Press, 1979), chaps. 5, 6.

7. A Usually Reliable Source

1. Monthly intercept totals often vary according to the source. I depend on the most conservative reports. See SRH 349, "Achievements of the Signal Security Agency in World War II," pp. 12–13.

At the end of the war the Signal Security Agency operated the following fixed intercept stations: 1. Vint Hill Farms, Virginia; 2. Two Rock Ranch, California; 3. Indian Creek Station, Florida; 4. Asmara, Eritrea; 5. Fort Shafter, Hawaii; 6. Amchitka, Aleutian Islands; 7. Fairbanks, Alaska; 8. New Delhi, India; 9. Bellmore, New York; 10. Tarzana, California; 11. Guam.

2. For reports of Vatican attitudes, see Magic Diplomatic Summaries, 10 December 1942, 20 May 1943, 10 June 1943. For papal mediation, see Magic Diplomatic Summary, 12 July 1943.

3. Magic Diplomatic Summaries, 26 and 29 July 1943.

4. Magic Diplomatic Summaries, 26 August 1944, 27 September 1944, 11 November 1944.

5. One can follow the Japanese "peace messages" in the Magic Diplomatic Summaries beginning with the summary of 12 July 1945. For an insightful perspective on Japanese policy making in the last weeks of the war, see Herbert Bix, "Japan's Delayed Surrender: A Reinterpretation," *Diplomatic History* 19:2 (Spring 1995): 197–225.

6. Information from Frank Lewis and Cecil Phillips.

7. David Kahn, "Epilogue," in Frank Rowlett, *The Story of Magic: Memoirs of An American Cryptologic Pioneer* (Laguna Hills, Calif.: Aegean Park Press, 1998), p. 253.

8. "SSA, General Cryptanalysis Branch, Annual Report, July 1944–July 1945," p. 2, box 1380, HCC.

9. Intelligence Division Executive Council, Minutes of Meeting of 22 March 1945, box 995, HCC.

10. Major Frank Stoner to Colonel Hatch, 26 April 1945, Top Secret Intelligence Files, 1942–1945, box 4, Records of the Office of the Chief Signal Officer, Record Group 111, NARA.

11. Stephen Schlesinger, "Cryptanalysis for Peacetime: Codebreaking and the Birth and Structure of the United Nations," *Cryptologia* 19:3 (July 1995): 223; Townsend Hoopes and Douglas Brinkley, *FDR and the Creation of the U.N.* (New Haven, Conn.: Yale University Press, 1997), p. 190.

12. Schlesinger, "Cryptanalysis for Peacetime," 227–229; Hoopes and Douglas, *FDR and the Creation of the U.N.,* p. 199.

13. Mark Stoler, *The Politics of the Second Front: American Military Planning and Diplomacy in Coalition Warfare, 1941–1943* (Westport, Conn.: Greenwood Press, 1977), pp. 32, 36, 116–117.

14. For an example of this approach, see Bruce Lee, *Marching Orders: The Untold Story of World War II* (New York: Crown Publishers, 1995).

15. See, for example, "Cryptanalytic Branch, Signal Security Service, Annual Report, July 1, 1942, to June 30, 1943," p. 5, box 2, Yardley Collection.

16. David Kahn, *The Codebreakers: The Story of Secret Writing* (New York: Macmillan, 1967), p. 24.

17. Magic Diplomatic Summary, 26 July 1945.

18. For a case study of the influence of midlevel officials on wartime diplomacy, see David Alvarez, *Bureaucracy and Cold War Diplomacy: The United States and Turkey, 1943–1946* (Thessaloniki: Institute for Balkan Studies, 1980).

19. This discussion of the navy's distribution of diplomatic sigint depends on "Navy Route Sheets and Outgoing Logs for White House Interest Material (1943–1945)," box 601, HCC.

20. Items sent to the president have been identified by comparing the translations marked for the White House on the route sheets in box 601, HCC, with the translations in "Diplomatic Message Translations," box 373, HCC.

21. Calculated from materials in "Diplomatic Translations of White House Interest," box 833, HCC. The three folders in this collection contain the surviving examples of sigint material passed to the White House. They cover the period September 1942 through June 1943, although there are some gaps. White House materials were usually burned upon their return from the president's naval aide.

The number of messages translated by Arlington Hall in June 1943 is taken from "Cryptanalytic Branch, Signal Security Service, Annual Report, July 1, 1942, to June 30, 1943," p. 19, box 2, Yardley Collection.

22. David Kahn, "Roosevelt, MAGIC, and ULTRA," *Cryptologia* 16:4 (October 1992): 307.

23. Carl Boyd, *Hitler's Japanese Confidant: General Oshima Hiroshi and Magic Intelligence, 1941–1945* (Lawrence: University Press of Kansas, 1993), p. 103.

24. Ibid., pp. 109–111; Kahn, "Roosevelt, MAGIC, and ULTRA," pp. 307, 309.

25. Kahn, "Roosevelt, MAGIC, and ULTRA," p. 311.

26. For the impact of Roosevelt's health on his work habits, see Robert Ferrell, *The Dying President: Franklin D. Roosevelt, 1944–1945* (Columbia: University of Missouri Press, 1998).

27. Kathryn E. Brown, "The Interplay of Information and Mind in Decision-Making: Signals Intelligence and Franklin D. Roosevelt's Policy-Shift on Indochina," *Intelligence and National Security* 13:1 (Spring 1998): 128.

28. Mark M. Lowenthal, "Searching for National Intelligence: U.S. Intelligence

and Policy Before the Second World War," *Intelligence and National Security* 6:4 (October 1991): 745.

29. Christopher Andrew, *For the President's Eyes Only: Secret Intelligence and the American Presidency from Washington to Bush* (New York: HarperCollins, 1995), p. 139. Almost nothing is known about the attitudes toward diplomatic signals intelligence of other foreign policy authorities. Like Roosevelt's earlier vice presidents, Harry Truman had been excluded from policy making and was unaware of the very existence of signals intelligence when he assumed the presidency upon Roosevelt's death on 12 April 1945. Concerned about the security consciousness of Truman's military aide, the voluble Colonel Harry Vaughan, the armed services did not reveal the precious secret to the new commander in chief until 17 April, when General Marshall submitted a memo (marked "For President's Eyes Only") outlining the signals intelligence program. There is little evidence, one way or the other, to indicate Truman's attitude toward sigint in the remaining months of the war, although his initial response seems to have been nonchalant. Ibid., p. 151.

BIBLIOGRAPHY _____

Unpublished Documents

National Archives and Records Administration, College Park, Maryland
    Record Group 111. Records of the Office of the Chief Signal Officer
        Top Secret Intelligence Files
    Record Group 173. Federal Communications Commission
        Records of the Radio Intelligence Division
    Record Group 226. Office of Strategic Services
    Record Group 457. National Security Agency
        Historic Cryptographic Collection
        Herbert Yardley Collection
        Magic Diplomatic Summaries
        Special Research Histories (SRH)
Public Record Office, Kew
    HW 14. Government Code & Cipher School: Directorate: Second World War
        Policy Papers
George C. Marshall Library, Lexington, Virginia
    William Friedman Papers
Franklin D. Roosevelt Library, Hyde Park, New York
    President's Secretary File
    Adolf Berle Papers

Interviews and Correspondence

Robert Louis Benson	Dale Marston
Ann Caracristi	Juanita Moody
Constance Clarke	Cecil Phillips
Ralph Erskine	Frank Rowlett

Kathleen Fenton   Katharine Swift
Arthur Levenson   Samuel Snyder
Frank Lewis   Milton Zaslow

Oral Histories, Center for Cryptologic History, National Security Agency

Earle Cook, OH-14-82   William Lutwiniak, OH-10-81
Prescott Currier, OH-38-80   Leo Rosen, OH-16-84
Rudolph Fabian, OH-09-83   Frank Rowlett, OH-01-74
Russell Horton, OH-06-82   Robert Schukraft, OH-36-80
Harold Jones, OH-26-83   Norman Willis, OH-34-80
Solomon Kullback, OH-17-82

Books

Alvarez, David, ed. *Allied and Axis Signals Intelligence in World War II.* London: Frank Cass, 1999.

Andrew, Christopher. "The Making of the Anglo-American Sigint Alliance." In *In the Name of Intelligence: Essays in Honor of Walter Pforzheimer,* edited by Hayden Peake and Samuel Halpern, pp. 95–110. Washington, D.C.: NIBC Press, 1994.

———. *For the President's Eyes Only: Secret Intelligence and the American Presidency from Washington to Bush.* New York: HarperCollins, 1995.

Bamford, James. *The Puzzle Palace: A Report on America's Most Secret Agency.* Boston: Houghton Mifflin, 1982.

Barker, Wayne G., ed. *The History of Codes and Ciphers in the United States Prior to World War I.* Laguna Hills, Calif.: Aegean Park Press, 1978.

———. *The History of Codes and Ciphers in the United States During the Period Between the World Wars.* Part 1, *1919–1929.* Laguna Hills, Calif.: Aegean Park Press, 1979.

———. *The History of Codes and Ciphers in the United States During World War I.* Laguna Hills, Calif.: Aegean Park Press, 1979.

Barros, James, and Richard Gregor. *Double Deception: Stalin, Hitler, and the Invasion of Russia.* DeKalb: Northern Illinois University Press, 1995.

Bath, Alan Harris. *Tracking the Axis Enemy: The Triumph of Anglo-American Naval Intelligence.* Lawrence: University Press of Kansas, 1998.

Bennett, Ralph. *Behind the Battle: Intelligence in the War with Germany, 1939–45.* London: Sinclair-Stevenson, 1994.

Benson, Robert Louis. *A History of U.S. Communications Intelligence During World War II: Policy and Administration.* Fort Meade, Md., National Security Agency, 1997.

Benson, Robert Louis, and Michael Warner, eds. *Venona: Soviet Espionage and the American Response, 1939–1957*. Washington, D.C.: National Security Agency and Central Intelligence Agency, 1996.

Boll, Michael. *Cold War in the Balkans: American Foreign Policy and the Emergence of Communist Bulgaria, 1943–1947*. Lexington: University of Kentucky Press, 1984.

Boyd, Carl. *Hitler's Japanese Confidant: General Oshima Hiroshi and Magic Intelligence, 1941–1945*. Lawrence: University Press of Kansas, 1993.

Brown, Anthony Cave. *The Last Hero: Wild Bill Donovan*. New York: Times Books, 1982.

Bryden, John. *Best-Kept Secret: Canadian Secret Intelligence in the Second World War*. Toronto: Lester Publishing, 1993.

Dallek, Robert. *Franklin D. Roosevelt and American Foreign Policy, 1932–1945*. New York: Oxford University Press, 1979.

Davis, Lynn Etheridge. *The Cold War Begins: Soviet-American Conflict over Eastern Europe*. Princeton, N.J.: Princeton University Press, 1974.

Denniston, Robin. *Churchill's Secret War: Diplomatic Decrypts, the Foreign Office and Turkey, 1942–44*. New York: St. Martin's Press, 1997.

De Santis, Hugh. *The Diplomacy of Silence: The American Foreign Service, the Soviet Union, and the Cold War, 1933–1947*. Chicago: University of Chicago Press, 1979.

Dorwart, Jeffrey. *Conflict of Duty: The U.S. Navy's Intelligence Dilemma, 1919–1945*. Annapolis, Md.: Naval Institute Press, 1983.

Drea, Edward. *MacArthur's Ultra: Codebreaking and the War Against Japan, 1942–1945*. Lawrence: University Press of Kansas, 1992.

Gellman, Irwin. *Good Neighbor Diplomacy: United States Policies in Latin America, 1933–1945*. Baltimore, Md.: Johns Hopkins University Press, 1979.

Hinsley, F. H., et al. *British Intelligence in the Second World War*. London: HMSO, 1979–1988.

Hinsley, F. H., and Alan Stripp, eds. *Codebreakers: The Inside Story of Bletchley Park*. Oxford: Oxford University Press, 1993.

Hoopes, Townsend, and Douglas Brinkley. *FDR and the Creation of the U.N.* New Haven, Conn.: Yale University Press, 1997.

Kahn, David. *The Codebreakers: The Story of Secret Writing*. New York: Macmillan, 1967.

Kimball, Warren. *The Juggler: Franklin Roosevelt as Warrior Statesman*. Princeton, N.J.: Princeton University Press, 1991.

———. *Forged in War: Roosevelt, Churchill, and the Second World War*. New York: William Morrow, 1997.

Kuniholm, Bruce. *The Origins of the Cold War in the Near East*. Princeton, N.J.: Princeton University Press, 1980.

Lewin, Ronald. *The American Magic: Codes, Ciphers and the Defeat of Japan*. New York: Farrar, Straus and Giroux, 1982.

Matthews, Tony. *Shadows Dancing: Japanese Espionage Against the West, 1939–1945.* London: Robert Hale, 1993.

Parker, Frederick. *Pearl Harbor Revisited: United States Navy Communications Intelligence, 1924–1941.* Fort Meade, Md.: National Security Agency, 1994.

Parrish, Thomas. *The Ultra Americans: The U.S. Role in Breaking the Nazi Codes.* New York: Stein and Day, 1986.

Prados, John. *Combined Fleet Decoded: The Secret History of American Intelligence and the Japanese Navy in World War II.* New York: Random House, 1995.

Rowlett, Frank. *The Story of Magic: Memoirs of an American Cryptologic Pioneer.* Laguna Hills, Calif.: Aegean Park Press, 1998.

Sigal, Leon. *Fighting to the Finish: The Politics of War Termination in the United States and Japan, 1945.* Ithaca, N.Y.: Cornell University Press, 1988.

Smith, Bradley F. *The Shadow Warriors: OSS and the Origins of the CIA.* New York: Basic Books, 1983.

———. *The Ultra-Magic Deals and the Most Secret Special Relationship, 1940–1946.* Novato, Calif.: Presidio Press, 1993.

———. *Sharing Secrets with Stalin: How the Allies Traded Intelligence, 1941–1945.* Lawrence: University Press of Kansas, 1996.

Stafford, David. *Churchill and Secret Service.* Woodstock, N.Y.: Overlook Press, 1997.

Stoler, Mark. *The Politics of the Second Front: American Military Planning and Diplomacy in Coalition Warfare, 1941–1943.* Wesport, Conn.: Greenview Press, 1977.

Walker, J. Samuel. *Prompt and Utter Destruction: Truman and the Use of Atomic Bombs Against Japan.* Chapel Hill: University of North Carolina Press, 1997.

Weinberg, Gerhard. *A World at Arms: A Global History of World War II.* New York: Cambridge University Press, 1994.

West, Nigel. *The Sigint Secrets: The Signals Intelligence War, 1900 to Today.* New York: William Morrow, 1988.

West, Nigel, and Oleg Tsarev. *The Crown Jewels: The British Secrets at the Heart of the KGB Archives.* London: HarperCollins, 1998.

Wilcox, Jennifer. *Sharing the Burden: Women in Cryptology During World War II.* Fort Meade, Md.: National Security Agency, 1998.

Winks, Robin. *Cloak and Gown: Scholars and the Secret War.* New York: William Morrow, 1987.

Yardley, Herbert O. *The American Black Chamber.* 1931. Reprint, Laguna Hills, Calif.: Aegean Park Press, n.d.

Articles

Alvarez, David. "No Immunity: Sigint and the European Neutrals, 1939–1945." *Intelligence and National Security* 12:2 (April 1997): 22–43.

———. "Axis Sigint Collaboration: A Limited Partnership." *Intelligence and National Security* 14:1 (Spring 1999): 1–17.

Angevine, Robert G. "Gentlemen Do Read Each Other's Mail: American Intelligence in the Interwar Era." *Intelligence and National Security* 7:2 (April 1992): 1–29.

Benson, Robert Louis. "VENONA and More: Declassifying Historical Counterintelligence." *Counterintelligence Digest* (Spring 1998): 23–27.

Bernstein, Barton J. "The Perils and Politics of Surrender: Ending the War with Japan and Avoiding the Third Atomic Bomb." *Pacific Historical Review* 46:1 (February 1977): 1–26.

———. "Understanding the Atomic Bomb and the Japanese Surrender: Missed Opportunities, Little-Known Near Disasters, and Modern Memory." *Diplomatic History* 19:1 (Spring 1995): 227–273.

Bix, Herbert. "Japan's Delayed Surrender: A Reinterpretation." *Diplomatic History* 19:2 (Spring 1995): 197–225.

Brown, Kathryn E. "Intelligence and the Decision to Collect It: Churchill's Wartime Diplomatic Signals Intelligence." *Intelligence and National Security* 10:3 (July 1995): 449–467.

———. "The Interplay of Information and Mind in Decision-Making: Signals Intelligence and Franklin D. Roosevelt's Policy-Shift on Indochina." *Intelligence and National Security* 13:1 (Spring 1998): 109–131.

Chapman, John. "No Final Solution: A Survey of the Cryptanalytical Capabilities of German Military Agencies, 1926–35." *Intelligence and National Security* 1:1 (January 1986): 14–47.

Croft, John. "Reminiscences of GCHQ and GCB, 1942–45." *Intelligence and National Security* 13:4 (Winter 1998): 133–143.

Currier, Prescott. "My 'Purple' Trip to England in 1944." *Cryptologia* 20:3 (July 1996): 193–201.

Erskine, Ralph. "Churchill and the Start of the Ultra-Magic Deals." *International Journal of Intelligence and Counterintelligence* 10:1 (Spring 1998): 57–74.

Ferris, John. "Whitehall's Black Chamber: British Cryptology and the Government Code and Cypher School, 1919–29." *Intelligence and National Security* 2:1 (January 1987): 54–91.

Kahn, David. "Pearl Harbor and the Inadequacy of Cryptanalysis." *Cryptologia* 15:4 (October 1991): 273–294.

———. "Roosevelt, Magic, and Ultra." *Cryptologia* 16:4 (October 1992): 289–316.

Kruh, Louis. "Stimson, the Black Chamber, and the 'Gentleman's Mail' Quote." *Cryptologia* 12:2 (April 1988): 65–89.

Langbart, David. "Spare No Expense: The Department of State and the Search for Intelligence About Bolshevik Russia, November 1917–September 1918." *Intelligence and National Security* 4:2 (April 1989): 316–334.

Linsenmeyer, William. "Italian Peace Feelers Before the Fall of Mussolini." *Journal of Contemporary History* 16:4 (October 1981): 649–662.

Lowenthal, Mark M. "Searching for National Intelligence: U.S. Intelligence and Policy Before the Second World War." *Intelligence and National Security* 6:4 (October 1991): 736–749.

Schlesinger, Stephen. "Cryptanalysis for Peacetime: Codebreaking and the Birth and Structure of the United Nations." *Cryptologia* 19:3 (July 1995): 217–234.

Wark, Wesley. "Cryptologic Innocence: The Origins of Signals Intelligence in Canada." *Journal of Contemporary History* 22:4 (October 1987): 639–667.

Warner, Michael, and Robert Louis Benson. "Venona and Beyond: Thoughts on Work Undone." *Intelligence and National Security* 12:3 (July 1997): 1–13.

INDEX